Stephan Martin's book *Cosmic Conversations* makes an excellent contribution to the philosophical revival that is taking place in the marketplace of ideas. Stephan's searching and heartfelt questions bring out the best of the authors he interviews. The book is full of intriguing ideas and meaningful answers to some of life's most important questions. I recommend this book to anyone interested in the developing dialogue about meaning in our universe.

— Steve McIntosh, author of *Integral Consciousness and the Future of Evolution*

Cosmic Conversations offers the reader a chance to eavesdrop on a handful of deeply satisfying conversations that mesmerize, stimulate, and entertain at the same time. If science were a jungle, Steve Martin would be the Harrison Ford character you'd want by your side. He serves as an eloquent but tough-minded guide through the complexities of some of the most compelling, cutting-edge ideas about who we are and what kind of world we live in. This is a daring book—and a great read!

— Glenn Hartelius, Ph.D.

Imagine sitting around a camp fire with some of the world's leading scientific and spiritual wisdom keepers, warmed by the glow from the primal flaring forth of the cosmos, with friendly spirits and even the stars bending down to listen in... Read this book and take your place by the fire!

-Sean Kelly, Ph.D., Professor of Religious Studies, Philosophy, Cosmology, and Consciousness Program, California Institute of Integral Studies, and author of *Individuation and the Absolute: Hegel, Jung, and the Path Toward Wholeness* and co-editor of *Ken Wilber in Dialogue: Conversations with Leading Transpersonal Thinkers*.

D0381346

Cosmic Conversations

Dialogues on the Nature of the Universe and the Search for Reality

By Stephan Martin

New Page Books
A Division of The Career Press, Inc.
Franklin Lakes, NJ

COSMIC CONVERSATIONS
EDITED AND TYPESET BY GINA TALUCCI
Cover design by The Book Designers
Printed in the U.S.A. by Courier

To order this title, please call toll-free 1-800-CAREER-1 (NJ and Canada: 201-848-0310) to order using VISA or MasterCard, or for further information on books from Career Press.

The Career Press, Inc., 3 Tice Road, PO Box 687,
Franklin Lakes, NJ 07417
www.careerpress.com
www.newpagebooks.com

Library of Congress Cataloging-in-Publication Data

Data availabl e upon request.

Dedication

To my parents and grandparents, who encouraged my love of nature and wonder at the night sky.

Acknowledgments

If it takes a village to raise a child, it takes a universe of people to write a book. My thanks go first and foremost to my contributors, who allowed me to interview them on such an arcane and grand subject as the universe, and without whom this book could not exist.

Great appreciation goes to my stellar literary agent Lisa Hagan at Paraview, who believed in the project from the beginning, and whose support and hard work was integral to this book's publication. Tremendous thanks also go to Ron Fry, Michael Pye, Jeff Piasky, Kirsten Dalley, Gina Talucci, Laurie Kelly-Pye, and the whole publishing team at New Page Books for their professional and skillful treatment of the manuscript throughout the entire publishing process. I would also like to express heartfelt gratitude to all those who helped edit and improve the introductory and end matter, particularly David Carr and Laurie Ross, without whose expert editorial advice, corrections, suggestions, improvements, and most importantly, friendship, this book would not be in the form it appears today. Thanks also go to fellow writers Michaela Aizer, Paul Coren, Glenn Hartelius, and Bruce Thompson, whose friendship, encouragement, and "compassionate critique" of my writing on this project and others has made all the difference.

I would also like to thank all those who spent long hours transcribing, and in some cases, translating, the interviews for this book. Thank you Dannhae Herrera-Wilson, Beth Hooper, Alexi Meyer, Amanda Postula, Tom Purton, and Stacy Simone for all your hard work, diligence, and effort.

It is also important to acknowledge and thank the faculty, staff, and students of the Philosophy, Cosmology, and Consciousness program at the

California Institute of Integral Studies for the creativity, guidance, and academic excellence they inspired in me during my time there. Their support for exploring bold new ideas toward a more integral and sustainable world has shaped my worldview and work in the world immeasurably.

Thanks as well go to all my students and fellow faculty for the shared adventure of learning about the universe and our place in it.

I would also like to thank all my teachers and fellow companions in the Ridhwan School for their love, support, and dedication to authenticity, truth, and the deeper reality.

I would also like to express loving thanks to my family and friends, without whose enduring support this book certainly could not have been written. These include my parents, Ed and Judy Martin, my brother Gregory Martin, and my long-time friends and family Mark Wheeler, Art Peña, Cristin DeVine, Lee Brewster, Patrick Wood, Scott Hill, Mary Reynolds Thompson, Bryan Johnson, Melissa Patterson, Jan Hodgman, Dorothy Orzulak, the CHE faculty and students at New College, and so many others who continue to add richness, depth, and fun to my life in so many ways.

Lastly I would like to thank my wife, Kim Bella, for her love, support, and encouragement as my biggest fan. I'm grateful every day for her as my companion on our shared journey in a creative and mysterious universe.

Contents

Part 3: The View From Culture

Introduction

What Is the Universe?

On a clear night, step outside beneath the star-flecked sky and listen. If you are far enough from the urban undertow of modern life and stand still long enough to let your thoughts settle, you might feel yourself enveloped in the universe's majestic depth and beauty. As you swim in the luminescent blackness among the uncountable stars, you may begin to feel dizzy or disoriented, perhaps feeling your familiar sense of self dissolving or diffusing out into the enormity of space.

At first this might feel disquieting, but if you let the immensity of the silence speak to you, questions may spontaneously appear. What is all this? Where did it all come from? What's it all about? What is it telling me? People have been asking questions like these for at least as long as there have been people looking up at the night sky. Our wonder and our questions, our innate curiosity about the world around us, and our role in it, are part of our humanness.

Every culture has been awed by the heavens and asked, "What is the universe?" How a culture—or individual—answers this question becomes the source of their myths, beliefs, and creation stories, which influences how they live in the world. The Wari people of the western Amazon see the cosmos (and particularly the natural world) as imbued with endlessly flowing energy, spiritual intelligence, and power. Time, space, and matter appear fluid to them, alterable through language, music, and ritual. Contemporary Western scientists view the universe as the interplay and exchange of matter and energy, combining, changing, and evolving through predictable and comprehensible physical laws. And Vajrayana Buddhism of Tibet discerns multitudes of universes and worlds within worlds, all interpenetrating and appearing as forms of awareness in an infinite and eternal Mind.

Yet they are all talking about the same thing, aren't they? This collection of conversations explores the question: "What are we talking about exactly when we talk about, look at, or inquire into the nature of life, the universe, and everything?" Is it matter, energy, God, spirit, or Mind? Is its occurrence random, purposeful, intelligent, meaningless, or beyond the imagination? The great philosophers, scientists, and poets throughout human history have asked and answered these questions, so why do we continue to address these same mysteries today? Some of my guests suggest that our questioning is of the very nature of the universe.

Our answers and formulations to these questions are personally relevant. How we conceive the universe guides our efforts to find and make meaning in our own lives. How we answer these questions on an individual, cultural, or global level—whether consciously or unconsciously—not only forms the basis of our philosophical view of the world, but also influences the ways we act on it and in it—the patterns and rhythms of our daily life. Where our attention is drawn moment to moment is largely based on our values, which ultimately arise from our beliefs about the universe. Where we place our attention day to day guides how we act in the world and creates the underlying fabric of our lives.

Why we continue asking has a practical underpinning. Stop reading and look around you right now. Anything fabricated that you see represents a particular worldview realized into material form. Each crafted object begins as an idea, which is formed and shaped according to the skills of people with a specific worldview and set of values. If the principles of physics were not valued by people in modern industrialized societies, there would be no television sets, computers, or airplanes. If the Wari of the Amazon did not value different principles of existence, they would not create their ritual staffs, masks, and earth shrines. The variety of art, architecture, and crafts among cultures and throughout time express, the many different perceptions of the universe.

Beyond the philosophical and practical impulses behind the Big Questions lies another: the impulse for transformation. The very asking has the power to shift our worldview and change our lives in significant ways. By contemplating the responses and viewpoints of others, we can refine our understanding of ourselves and our unique place in the universe.

I invited my guests into conversation on this topic not in hopes of receiving final answers, but as a path of inquiry, a way of engaging fully with the mysteries of existence. This, for many, lies at the heart of a fulfilling life. As Emerson expressed, "Were I to hold the truth in my hand, I would let it go for the positive joy of seeking." As we begin asking these questions with a curious mind and a sincere heart, we may eventually find ourselves beginning to "live the questions," as Rilke suggested. We participate in the world more deeply, in seeking a meaningful relationship with the universe.

But if we begin to ask thoughtful questions such as, "What is the universe?" we must be prepared for profound, perhaps unsettling, answers. One individual who was not prepared for the answers the universe gave him in response to asking these kinds of questions was Albert Einstein. Above all the other reasons for his work in physics was Einstein's desire to "know the mind of God." With his general theory of relativity, Einstein had found a way to weave space, time, matter, energy, and gravity together into a coherent mathematical model, an unprecedented achievement in physics still celebrated today. Yet when he and the Dutch mathematician William de Sitter sat down in 1917 to try to apply Einstein's new theory to the structure of the universe, they discovered something unexpected and even more interesting: The universe seemed to be expanding.

In the early 20th century this idea was considered not only revolutionary but mind-boggling. Einstein had grown up during a time when the universe was generally considered eternal and unchanging. The idea of an expanding universe was initially too much for him, so he included a "fudge factor" in his mathematics, which canceled out the predicted expansion, allowing his equations to more closely match his beliefs about the universe. He had asked the question, "What is the universe?" but had been unable to believe the reply the universe had given him. He later called this the greatest blunder of his life!

A decade later the American astronomer Edwin Hubble measured the velocities of distant galaxies, empirically demonstrating that the universe was expanding. Soon after, the Belgian priest and astrophysicist Georges Lemaître proposed that not only was the universe expanding, but that what we see today is the "ashes and smoke of bright but very rapid fireworks"—the very beginning of the universe. The universe could no longer remain static and eternal. It was now perceived as dynamic, evolving, with even a beginning!

Enter now the theory of quantum mechanics to upend our ideas about the physical nature of the world. Physicists were discovering in their laboratories that the basic properties of atomic particles were being altered just by the simple act of measuring them. Soon after it was discovered that, in certain experimental arrangements, particles at the atomic level do not fully exist prior to being observed. The activity of conscious observation and measurement was actually bringing particles into full existence! This suggests that reality may not be pregiven and "objective," but rather that it is being continuously shaped by our interactions with it. Based on this surprising result and others, many scientists have been led to the intriguing conclusion that Mind or consciousness may lie at the foundations of the universe. As the physicist Sir James Jeans said nearly a century ago, the universe "seems to be more like a great thought than a great machine."

The answers to our simple question, "What is the universe?" have changed many times throughout the past hundred years, and are likely to continue evolving in surprising and intriguing ways each time we ask it.

Recent astronomical measurements have provided another unexpected response to this question by showing that the overwhelming majority of the universe is composed of two enigmatic and invisible components: dark matter and dark energy. In other words, the latest response to our question from the universe is that it is almost entirely something that we can't see, and offers us no idea of what it is! And so the mystery grows as we venture deeper into the universe with our questions, evoking new responses that may sometimes leave us feeling uncertain and shaky as we try to make sense of the insights and revelations of our continuing inquiry.

We might continue feeling dizzy if we join in the current cosmological speculation that our universe may be only one of many universes (multi-verses), eternally and endlessly inflating in a vast void, bubbling up as quantum fluctuations out of literally nothing. Additionally, there may be many more dimensions to our universe than meet the eye—as few as 11 or as many as 26, according to some theories. A recent survey of the scientific and philosophical literature by noted scholar and researcher Dr. Robert Lawrence Kuhn classified at least 27 different explanations for the current observed universe and why things are they way they are.[1] So…what *is* the universe?

One insight into how to approach multiple perspectives on the universe comes once again from Einstein. His special theory of relativity (a "special" case of the general theory) posits that space and time are not uniform everywhere in the universe, but strongly depend on the observer. Two people moving at different speeds relative to each other will actually see and experience space and time differently. How can the universe not only *look* different, but *be* different for different people? Don't we all live in the same universe? This is more than a scientific question—generations of artists, writers, and philosophers have been deeply affected by Einstein's insight.

Moving deeper into the unfamiliar, Einstein and de Sitter's discovery of the expanding universe implies that the universe is expanding everywhere, and yet has no center. In other words, everywhere is the center of the expansion of the universe (this view is called *omnicentrism*). This means that Chicago, the Andromeda Galaxy, and you are all the center of action for the universe. So modern cosmologists have proposed that the dynamics of the universe are equally present everywhere in the universe (an assumption consistent with current astronomical observations). Then, if every place in the universe is the center of its expansion and has the same laws and dynamics as everywhere else, we can learn about the universe from any particular place. We can study Mars or the Orion Nebula to learn about the universe, but we can also study our bioregion or even—ourselves. Every person and each part of the universe is a valuable source of information about its dynamics and nature. Each of us *is* the universe being expressed in a particular location in a specific way. We're all part of the same moving and evolving cosmos, but the view of it is unique from each of our respective locations. *Hold on to your seats!*

This suggests that the universe is not only omnicentric, but that it is also *multiperspectival*—there are many different, and equally valid, viewpoints on this mysterious phenomenon we call the universe. Astronomy, physics, chemistry, and biology each offer distinct perspectives on the universe, because each is attuned to a different class of phenomena within it. Then we have the gifts of music, literature, philosophy, religion, and the humanities—each also offering its distinctive and unique insights into this evolving universe that we all participate in. Don't forget to add in the insights of other cultures and religious traditions before we undertake any kind of "unified theory" of the universe!

The technique of seeing existence from many different angles in hopes of finding common ground in our shared experience while acknowledging the unique perspective each one brings to the whole, I refer to as "reality slicing." It's like slicing through a loaf of cinnamon swirl bread at different angles, revealing different patterns of swirl in each slice. So many different patterns and possibilities, all from the same bread!

So if it is true, as it seems to be, that the universe is more than what any one of us can say it is, then in order to bring together diverse perspectives toward a common understanding of the whole, we need to first acknowledge that our viewpoint may not be the only "correct" one. We must relax long-cherished preconceptions, beliefs, and certainties about ourselves and the universe, so that something new may inform them. If we can agree that different perspectives on the universe exist, and that each represents an equally valid viewpoint, then what does this say about the universe we live in? What is the cosmos telling us about itself through the existence of so many different perspectives on itself? How is it that so many people can see the world so differently when we're all part of the same evolving universe? Now wouldn't it be interesting to inquire with people about their diverse viewpoints to find out more about the nature of the universe?

I thought so. I sought them out in various fields and from a range of diverse backgrounds. We met in offices, laboratories, living rooms, cafes, and even parking lots. We talked by phone, exchanged e-mail and letters, and shared insights garnered throughout the course of entire lives and careers dedicated to asking these kinds of questions. We spoke from theory and experience, about data and speculation, and out of belief and personal revelation. We explored the universe as matter and energy, as form and emptiness, as spirit and consciousness. Our conversations spanned the depth and breadth of space, time, and human history, entwining the nature of the cosmos with the threads of science, culture, and the most profound questions of human existence.

As I joined in conversation with my guests—spacious thinkers, disciplined researchers, and courageous explorers of the intimate and infinite, I found my own beliefs challenged, my preconceptions revealed, and my viewpoint transformed. These conversations made clear to me that not only does the researcher influence the outcome, but the outcome also influences the researcher. With each dialogue, I felt as if my familiar self and worldview were being softened and reshaped like wax in the sunlight, twisting my perception askew so as to see the world afterward in a different light. It was as if I was morphing and growing with each conversation, leaving each interview in a larger space of uncertainty than when I had first arrived, yet with access to more possibilities. What I lost in certainty through these conversations, I gained in awe, wonder, and curiosity.

The final result of these dialogues and explorations is what is found in this book. For convenience, these various perspectives are grouped into three broad perspectives: science, spiritual traditions, and modern cultural thought. None of these categories is by any means completely or fairly represented here, and in many cases my guests span two or more categories with the breadth of their perspective, experience, and vision. Many of them are exemplars of interdisciplinary thinking that synthesizes the results of their field, culture, or tradition with those of diverse and sometimes seemingly conflicting perspectives into a coherent vision. Others have traveled deeply in their specialization, discovering universal truths that interconnect their fields with those of others. Each one brings new insights about the universe, spotlighting our world in a slightly different hue.

These interviews are an invitation to ponder these big questions for yourself, to have your worldview challenged, enlarged, and transformed. Perhaps you will find yourself asking, "If this is true about the universe, what does it mean about me and my participation in it?" We are each on a journey of discovery, and as you travel this path you may find that asking the right questions can be just as important as finding the right answers. May your inquiry into and engagement with these questions carry you deep into the heart of the universe and the mystery of your own life as it has for me.

Part 1

The View From Science

When Galileo Galilei first turned a telescope toward the heavens in 1609, our mode of understanding the universe was changed forever. The systematic investigation of reality through physics, astronomy, chemistry, biology, and their sister sciences has become an integral part of the modern worldview—to such an extent that the scientific method is now the primary source of insight into the nature of reality and the primary mode of engagement with the universe for modern culture. What children are taught in school about themselves and their relationship to the world is generally drawn from the tremendous well of knowledge that science has tapped throughout the past 400 years. Advances in technology, medicine, and engineering all represent the practical applications of our scientific approach to understanding the world. For many of us, the houses we live in, the cars we drive, the tools of our professions, and even the foods that sustain us all represent modern scientific understanding of the universe realized in material form.

The remarkable thing is that it seems to work so spectacularly well. The universe seems endlessly receptive to discovery through the scientific method, and many suggest that the development of science represents one of the crowning achievements of Western culture. With exponentially growing reservoirs of data flowing in every year, science's capacity to increasingly reveal ever more about the universe offers great confidence in our ability to fully understand reality from a scientific perspective. The success of science in describing the physical world has even led to attempts to apply scientific theories from fields such as evolutionary biology and neuroscience to traditionally more qualitative realms of human experience such as social psychology and consciousness studies.

Yet as compelling as the scientific perspective is, can science answer everything? Does the scientific worldview offer us a complete picture of reality, or can science ask questions about the universe that it ultimately cannot answer? Are our most profound questions about the cosmos and human meaning answerable through science? On this point, scientists are divided. Some believe that all phenomena in the cosmos (including human experience) can be reduced to fundamental forces interacting, and they dream of grand unified theories as compelling explanations for why the world seems to be the way it is. Others question this assumption and turn to the world's cultural and spiritual traditions for insights into aspects of human experience that seem to elude or lie in the gaps of our current scientific understanding. Still others see science as one mode of relating to the universe among many, providing insights not necessarily about nature herself, but, as Heisenberg discerned, "nature exposed to our method of questioning."[2]

Whatever science's ultimate relationship to reality, scientists themselves have a tremendous amount of insight, perspective, and even wisdom to offer about the universe and our role in it. The scientists interviewed in this section represent some of the cutting-edge thinkers and researchers working in their fields today. Many of them are pressing the boundaries of conventional scientific thinking, challenging us to consider fresh paradigms in light of radical discoveries about the nature of space, time, and the overall structure of the universe. This new data suggests that our beliefs about the universe that derive from everyday human-scale experience may be naïve, and that the universe may be much more creative, mysterious, and participatory than had previously been considered.

Because my formal background and training are in science, I felt a natural rapport with the individuals interviewed in this section as well as the topics and material we explored together. Contrary to the popular stereotypes of scientists in white laboratory coats coolly detached from their experiments, the men and women I interviewed in this section were warm, engaging, and enthusiastic about their work. Science, after all, is a very human activity, and although the ability to be a good scientist takes years of training, discipline, and insight, more than any of these it takes a passion for discovery and an innate sense of wonder about the cosmos. The capacity to be continually amazed by the universe is one of the qualities that often sets scientists apart from those in other fields, and this fascination with discovery is one of the threads that comes through most strongly in this set of interviews.

This set of conversations begins with cosmologist Brian Swimme, where we find that scientific insights about the nature of the universe challenge us to reimagine the nature of the human as creative, evolutionary, and sustainable. With physicist Joel Primack and cultural historian Nancy Abrams we explore how discovering our place in the cosmos can be a rich source of human meaning that orients us in a way that can be globally unifying, as well as personally satisfying. In conversation with astrophysicist Bernard Haisch, we discover intriguing results from scientific inquiry that parallel the world's spiritual and mystical traditions. With complexity theorist James Gardner we explore the radical idea that life itself may play a central and shaping role in the future and destiny of the cosmos. The mysteries deepen as physicist Fred Alan Wolf and I discuss the paradoxical findings of quantum physics. We close this section with parapsychologist Dean Radin, who points out how the results of consciousness research not only challenge the methodologies and assumptions of contemporary science, but also reveal how much we have yet to learn about both the human mind and the universe.

Chapter 1

The Creative Cosmos: An Interview With Brian Swimme

Talking with Brian Swimme about the universe is itself a cosmic event. His sense of wonder and amazement about the universe and his enthusiasm for it are contagious, inspiring, and transformative. Dr. Swimme is a mathematical cosmologist and core faculty in the Philosophy, Cosmology, and Consciousness graduate program at the California Institute of Integral Studies in San Francisco. His primary fields of research are the nature of the evolutionary dynamics of the universe, the relationship between scientific cosmology and more traditional religious visions, the cultural implications of the new evolutionary epic, and the role of humanity in the unfolding story of Earth and cosmos. Central to Swimme's work is the nature of the human as an emergent being within the universe and Earth, and the role of the human within the Earth community.

He is the author of *The Hidden Heart of the Cosmos* (Orbis, 1996), *Manifesto for a Global Civilization* (with Matthew Fox) (Bear and Company, 1983), *The Universe is a Green Dragon* (Bear and Company, 1984), and *The Universe Story* (Harper, 1992), which is a culmination of a

10-year collaboration with the well-known cultural historian Thomas Berry. His media credits include the video series *Canticle to the Cosmos*, *The Hidden Heart of the Cosmos*, *The Earth's Imagination*, and *The Powers of the Universe*.

Brian Swimme received his PhD in 1978 from the University of Oregon, specializing in gravitational dynamics. He was a faculty member in the Department of Mathematics at the University of Puget Sound in Tacoma, Washington, from 1978 to 1981, and a member of the faculty at the Institute for Culture and Creation Spirituality at Holy Names College in Oakland, California, from 1983 to 1989. In 1989 he joined the faculty at the California Institute of Integral Studies in San Francisco, where he continues to teach today.

Swimme lectures worldwide and has presented at conferences sponsored by the American Association for the Advancement of Science, The World Bank, UNESCO, The United Nations Millennium Peace Summit, and the American Natural History Museum.

Stephan Martin: In your work you've expressed the view that the universe is not evolving randomly, but is instead making choices in search of something. I wonder if you could say more about what that something is. If it's not teleology, then what is the universe aiming at through this ongoing process of evolution?

Brian Swimme: One of the stunning developments of 20th-century science is that we can actually say that the universe seems to be in search of complexity. What complexity means is an interesting question, as is what it means to say that it's in search of something. The difficulty when we use language like this is that it sounds like anthropomorphism.

So when we say "the universe" is seeking, it sounds as if we're thinking of the universe as a person, and we're not. The universe is not a person, it's something vastly greater than we are, and we're attempting to say something about that which gave birth to us. We're reflecting on a reality that has brought us forth, and we're using language like the English language, which doesn't really have the capacity to describe the universe fully. Not at all, because a lot of the scientific discoveries about the universe that we're making are very recent, and they run counter to the mentality that humans had when the English language was invented and shaped.

So we're in this really awkward situation of having amazing insights into the universe and yet not having the capacity to fully express those insights in language. Sometimes we can capture some of them in mathematics and that's great, but even then it's a challenge.

So for me, there's this overall sense of the universe trying to get somewhere. What we can say with some certainty is that the sense of the universe being entirely random would lead to the expectation that after 14 billion years there wouldn't be much complexity in the universe. So it's interesting that whatever it is that we're enveloped in is getting somewhere more quickly than it would if it were simply random. That's very interesting!

So that's what I mean when I say the universe is seeking or searching for the complex. Complexity itself is another mystery, and what I mean by complexity is that we have evidence now that the universe 14 billion years ago was very simple in terms of structure—just elementary particles and photons, and now we find all these complex structures like galaxies and people.

At the same time—and I know this is one of the things you're interested in—if it's not just random, is it *also* random? We've been discovering that it's not just random, but I want to emphasize the fact that it's also random. It's both random and non-random, and the relationship between these two is the actual unfolding of the universe. There's a way in which the structure of the Milky Way reflects both the random dimension of the universe and the non-random. Both are extremely important. The thinker who understands as well as anyone is Edgar Morin. Your readers might want to explore his book, *On Complexity*.

Now even if we're moving away from the idea of things being totally random, we're not moving toward the idea that the universe was *designed* from the beginning to be just as it is now. That, I think, is a very weak interpretation of the universe. The universe is an exciting, chaotic process that is in search of a mysterious something that we can just point to with a word like *complexity*.

We often associate the idea of randomness with total chaos, yet there are new fields of science such as complexity theory and chaos theory, where there seems to be a certain kind of emergent order that comes out of chaotic systems spontaneously. I wonder if *spontaneity* would be another word to use in addition to *randomness*?

Yes, yes, that's a great word. The spontaneity of the universe includes both some sort of ultimate order and also chaos. Simultaneously. I love the ideas of complexity and chaos science, where order and chaos are entwined mysteriously.

And they seem to arise out of each other, without a pre-existing plan, which is more stunning than if it had a plan that was unfolding.

Exactly—it's way more stunning! Right now when we're discovering that things aren't totally random, we're looking around for a way to express it, and so some people have locked onto this idea that "Oh, it must have been *designed*." In the English language we have phrases such as design, intelligent design, and intelligent designer, but that isn't anywhere near as exciting as what's actually happening. We don't have a readily available phrase in English to capture all that we're saying here, but all of it is way more exciting than simply saying it was designed.

Yes, it's really an approximation because we really can't reach for the right word. That's why people throughout history have fallen back on poetry and metaphor to describe the universe.

We're in a moment in our understanding of the universe where the human imagination has to plumb its depths to bring forth new images, new poetry, and new insights to describe reality. Language has to be recreated if we're to express what we're discovering about the universe. So it's a time for the poets and for the imagination.

Some people are depressed by the fact that the English language does not contain the necessary words for us to express ourselves fully, but other people are thrilled by it, because it means that we're giving birth to new language. The English language is going to be so different in a couple of centuries than it is right now.

Right, and it won't just be different vocabulary, but maybe the structure of it will be different as well. One thing I heard recently is that people are approaching indigenous cultures who have process-based languages for talking about the results of quantum theory, since

quantum theory strongly suggests that the universe is not a thing, but a process, and so this way of speaking about things naturally makes sense to these peoples.

Yes, and the indigenous languages, certainly those of North America, are much more process-oriented than English. English is heavily noun-based, because the English language reflects the fundamental cosmology of English-speaking people. In the modern period, Newtonian cosmology was based on the idea of substance, the idea that everything is made up of particles and atoms. So naturally if atoms and particles interacting with each other are seen as the building blocks of the world, then our language will reflect that with nouns and verbs interacting with each other in a similar way. We have more nouns in the English language than any language we know of throughout all of history, and this reflects the belief of Western peoples that the world is made up of objects.

It's amazing, really, to think of how cosmology seeps into language, so that when you're speaking English, basically you're speaking Newtonian cosmology. But now what we've discovered through quantum physics is that everything is fundamentally a process, yet we're still trying to use English nouns to describe it. This type of process thinking seems to have been present in earlier and current indigenous peoples. Hopi, Navajo, and many indigenous languages reflect a very different cosmology, so there's a fertile interaction happening between modern languages and those of ancient and traditional cultures right now. Nancy Maryboy and David Begay explore these ideas in their work relating Dine and Western cosmologies. The physicist David Peat and his book *Blackfoot Physics* might also be mentioned here. It's an ongoing endeavor that I think is going to be increasingly important as we move further into this challenge of re-creating language.

It seems like language is fundamental because it is such a shaping force in our interaction with the universe. As you said, escaping out of the Newtonian framework and out of the subject-object split requires a transition from thinking of the universe as a collection of objects to a communion of subjects, as you and Thomas Berry have phrased it.

Yes, that's one way to articulate the major challenge before us as humans. Scientists originally felt that they had all the truths, but now there's the growing realization that there are deep, deep truths about cosmic process embedded in indigenous languages. It's a thrilling exploration for those who have the sense of this. We were so certain in modern science that we really had the final say on the nature of the world—just so certain—and then to have all that break apart has been not only sobering, but liberating.

It seems like we're in a similar place now with our scientific culture as we were just before quantum physics shattered the mechanistic view of the world nearly a hundred years ago. What comes to mind is John Horgan's book *The End of Science*, where he suggests that we're at the end of the era of great discoveries about the nature of the universe. It reminds me so much of Lord Kelvin's statement at the end of the 19th century where he says something like "Don't go into physics anymore—it's all done." And so I wonder, are we on the edge of some great initiation into some new aspect or dimension of science right now? What direction will 21st- and 22nd-century science take?

It seems very clear that it will not be the direction of the 17th, 18th, 19th, and 20th centuries where science aimed at discovering the "fundamental" equations that governed particular phenomenal domains. A number of leading scientists believe that search is over and done with. So what new way of interacting with the universe will surface, especially in terms of scientific investigation of the universe? We only have intuitions, surmises, and my personal favorite, which is the one that believes 21st-century science will be focused on the study of complex systems. I think scientists will increasingly focus on very particular systems such as Earth's climate, or a spiral galaxy, and will attempt to learn not the fundamental equations, but the basic *habits of behavior* of such systems. But that's just a guess. What will actually take place nobody knows.

It seems like we're in an era where we're letting go of our old ideas about what the universe is, as well as reconsidering our relationship to it. It's a pretty recent discovery that we can say that we are not walking around *in* the universe, but that we *are* the universe itself. As increasing numbers of astronomers, philosophers, and others are now saying, we seem to be the self-reflexive capacity of the universe to reflect on itself.

Yes, that would be one way of characterizing the deepest contribution that Western science has made to the world. We can say simply that "we *are* the universe."

Clifford Matthews, professor of chemistry at the University of Illinois, says that the way to summarize everything we've learned through science about the universe in four words is: "we are recycled stardust." It's just so great! In terms of science and empirical knowledge, this was completely unknown a few centuries ago.

Now we realize, with our observational methods and our theoretical formulations, that the stars have given birth to us. It's an incredible discovery. So we can say with absolute scientific certainty, as you said, "We *are* the universe," and notice how profoundly that breaks us out of the subject-object relationship. There's no object in a certain sense—it's all one vast communion of subjects that gave birth to us.

How to take that fundamental insight, which has required millions of humans with their observations and thought and experiments, and work it into the grammar of daily life? That's the task we have before us. To live in a way that's in alignment with our deepest understanding. That's why it's so great to be alive right now! [laughs] All of the old certainties are being broken apart, and so we're in this thrilling moment of giving birth to this new way of being human.

I should say right away that a lot of these insights have parallels and are mirrored in other cultural traditions. We've been talking about the indigenous traditions, and many of them would be completely at home with the insight that "We are the universe," or that "We come from the stars." They've understood themselves that way for millennia. Even in the classical religions of Taoism, Confucianism, and Hinduism they would be at home with these ideas.

It's the West—the industrial West—that needs to understand this. As industrial Western ways of knowing embrace this understanding, it will enter more deeply into a dialogue with the other traditions of the world. It's a planetary movement and together we're going to find our way into what it means that we are deeply interconnected with everything. What kind of economics do you build when you start off with such an idea? What kinds of religions do you have?

Yes, and all of it has to be recycled from the foundations in a sense, and re-envisioned from the perspective "We are Universe." We can't even say "We are *the* universe," because that implies a separation, so we have to say "We are Universe."

Yes! Exactly. We are Universe!

So does this lead you to any insights about the human's role in this transformational process that is occurring? It seems like we have such an impact on this planet, and that we have so many gifts to offer.

Absolutely. The first part would be that if we start with the insight "We are Universe," then we have a base upon which to criticize other inadequate formulations of the human. The one that's most current in industrial society would be something like "We are consumers."

Our society is basically about using natural resources to make commodities that lead to human comfort. Unfortunately, this view of the planet as a resource bin is what's leading to the destruction of all the ecosystems around the planet. We need to get some distance from what I call this "use cosmology," the idea that the universe and the earth are here only for our use. But if we're not here just to be consumers, what is our role?

One idea comes from noting that the human is certainly a place in the universe where the entire vast story can burst into awareness of itself. The human is this place where 14 billion years of evolution is reflecting upon itself. One way to think about us is to think that we are the way Universe reflects upon its own majesty and mystery.

It means that it's possible that our primary role as humans is that of celebration. We have this destiny—and even duty—to become astonished by the universe! [laughs]

It sounds almost ridiculous to say this when our industrial society is oriented toward getting a job and producing stuff. But it's a perspective that we need to take seriously. What if we began to organize our school system and educational process so that humans could move more deeply into an understanding and celebration of existence itself? What's interesting is that to call consumer society into question is difficult because it's so ingrained in each of us, and so it sounds as if I'm pitting myself against all of the benefits of industrial society, but I'm not.

What I am saying is that we might begin to take seriously the idea that it's in the arts, it's in the sciences, and it's in the religions and the humanities, where we can find the deeper roles of the human, including the idea that we are here to marvel over existence and to celebrate it and to extend to those less fortunate the great privilege of being alive and healthy.

So, there's one idea. That we are here to celebrate the magnificence of being. And to work so that others might share in this joy. That's different than just being a consumer. In any event, we need to reimagine in a radical way what it means to be human.

Yes, and in this reimagining we cannot settle for small or pat answers, because part of the danger of materialism is getting sucked into thinking we know the basic nature of the universe. Calling humans consumers isn't necessarily a bad label, but it's just one that's way too small for what we truly are. It simply isn't satisfying.

Absolutely. That's why some people regard this moment as philosophically similar to the pre-Socratics, going all the way back to Pythagoras, Heraclitus, Parmenides, and others who were just freshly wondering about great questions like "What does it mean to be human?" We've developed a particular set of answers, and we've tried them out for a few thousand years, and now that we're coming to the end of that particular experiment, we're thrown back into a deep sense of questioning and wonder.

It seems like cultures have to go through this process of questioning every now and then when they've gotten too small for what they truly are.

Our planet is falling apart. That's a horrible thing, but one of the opportunities is that as we get in touch with the misery we are causing, we can find the energy to actually ask these radical questions at a level that's deep enough, as you say, to confront the tiny role of the consumer. We can be critical of our current role because we find ourselves in the midst of this vast firestorm taking place all around the planet with so many other species disappearing because of us.

Given this situation, what are the sources of guidance that people can have in these times? What can they rely upon to see them through this transformation that's happening in our culture right now?

Let me quote the economist Hazel Henderson, because she's really good on this. She's one of these cutting-edge thinkers who are trying to find their way out of industrial society into a more vital way of being human. She said simply, "I rely on my senses." She relies on her direct experience. She was trained in classical economics—it was her education, her philosophy, her cosmology, her whole way of seeing the world, and yet she found that she could not rely upon it for a new perspective. She had to return to her body and to her own deepest experiences to find the new truths. By returning to what she was experiencing in her body, she began to formulate new ideas about economics, contributing to a wide body of thought that "biologizes" civilization. In economics we have Henderson and such people as Herman Daly and Richard Norgaard. In technology we have Jenine Benyus and Hunter Lovins. In agriculture, Wes Jackson, in city planning, Richard Register. These are the geniuses who are providing us with the guidance we need to build a new civilization. And all of them began by throwing out the axioms of industrial society and thinking anew from their own experiences.

Yes, It makes me think of the recent turn in modern philosophy toward phenomenology—the return back to the actual phenomena of experience, because what is the universe but these basic elements of experience? In closing, I wonder if we could talk briefly about what's coming into the universe right now that's new. What is being born and is newly emerging in this stage of cosmic evolution?

That's a great question. The context for answering the question is that time can be talked about in different ways: linear time, cyclical time, organic time, mechanical time, and so forth. But in terms of the universe, time is newness. Time is creative emergence. What's really great is that the universe has this creative sense of time. Earlier in the universe it was the time of atoms—that's what was newly emerging into existence! Later it was the time of galaxies—that's the time they came forth. And once the galaxies came in and perdured, it became the time of planets. And then the first cells of life—new again, and so forth.

On the planet today, certainly one of the newest species is our own. The white shark is fantastic, but it attained its physical form a long time ago, and it continues in this same form today. Likewise, our Sun arrived at its stable form a long time ago. The cactus continues to change a little bit, but it's been in its form a long time. But the human has just arrived, and we are still attempting to find our form. So it is the human that is new in the universe right now.

In our emergence on Earth, what is new about the human? It's not our feet or our lungs or our heart—all of these things have been around for a long time through other organisms. It's not even our brain, because even though our brain is larger than other primates, it's very similar in form to other primates. What's new with the human is thought, and by thought I mean two things. I mean consciousness reflecting upon itself, so that conscious self-awareness is new. We're not the only species that has this, but we're the species that it has taken hold in most profoundly.

The other capacity of thought is the ability to hold conscious self-awareness in a form that is exterior to the human body, and more particularly in language that can be given cultural forms, such as paintings, books, and libraries. This change can be talked about in various ways, but one way to say it is that the DNA, which has operated brilliantly for three and a half billion years, has through the human spilled out into an exterior trans-genetic form that we call culture.

So that is what is new on the planet right now. If you're a baby white shark, you have a tremendous amount of information in your DNA, and you also have information from learning experiences in your environment, but what you don't have is all the detailed experience from previously existing individual white sharks—that's all gone.

With the human so much of it is there, captured in our languages. The difference then for the human is that even if we live to be a hundred years old, it's not fair to say that we have a hundred-year-old mind. Rather, even when we are young children, we are involved with a mind that is a hundred thousand years in the making. Through cultural artifacts, we enter into a continuously accumulating mind called humanity. In a real sense that continuously accumulating mind is currently shaping the planet more powerfully than anything else in nature.

This brings us back to the beginning of our conversation. What's the most powerful way of entering into the shaping of the planet? It is through the invention of new symbols and new modes of expression, because that is what is new right now. The entire planet is being organized by symbolic forms called English, Japanese, mathematics, Picasso, music of all sorts. This ongoing flow of language and symbolic expression is what is shaping all of the species of our planet right now.

That's why there is this impulse that people have, that you have in creating this book, and that people who are reading your book have—this impulse to give birth to new language and ideas. That's the very center of evolution, the spirit of the universe, the élan vital, the zest, it's the way in which Universe is attempting to bring itself forth newly. Our burning energy to create symbolic forms is the same burning energy 12 billion years ago when Universe was constructing galaxies. Same urgent creativity, different form.

Wow. It's quite a gift.

The most amazing we have.

Chapter 2

The View From the Center of the Universe: An Interview With Joel Primack and Nancy Abrams

W hy does it matter what kind of universe we live in? Does our cosmology affect how we live our lives day to day? Primack and Abrams would argue that it does. "To act wisely globally, we must think cosmically," they suggest in their 2006 book *The View from the Center of the Universe*. Understanding our role in the cosmic perspective is not only tremendously inspiring and meaningful, but it may be an essential part of solving the large-scale problems and crises that our species currently faces on this planet. As we will see, the new view of the universe currently emerging from modern cosmology has the potential to be both scientifically accurate, as well as spiritually satisfying.

Dr. Joel Primack is a professor of physics at the University of California at Santa Cruz. The author of more than 200 technical and popular articles, Dr. Primack has been a leading researcher in the fields of observational cosmology, particle astrophysics, and relativistic quantum field theory for more than three decades. In the 1970s he helped create what is now known as the Standard Model of particle physics, and in the 1980s he was one of the primary originators of the Cold Dark Matter theory, one of the leading models of cosmological dark matter today. He has been director of the Theoretical Advanced Study Institute at UCSC, codirector of the Enrico Fermi school on dark matter in Varenna, Italy, and helped create the Scientific Visualization Laboratory and UpsAnd Beowulf Computer Laboratory at UCSC. He is also interested in science and technology policy, and is the coauthor of *Advice and Dissent: Scientists in the Political Arena.*

Nancy Ellen Abrams is a lawyer, writer, and former Fulbright scholar with a long-standing interest in the history, philosophy, and politics of science. While on staff at the Office of Technology Assessment of the U.S. Congress, she co-created a method called "Scientific Mediation" for guiding government agencies in making wise policy decisions in cases involving scientific uncertainty. She has consulted on the use of this novel procedure with corporations, as well as state and national governments around the world. She has been interested in the interface between myth, cosmology, and culture since studying with religious scholar Mircea Eliade at the University of Chicago. Her articles on science policy, space policy, and the cultural implications of modern cosmology have appeared in journals and magazines such as *The Bulletin of the Atomic Scientists*, *Environment*, *California Lawyer*, and *Science and Global Security*. With Joel Primack, she coauthored a prize-winning article on quantum cosmology and Kabbalah that was featured in the magazine *Tikkun*. An accomplished songwriter and musician, Abrams has also released three albums and has performed in more than 18 countries.

Together, Abrams and Primack have coauthored articles that have appeared in many scientific and popular journals and magazines, and have given invited talks and presentations on the cultural implications of modern cosmology around the world. For the past 10 years they have co-taught an award-winning course titled Cosmology and Culture at UC Santa Cruz. Their coauthored book *View From the Center of the Universe* has won widespread acclaim for presenting a new positive vision of human culture's place in the universe, and they continue to write, present, and work together on a diverse variety of topics related to science, spirituality, and the interface of cosmology and culture.

Stephan Martin: In your book *View from the Center of the Universe*, you make the case that widespread cultural indifference to the universe is one of the biggest handicaps we face today in solving our global problems. Why is it so important that we understand what the universe is at this time in our culture?

Joel Primack: The problem is not so much in understanding the universe as something that's out there beyond the earth, but it's a basic lack of understanding about how things really work, about the connections between the various properties of the world and ourselves. For example, if people don't have a real understanding of what science tells us and how technology works then they can't make realistic decisions, and so many of our current energy problems are based on unwillingness to face the facts in a realistic way.

The human race is entering a period during which we are going to have to make some very fundamental changes in our relationship to the world, and to navigate these changes successfully we need to understand the way the physical and biological world really works.

We have become used to the idea that the amount of resources that we use and our impact on the planet can grow indefinitely, as we've believed in the past. This idea that we can just keep going on as before is so completely out of sync with reality that people are just going to have to learn what is really going on and come to terms with it.

Another way of saying it is that these tremendous global problems that we currently face are really our negotiation with the universe, with the basic physical laws and biological laws of existence. Our problem is not so much with the other humans on Earth as it is in negotiating a proper relationship with the really big picture.

You suggest in your book that many people today are actually living according to a cosmology that is hundreds, if not thousands of years out of date. As you point out, our current ideas about the way the world works have come from a time when we lived in much smaller societies, where we did not see as big an impact on the planet as we are having now.

JP: The widespread uncertainty in the United States over fundamental issues like the energy crisis is a sign of this, since the scientific consensus on this topic has really been quite solid for some time. Yet current polls show that something like 44 percent of Americans still haven't accepted the basic validity of Darwinian evolution, and still think the entire universe is less than 10,000 years old. This seems to be symptomatic of how out of touch people are with the basic facts of science that underlie our technological world.

Do you see this as a limitation of science education or is it a lack of interaction with the universe in a meaningful way?

JP: It's both. If people haven't learned the basic facts of how the universe works and the relationship of the Earth to it, then how can they have an appreciation of their relationship to the planet and the larger universe? For that matter, how can people appreciate the relationship of different cultures and different people to each other without this basic understanding of relationships?

Obviously, science education is not so great in this country. Part of the problem is that education today is so pragmatic and really isn't taken very seriously until the college level. The American college education system is widely regarded as one of the best in the world, but our K–12 education is somewhere between awful and poor.

Now of course, the fact that the American government throughout the past decade has so thoroughly discounted science and rejected scientific findings is another reason why Americans have taken a long time to come to terms with modern science.

Nancy Abrams: But you know, just because people say that they believe in evolution does not mean that they actually do. In David Sloan Wilson's book, *Evolution for Everyone*, he explains that while many humanists believe in evolution in the abstract, when it comes to art and culture and so forth, they don't believe these activities are actually serving some kind of evolutionary goal. They think that there is something special about humans that allows them to create art, and that art has no connection to the evolutionary process.

So there's a cognitive disconnect there. A lot of people would like to believe in evolution, but they don't really know how it works, and so they're not able to apply these kinds of ideas to other parts of their lives.

You two have made the point that scientific thinking about the universe is not only socially valuable, but that it's essential for our culture right now. We really need a social consensus on the nature of the universe, so that we can come together on common ground on the problems we are currently facing as a species.

NA: It seems absolutely crazy, but our society is currently divided in coming to a shared agreement about what actually exists. In ancient societies, nobody really questioned the flat picture of the Earth. Even if they had the wrong model of what existed, they at least agreed on it in a more or less unified way. Today we don't have that common agreement about what physically exists. It's a very strange situation.

You make the point that a scientific cosmology is one way of putting a framework around the universe so that we can talk about it in a common way from a place of universal agreement. But why is cosmology so relevant to everyday life? Why would the average person need to know about their place in the universe?

NA: You might also ask the question, "Why does the average person need to have a religion?" Many people want to have some sort of deeper meaning to understand the purpose of our lives and how we spend them. The idea of a spiritual quest or a search for meaning and personal understanding is a very ancient part of what makes us human. People have a innate natural urge to learn more about themselves and to understand their place in things.

If we didn't have this drive to understand and undertake these quests for meaning we would have never made the kind of cultural progress we have made throughout the past few millennia. Now we've discovered that we cannot find answers about the larger meaning of things and our role in the world without science.

So what can science provide for people's search for meaning and their quest to understand themselves in relation to the universe? You go into great detail in your book about how humans aren't meaningless, but are central in the universe.

NA: This new picture of cosmology provides a wonderful way of looking at our meaning. It certainly isn't the only way, but it's one where large numbers of people can agree on the basic data and perspective.

JP: We find that it's very helpful to have symbols to encapsulate a lot of this information and perspective. For example, in our book we use the symbol of the ouroboros to represent all the different sizes in the universe and the reciprocal relationship between things at very large and very small scales. It's interesting that humans are right in the middle of all possible sizes, and this range is the only place where really complex things can exist.

Another example is the cosmic density pyramid, where we show that humans are made of the rarest stuff in the universe—heavy elements. Once again, this is the only kind of stuff that really complex things can be made from because of the very complicated chemistry which underlies life.

As we learn about these things we come to understand how we really fit into the universe. Now any individual's identity is really the history of that individual, so understanding the biological and the physical evolution of the universe is a way of reclaiming this very large sense of who we really are. The more of that cosmic identity that we can claim, the bigger we are.

Do you mean understanding our connection to the chain of evolution in terms of a shared common ancestry?

NA: Yes, because if you go back far enough we all have exactly the same ancestry. All the things people fight about are relatively recent and small compared to who we really are. If you can start to understands this from a much larger perspective, you can then realize the trivial nature of our differences.

And you begin to see that our differences are really very small compared with this grander perspective. We really have a much smaller

identity of who we think we are than who we really are. It also seems like you are proposing that our identity is really with the entire cosmic process up to this point.

NA: Yes, because each one of us is the result of an unbroken chain of events starting from the Big Bang. We couldn't be here without every single one of those things happening at just the right rate and in just the right order. First there had to be galaxies, then stars forming in the galaxies, and so on, and that's why we say we are really supported by the entire cosmic density pyramid. It is not just a random occurrence that we are made of the rarest material, but we're supported by this immense base of cosmic history.

Now if it's true that there are infinite other universes in a superuniverse of eternal inflation, then this universe is also incredibly lucky because it is sustaining itself long enough for fascinating things to happen. In many other universes things might not work out just right for things like us to be here.

You term it in your book as having hit the cosmic jackpot with the current universe we live in.

NA: Every living human being who is alive has hit the cosmic jackpot just by being born. Think of the probabilities. Just between your two parents, what were the probabilities that you would be the one born? Considering the number of eggs your mother had, and God knows, the number of sperm your father had, think about the probability that you would be born from all the possible combinations? Then think of the probability that they would have even met, and if you add up all the probabilities, it is phenomenally small that any one of us would have come into existence. Yet here we are.

Yes, exactly. And, how do we explain that?

NA: It's not really a question so much of explanation as appreciation. If you don't appreciate that this existence is really an incredible gift from the universe, you have not really gotten it.

JP: One quote attributed to Einstein is that, "There are only two ways to live your life. One is as though nothing is a miracle. The other is as though everything is a miracle." Einstein apparently recommended the miracle approach.

So a cosmic or reality-based perspective is important for people to understand how they fit into the universe, but it can also change their attitude toward everything they do.

Now, because humans are central and co-emergent with the universe, can either of you speculate about what humans contribute to the universe? What is it that we bring to the cosmos that is new?

JP: As far as we know, the human is the only intelligence of our kind in our part of the galaxy and perhaps our whole galaxy. Since we haven't found evidence of other advanced civilizations in our galaxy, then we might very well be the first. And the tremendous number of lucky accidents that seem to have happened in our history suggest that intelligent life may be very, very rare in this universe. So, we may very well be the consciousness in the universe, at least in our part of it.

Furthermore, if the dark energy is anything like a cosmological constant then the future of the universe is such that many parts are going to eventually become causally disconnected. Our local region of the Milky Way galaxy, the Andromeda galaxy, and all the other smaller nearby galaxies will all eventually combine together to form a giant galaxy that we sometimes call Milky-Andromeda. That will be the entire future of the visible universe far into the future. And we might be the only intelligent species in this entire region. We have no evidence that there are any other ones, so we might as well act as if we are it.

So if you look at things from this perspective, what we do in the next few years to get through this very challenging time of coming to grips with the end of exponential expansion of the impact of humans on the earth could have consequences for the entire future of the visible universe.

Wow! That's an amazing perspective on our situation, and it really highlights the importance of what we are currently facing on our planet right now.

JP: So, what difference do humans make? This is the most grandiose story that I can think of!

NA: And it has to be grandiose, because we're talking about things on the scale of the universe, which always sounds grandiose.

It is quite a poignant possibility that what we do on Earth may matter for the entire visible universe in a big way.

JP: Another point we make in the same context is with the idea of sin. Augustine introduced the idea of original sin into Christianity as a consequence of Adam and Eve disobeying God's order not to eat from the tree of knowledge of good and evil. This was the beginning of the idea that humans are all basically evil and flawed from the beginning, and therefore need the Church to correct this. Jesus's sacrifice is Augustine's answer to that.

Well, we are Jews, and the Eden story is our story, and I think Jews in general find the Christian interpretation to be completely bizarre. The really terrible sin would be to wipe us out for essentially trivial reasons. This would be the final sin.

Yes, to wipe out something so precious and rare in our cosmos as human existence.

JP: And of course, we are developing all sorts of technological ways of doing exactly that, with nuclear weapons and other weapons of mass destruction.

This is why it would be wise to cultivate this notion of final sin, that this is a really terrible thing to do and that we should not be walking in that direction.

And also not relying on something from the outside to come and rescue us. I think a lot of people hold on the unconscious belief that maybe someday aliens or God will come and rescue us from ourselves.

JP: I think that people have to understand that it is really up to us. And there is no law of physics that says we have to fail. As H.G. Wells said, "History is a race between education and catastrophe." That has never been more true than it is right now.

As the two of you share in your book, you have moved from a very existential view of the universe to one where your scientific, personal, and spiritual lives have become integrated in a harmonious, satisfying, and meaningful way. Could you talk about what has shifted for you in this journey, and what you've discovered is at the heart of a meaningful relationship with the universe?

JP: In teaching our course on Cosmology and Culture for the past decade we have been continually challenged to explain all these things to undergraduates. What we found was that instead of looking at the universe in a way that emphasizes our smallness and insignificance, if you look at things from the another perspective you find that we are made from the rarest and most complex stuff in the universe, and this makes us very special and precious. Then to see that the whole history of the universe was necessary for each of us to come into existence has really changed my attitude toward how we fit into the cosmic perspective.

NA: What I have found is that the outlook that you take on facts is a choice. It is largely determined by your own feelings of what you naturally gravitate toward. We have an incredibly important choice in the outlook we take on how we fit into the universe. Yet I would say that the vast majority of scientists who even understand this stuff do not take our outlook, but continue to see humans as small and insignificant in the big picture.

I just can't imagine why people would want to live with that outlook when it is totally unnecessary. This is really where people have to wake up. The facts are the facts. We do not have any control over them, but what do we do with them? How do we make the best that we can out of it, and how do we appreciate each other during this process? Our outlook is a choice, and what people mainly need to see is that there is another outlook besides the cynical one.

It's all about attitude, and seeing that some attitudes are really bad for the future of our species and the planet, and some of them could be incredibly constructive. So if it's a choice, why not go with the constructive one? It's so much more fun!

JP: It's like Pascal's wager. What have you got to lose?

Chapter 3

Living on a Sea of Light: An Interview With Bernard Haisch

C an science and spirituality be seen as two different, yet complementary ways of experiencing the universe? Is there an account of the
universe that can embrace both rational scientific investigation and a
spiritual worldview that includes consciousness and intelligence as fundamental aspects of the cosmos? Astrophysicist Bernard Haisch thinks so, and is not
afraid to explore the overlap between the two as he investigates some of the
most profound mysteries of cosmology today.

Dr. Bernard Haisch is an astrophysicist and the author of more than 130
scientific publications. He has been principal investigator on several NASA
research projects, and has served as deputy director of the Center for
Extreme Ultraviolet Astrophysics at the University of California, Berkeley, as
well as being a staff scientist at the Lockheed Martin Solar and Astrophysics
Laboratory. For more than a decade he was a scientific editor for the Astrophysical Journal and has also been editor in chief of the Journal of Scientific
Exploration.

Dr. Haisch's research has focused on solar-stellar astrophysics and stochastic electrodynamics, developing (along with Alfonso Rueda) a theory proposing that the electromagnetic quantum vacuum—the zero-point field—might provide a physical explanation for the origin of inertia.

Long interested in the relationship between science and religion, Haisch studied for the priesthood at the St. Meinrad Seminary prior to his career in science. His book, *The God Theory*, explores the mysterious connections between God, light, and the universe.

Stephan Martin: Your long and impressive scientific career has been focused on very traditional scientific disciplines such as physics and astrophysics, yet you've made some surprising discoveries that seem to have deep metaphysical or even spiritual implications for our understanding of the universe. Can you say a little about these discoveries and some of their implications?

Bernard Haisch: I've been doing mainstream astrophysical research for the past 20 years, researching x-ray emission from stars, the occurrence of flares on stars, and sometimes solar behavior. I was publishing in the prominent mainstream journals and also serving as one of the scientific editors of the *Astrophysical Journal*. It was pretty interesting science, but nothing that would win me any Nobel prizes, put it that way.

Then in the early 1990s I got involved with zero-point energy research, and published a paper in 1994 with Alfonso Rueda and Hal Puthoff, in which we proposed to have found a possible origin for the inertia of matter. I thought at the time that it would be really important, since there's been a long-standing question about where mass and inertia comes from. It's usually attributed to the Higgs field, and here we had a completely new and different approach to the origin of inertia.

We published our findings in the world's leading physics journal, the *Physical Review*, and received coverage in *Science* magazine as well as *Scientific American* and other magazines and newspapers in the popular press. But it was pretty much ignored in the physics community and no one else followed up on our work. We received a grant from NASA to continue our research, and this took me into the investigation of the quantum vacuum, also known as the electromagnetic zero-point field.

This research has been somewhat controversial, both because of the scientific implications of our research, but also because the concept of the zero-point field and zero-point energy has been usurped by many people who claim it's everything from a near-endless source of energy to the nature of God. It's not God [laughs], but it's a very interesting field of research nonetheless.

Yet this zero-point field is an actual phenomenon that exists everywhere.

It is, and it has measurable effects that come right out of the Heisenberg Uncertainty Principle. For example, the reason you can't freeze helium under normal pressures is because zero-point energy prevents it from solidifying at absolute zero. Yet the zero-point energy is not generally considered to be totally real, because, if it exists, it's predicted to contain enormous amounts of energy, enough to have completely blown up the universe early in its history.

Because it has anti-gravitational effects, it's also the perfect candidate for dark energy, except that there's way, way too much of it! So it's still a huge mystery about what it is exactly.

Still, it seems to have definite effects on everyday life. For example, you and Rueda derived Newton's Law of Inertia from it.

Indeed, it's interesting that inertia might be traced back to electromagnetism, which is very important because it's the basis of most of our technology. It implies that there may be a way to control inertia and gravitation, and that's really exciting!

Oh sure, not just for propulsion devices, but for energy sources and all sorts of other things! You mention in your book that the implications of this can change the way we see the world, particularly when you discuss matter as floating on a sea of light. It really challenges our concepts on what matter and energy really are.

Yes, it takes the emphasis away from matter as the fundamental stuff of the universe and points elsewhere.

Elsewhere being this sea of electromagnetic energy or light. That brings some interesting parallels with many of the world's spiritual traditions, which teach that the universe we see and experience all arises out of light.

The idea that light is at the origin of creation is a common theme throughout the religious traditions. In the Kabbalah, for example, creation is described as being brought about when a space of some sort is evacuated within an intelligence, variously described as God, the Godhead, Ein Sof, and so on.... Light then enters into this void and through that a series of worlds is created, one of which ends up being our universe.

These ideas are certainly part of the esoteric traditions of the world, and the most I can say is that things are pointing in that direction when we look at the possible role of the zero-point field in providing mass for matter. This is of course a very speculative thing to say, and it is by no means proven, but it suggests some interesting connections between fundamental physics and metaphysics.

You've also talked about the possibility of bringing science and spirituality together, not so much for proving each other, but as complementary approaches to discovery.

Yes, that's right. What I'm hoping is that it may become more respectable and possible to expand the techniques and the analytical tools and the frontiers of science to include things that right now lie outside the borders of mainstream science, and to reach out to some of the concepts within the metaphysical perspective of reality and existence.

I think it's something that's coming because clearly if there's any reality to the metaphysical perspective then we'll eventually wind up exploring it. But I think that will require a change, not just in enlarging the domain of science, but in the tools and the techniques that are considered valid for exploration. More importantly, it may involve an expansion of our concepts of what reality may consist of.

Do you have any ideas about the kinds of expansion that may be needed within science?

One thing would be to stop ignoring the reports of the mystics about their experiences of reality. For example, mystical traditions around the world describe a oneness that can be experienced, the unification of our essence with the intelligence that's behind it all. Because this is a recurrent theme, we might look at it not just on the basis of religious merit, but as something that we can scientifically analyze and recognize as worth studying. Opening ourselves to that kind of exploration and taking that kind of circumstantial evidence seriously might point to some new developments in physics as well.

In a sense the insights of the mystics might be considered a kind of scientific data about what we're talking about when we talk about the universe and reality. What I find intriguing, however, is that science and spirituality continue to view the universe so differently. It's almost as if they're living in different universes!

In a sense that's almost literally true. The spiritual or mystical traditions point to more than the physical universe as making up reality. They sometimes point to a hierarchy of realms along with a hierarchy of intelligences associated with those realms, with ourselves occupying the lowest one, often described as the densest one (whatever that means). There may be other worlds that are not investigated or even taken seriously by science, but that nevertheless have a role to play in the totality of things within the metaphysical traditions.

Now it's interesting that with string theory, there's the necessity of having additional dimensions, and even other realms or universes. There's talk of other brane universes which exist in what they call "the bulk," with universes even colliding and that sort of thing. Even though these concepts are not ones that I take all that seriously scientifically, since there's no evidence so far that string theory's correct, they still point to the idea within mainstream science of other realms of existence that have been previously viewed as pure science fiction.

I can think of another example with quantum inflation cosmology, with the entire universe arising as a quantum event. What happened before this event or outside the creation of time and space is also very speculative.

It is, and it's based on the assumption that a quantum fluctuation could arise as the original source. It seems to me that you still need a prime cause, and in this case you still need a preexisting quantum law to allow for the quantum fluctuation to arise in the first place, so where did the law come from? I don't think you can start with absolutely nothing and then get something. I think the critique that invoking an intelligence behind it all as unnecessary is not true, because you still need a quantum law or a pre-existing field to give rise to the fluctuations. I think Aristotle was basically on the right track when he said that we need a prime cause.

You describe the prime cause in your book as some kind of vast intelligence and consciousness, what we might call God.

Exactly, and there's evidence for that because if we look at the fine-tuning of the physical laws and the constants of nature in the universe, their precision taken all together is quite striking. It's a serious problem within astrophysics to explain this, and scientists who don't take the perspective that I do have to find ways to explain this differently. But we still have to take seriously the problem of why we live in an apparently finely tuned universe. It's a mystery.

Yes, how is it that we're here to have this conversation given all the parameters involved?

All parameters that could have been a lot different, for all we know.

Now when you propose this vast intelligence behind all things in your book, you are very careful to distinguish it from intelligent design. I wonder if you could distinguish your approach from that of intelligent design.

In intelligent design you're looking at the micro-engineering of life forms, saying that there's a tweaking of evolution by an intelligence or even a design of creatures by an intelligence. I don't think that's the case. In fact, I would say that in the case of the God Theory, you want to have Darwinian evolution or something similar because it's all about novelty.

What you don't want is an intelligence that is cookie-cutter stamping out creatures to walk on a stage called Earth and acting out something that's pre-ordained—what fun would that be? It would be like writing a play and having actors come out and read their parts, rather than creating a world and letting things happen. I think the novelty that is inherent in evolution would be an essential part of the plan of the intelligence that's behind the universe.

Another distinguishing characteristic between your approach and intelligent design is that some people feel that intelligent design places God outside the universe, as a controller of what happens, but removed from it.

That perspective doesn't make much sense to me because why would a deity do such a thing? I think the deity interested in experiencing its potential, and creating an environment where that potential arises naturally as much as possible, is a much more rational and sensible motivation than a predetermined approach.

It also seems to be a much more intimate and participatory concept of the divine that you're suggesting.

This is also the kind of thing that is supported by the accounts of the mystics, who are searching for God and searching for unity with God, and what they find when they have the transcendent experience is that there is nothing else but God, that there is no outside God. They would experience, as you and I would if we were in that mystical state, that "I am God! I've been looking for myself, and here I am!" So here is evidence that what we are is God experiencing the physical realm.

Another concept that you touched on before that you explore further in your book is the concept of novelty. Many people, including physicists, have speculated on the origins of novelty and creativity, and have begun to conclude that our universe is fundamentally creative at its foundations.

I think so, because if the universe is the creation of an intelligence that seeks novelty, then the characteristics and attributes of that intelligence will be the ones we'll find in the product itself. So if we are creative, then that's not surprising if we are individualized incarnations of a God who is also creative, since that's what we are. Since we share in the same nature as the divine, how could we be anything but creative?

I wonder if you have any thoughts on the relationship between creativity and the zero-point field.

I don't really know. I'm really torn there because on the one hand I want to be conservative and say that the zero-point field is a sea of virtual photons that arises out of quantum effects. We know that much. On the other hand, it's interesting to speculate further about whether this has some connection with references in the esoteric traditions about light, and maybe light is characteristic of God and so on, but this is purely speculative at this point. I don't see any direct connection between the zero-point field and creativity, because I see creativity as the expression of this underlying intelligence. The only thing I know for certain about the zero-point field is that it's a photon field and we don't generally think of photons as being creative. If everything is the product of consciousness, which I believe it is, then even a photon is conscious in some sense, although I doubt that they are aware of themselves.

So I wonder if photons are not by themselves creative but are instead the elements of creativity, being arranged in creative ways throughout the universe. Do you think it's possible to speculate on some of the properties of the zero-point field, such as creativity or intelligence? You mention in your book a relationship between the zero-point field and universal timekeeping.

That connection was drawn by astrophysicist Sir William McCrae, who asked the question, "What makes things happen?" in a lecture for the Royal Astronomical Society. This is a very good question. We know, for example, that radioactive materials decay. Imagine an atom of uranium, sitting there for a billion years and suddenly it decides to decay. Well, what makes it finally happen? Something nudges it, and I suspect along with McCrae that somehow the zero-point fluctuations are the thing that push time along and make things happen. It's a very interesting concept that you need something to make physical processes go.

Right, and we perceive them as happening in a particular sequence of development.

Yes, and what makes them happen at all? What finally tells a particle when it's time to decay?

So maybe that's where the idea of a universal pattern in the zero-point field may come in. Maybe there are patterns even below the level of the zero-point field that get expressed through it.

It actually gets even more specific than that. For example, if you look at the excitation and de-excitation of electrons in an atom, there are coefficients called Einstein coefficients that determine what the rate of excitation or decay is for a particular process. There are two processes that cause emission of a photon from an atom: spontaneous emission, due to an electron changing orbital states, and stimulated emission, where an electromagnetic radiation field (such as in a laser) "pushes" atoms to de-excite and emit photons. Now spontaneous emission can be seen theoretically as being stimulated by the zero-point field of the vacuum. So the zero-point field can serve as the vacuum counterpoint to the process that causes stimulated emission.

So the zero-point field is really the source of whether or not an atom decides to emit a photon.

That's exactly right, it serves as a timekeeper.

I can see that we're in the very early stages of understanding what the zero-point field truly is and what its possible properties might be. In conclusion, are there any experiments or recent developments in your research that you'd like to share?

A colleague and I have been issued a patent and are carrying out a zero-point energy detection experiment to see whether it's possible to tap into zero-point energy. We just got funding but haven't seen any positive results yet, so maybe a few years from now we'll be able to determine if the zero-point energy is tappable, which would, of course, have profound and revolutionary implications for our planetary technology. It's way too early to say whether it's possible at this point, but it's an exciting idea.

Chapter 4

Life, Intelligence, and the Emerging Mind of the Cosmos: An Interview With James Gardner

Are life and intelligence in the universe the product of random evolutionary processes, or are they inevitable? Did the universe in some sense know we were coming, or are we, as Stephen Jay Gould suggested, "the accidental result of an unplanned process"? James Gardner explores a third possibility in his work, one that balances the apparent fine-tuning of the constants of nature toward life (known as the anthropic principle) with the role that random variation and natural selection play in evolutionary processes on all scales. And as we will see, it's in between these two extremes that we discover some very interesting possibilities...

James Gardner is a complexity theorist who specializes in the evolutionary dynamics of the universe. His first two books, *Biocosm: Intelligent Life Is the Architect of the Universe* and *The Intelligent Universe: AI, ET, and the Emerging Mind of the Cosmos* explore an innovative approach to cosmology called the Selfish Biocosm hypothesis, which seeks to answer the question of why our universe is so finely tuned toward the existence of intelligent life. A widely published theorist, his work has appeared in *Complexity*,

Acta Astronautica, The Journal of the British Interplanetary Society, The International Journal of Astrobiology, and others. Gardner is also a practicing lawyer and a former Oregon state senator.

Stephan Martin: One idea that is central to your work is that life and intelligence are not meaningless accidents in an unfriendly and lifeless cosmos, but are deeply woven into its foundations. Could you say more about this and the role that life and intelligence play in the evolution of the universe?

James Gardner: Yes. Please bear with me because this will get a little complicated. At least it will sound complicated at first. After you get used to it, my central hypothesis—which I call the Selfish Biocosm hypothesis—is actually quite simple and straightforward.

The best way to answer your question is to give you a little history about how I first developed the hypothesis. I began developing the Selfish Biocosm hypothesis as an attempt to supply two essential elements missing from a novel model of cosmological evolution put forward by astrophysicist Lee Smolin. Smolin had come up with the intriguing suggestion that black holes are gateways to new "baby universes" and that a kind of Darwinian population dynamic rewards those universes most adept at producing black holes with the greatest number of progeny.

Proliferating populations of baby universes emerging from the loins (metaphorically speaking) of black hole–rich "mother universes" thus come to dominate the total population of the "multiverse"—a theoretical ensemble of all mother and baby universes. Black hole–prone universes also happen to coincidentally exhibit anthropic qualities, according to Smolin, thus accounting for the bio-friendly nature of the "average" cosmos in the ensemble, more or less as an incidental side-effect.

This was a thrilling conjecture, because for the first time it posited a cosmic evolutionary process endowed with what economists call a utility function (that is, a value that was maximized by the hypothesized evolutionary process, which in the case of Smolin's conjecture was black hole maximization). However, Smolin's approach was seriously flawed. As the computer genius John von Neumann demonstrated in a famous 1948 Caltech lecture entitled "On the General and Logical Theory of Automata," any self-reproducing object (mouse, bacterium, human, or baby universe) must, as a matter of inexorable logic, possess four essential elements:

1. A *blueprint*, providing the plan for construction of offspring.
2. A *factory*, to carry out the construction.
3. A *controller*, to ensure that the factory follows the plan.
4. A *duplicating machine*, to transmit a copy of the blueprint to the offspring.

In the case of Smolin's hypothesis, one could logically equate the collection of physical laws and constants that prevail in our universe with a von Neumann blueprint and the universe at large with a kind of enormous von Neumann factory. But what could possibly serve as a von Neumann controller or a von Neumann duplicating machine? My goal was to rescue Smolin's basic innovation—a cosmic evolutionary model that incorporated a discernible utility function—by proposing scientifically plausible candidates for the two missing von Neumann elements.

Very interesting. The four elements that you list are very much like a cybernetic version of many of the commonly agreed criteria among biologists for defining life. Do you think this is significant? Does the universe as a whole necessarily share the characteristics of its component parts?

Yes, this is extremely significant. And yes, I think the universe necessarily exhibits the basic characteristics of its components. One of the striking features of terrestrial evolution is the pervasiveness of evolutionary convergence. The same solutions to common challenges, such as morphological streamlining to permit rapid transit through water, appear repeatedly in unrelated species. Why? Because the laws of physics impose severe constraints on how an animal's body can be shaped so as to optimize the speed of transit through a high-resistance medium like water. Likewise, the essential elements of self-reproduction identified by von Neumann are, so far as we know, universal. Any replicator that reproduces itself must, as a matter of pure logic, possess the four von Neumann elements. Note that this is not true if the process we are talking about is not true self-reproduction, characterized by what Darwin called "inheritance" of traits, but is rather a chaotic generation of new entities possessing a random assortment of traits, such as the hypothesized process of eternal chaotic cosmic inflation that Andrei Linde talks about. No "memory" or heredity principle is needed to guide the process of eternal chaotic inflation.

How did you come up with the idea that life and intelligence might serve as the missing von Neumann elements in the process of cosmic reproduction?

The hypothesis I developed was based on a set of conjectures put forward by Martin Rees, John Wheeler, Freeman Dyson, John Barrow, Frank Tipler, and Ray Kurzweil. Their futuristic visions suggested collectively that the ongoing process of biological and technological evolution was sufficiently robust, powerful, and open-ended, so that, in the very distant future, a cosmologically extended biosphere could conceivably exert a global influence on the physical state of the entire cosmos. Think of this idea as the Gaia principle extended universe-wide.

A synthesis of these insights lead me directly to the central claim of the Selfish Biocosm hypothesis: that the ongoing process of biological and technological emergence, governed by still largely unknown laws of complexity, could function as a von Neumann controller and that a cosmologically extended biosphere could serve as a von Neumann duplicating machine in a conjectured process of cosmological replication.

It reminds me in some ways of a cosmic-scale Dyson sphere! I wonder if some of these unknown laws of complexity might be emergent organizational properties of the universe that emerge on large scales. Does the Selfish Biocosm hypothesis speculate on or predict any of these laws or feedback loops that might exist as part of this process?

The Dyson sphere is a great analogy. Yes, I believe there will be emergent properties of a self-organizing cosmos that will appear at future thresholds in the process of cosmic ontogeny. I obviously can't predict precisely what those properties will be since they are emergent, and, thus, by definition, inaccessible to us in any detailed way. However, in a very broad sense, I can predict that, if my hypothesis is correct, the universe will literally come to life. It will eventually experience a transformation from a largely inanimate pile of dead matter into a vast cosmic mind. You can think of this end-state of the cosmos as a universe-wide AI as powerful as the laws of physics will allow.

Can you say a little more about the process of cosmic reproduction that you hypothesize and specifically the role that life-friendly physical laws and constants play in this process?

I have speculated that the means by which the hypothesized cosmological replication process could occur is through the fabrication of baby universes by highly evolved intelligent life forms. These hypothesized baby universes would themselves be endowed with a cosmic code—an ensemble of physical laws and constants—that would be life-friendly so as to enable life and ever more competent intelligence to emerge and eventually to repeat the cosmic reproduction cycle. Under this scenario, the physical laws and constants serve a cosmic function precisely analogous to that of DNA in earthly creatures: they furnish a recipe for the birth and evolution of intelligent life, and a blueprint, which provides the plan for construction of offspring.

This is fascinating. It sounds as though the blueprint for life is woven into the physical constants of nature, waiting for the right cosmic conditions for its emergence.

Precisely so. To paraphrase Paul Davies, my view is that the laws of the universe are cunningly contrived to coax life and intelligence into being against the raw odds. This means that life and intelligence are cosmic imperatives rather than improbable accidents. It means that the laws of physics have almost miraculously engineered their own comprehension through the medium of our human minds (and through more powerful minds soon to appear in the form of artificial intelligences). It means that the emergence of life and intelligence was written into the cosmic playbook from the very first moment of the Big Bang. And it means that life was destined, from that very first moment, to ultimately dominate the universe, to infuse it with massive intelligence, and ultimately to serve as the instrument of cosmic reproduction.

So in this view the universe is not simply anthropocentric, that is, friendly to humans, but biocentric, friendly to life itself. Can you say more? Is life inevitable in the universe?

Under my scenario, the cosmos is not anthropocentric at all. It is biocentric. Is life inevitable in the universe? Perhaps it's not strictly inevitable, although it is highly probable. There could conceivably be the equivalent of a birth defect in the cosmic reproduction cycle—some failure to transmit accurately the cosmic DNA from mother to baby universe—and one of the baby universes could be still-born.

Some researchers and philosophers have suggested that if our cosmos is patterned and embedded with the constants of nature then perhaps there is a metacosmos that is the larger context and source of this pattern. Any thoughts or speculation on this? Could this "superspace" be the mechanism by which the cosmic DNA is passed on from universe to universe?

There is a lot of speculation about this by the string theory and M-theory cosmology crowd. I agree with the critics of this approach. The string theory cosmologists seek to "explain" the bio-friendliness of the laws and constants of physics that we observe by postulating the existence of a vast so-called "landscape" of vacuua—vacuua correspond to pocket universes in the multiverse supposedly generated by eternal inflation—one of which "just happens" to be bio-friendly. This approach is unscientific in the extreme because there is no possibility in principle of falsifying the explanation. It's not even decent metaphysics. It's just hoisting a white flag of surrender in the face of a daunting mystery. And surrender is not an option for those of us who wish to think seriously about the nature of the universe. We are obliged to step forward with serious hypotheses that, while possibly radical, are falsifiable.

That's not what the string theory cosmology crowd is doing. They are saying that the best we can do is to assume that we happen to inhabit, purely by chance, an obscure and out-of-the-way valley in the string theory landscape that happens, for no reason that science can fathom, to be life-friendly. This is a restatement, in fashionable string theory terminology, of the purely tautological weak anthropic principle, which most serious scientists despise as a non-explanation. In my view, the string theory cosmologists have simply given up the fight for a predictive, explanatory, and falsifiable hypothesis. That's just plain wrong. And it is unscientific in the extreme. The necessity to search tirelessly for falsifiable hypotheses that actually explain profound observational mysteries should remain the fundamental credo of science.

That being said, I do think that the core notion of eternal inflation—that there is a basic process by which new universes sprout off continuously and eternally from "mother" universes and create a multiverse ensemble—is totally congruent with my hypothesis. Where I part company with the string theory cosmology crowd is their insistence that eternal inflation plus the weak anthropic principle offers a scientifically satisfying explanation for the life-friendly aspects of our cosmos.

If the universe is evolving through various stages of evolution, what do you see as emergent and new in the cosmos at this stage in its evolution?

Collective intelligence—what some have called a hive mind—and true general artificial intelligence. Like my friend Ray Kurzweil, I believe the so-called Singularity—the moment when AI begins to progress exponentially beyond our human intellectual capabilities—may be just around the corner (meaning no more than half a century away). In fact, the eventual emergence of the Singularity is one of the falsifiable implications of my hypothesis.

Collective intelligence in many cases leads to collective levels of higher organization and complexity. Do you see life as transcending biology at the Singularity point, as Kurzweil does? Is the merging of the animate and the inanimate in some way the next stage of evolution for both? Do you see life, intelligence, and technology as seamlessly merging together at some future point?

I totally agree with Ray Kurzweil that evolution is headed toward what he and others call the Singularity. Indeed, the eventual emergence of transhuman intelligence is a key falsifiable implication of the Selfish Biocosm hypothesis. The emergence of artificial general intelligence will be the next stage of terrestrial macro-evolution. It will be the means by which life will acquire the ability to transcend the limits that biology has placed on our human intelligence. It will be the next stage of the growth and spread of intelligence in our corner of the cosmos.

As to the eventual merger of the animate and the inanimate—of life, intelligence, and technology—yes, I think that is coming. Indeed, I think that the best way to think about life, intelligence, and the universe is that they are not separate things, but are rather different aspects of a single phenomenon. To take liberties with a popular ballad, "We are the world, we are the people, *and* we are the universe." To state the proposition from the opposite perspective, the universe is coming to life and waking up through the processes of our lives and thoughts, and, very probably, through the lives and thoughts of countless other intelligent beings scattered throughout the cosmos.

What is the universe aiming at, if it's directed toward greater levels of intelligence and life? Is there a final goal or purpose for the cosmos that we are all participating in? What is the functional role of humans for the universe?

This may be a kind of anthropomorphic way of putting it, but here goes. I think the universe is trying to come to life so that it can reproduce itself. Cosmic replication is the cosmic utility function. Why is it trying to do this? Because replication is what replicators strive to do. The idea is very much like that of Richard Dawkins's concept of the selfish gene. The functional role of human beings in this process is to participate in it in much the same manner that the cellular organelles called mitochondria participate in the life of a cell, in the life of a multicellular creature, and ultimately in the grand spectacle of terrestrial evolution, which I postulate is merely a minor subroutine in an overarching process of cosmic ontogeny. Human beings are part of what can be thought of as a vast cosmic community—or a cosmic ecosystem if you like—that is coaxing the still largely inanimate universe into pervasive life.

It's a wonderful idea that we may be the midwives of the future evolution of the universe. Do you see a breakpoint in complexity, which the universe in the future springs fully to life? Many biologists, for example, place the living complexity threshold at bacteria. Do you see a living threshold for the universe on a cosmic scale?

Under my hypothesis, there must exist a threshold at which the cosmos has become sufficiently alive and self-aware and sufficiently intelligent to reproduce itself. It is unclear to me how distant in the future that point might be. Conceivably it is not that far away. One of the amazing things I discovered when I was doing the research for my second book (*The Intelligent Universe*) was that a Japanese research team was already planning to attempt to create a baby universe in the lab. As outlined in a recent scientific paper published in the prestigious scientific journal *Physics Review D* entitled "Is it possible to create a universe out of a monopole in the laboratory?" the team contends that it is possible to create a new inflationary universe out of a stable subatomic particle in the laboratory by inflating a theorized but never-yet-observed elementary particle called a magnetic monopole. Astonishingly, the team is now designing an actual experiment that will attempt to do precisely that. If the Japanese experiment succeeds (which is obviously a long shot), then a central and highly controversial implication of the Selfish Biocosm hypothesis will have been validated. Amazingly, this would constitute laboratory proof of one of the central claims of the hypothesis—that life and intelligence (in the form of the Japanese research team) can develop the capacity to mediate the fabrication of a new baby universe. But even if the Japanese experiment succeeds, we will still be very far from acquiring the capacity to actually engineer the laws and constants of the newly created universe to ensure its life-friendliness.

Current cosmological models predict that the universe may end in one of two ways: fire, a Big Crunch in which gravity condenses the contents of the universe back into a primordial state; or ice, the endless expansion and cooling of the universe into oblivion. But you suggest a third possibility: that the universe might end in intelligent life. Can you say more about this third possibility that you propose?

This is the essence of the Selfish Biocosm hypothesis—that intelligent life plays an essential role in the process of cosmic reproduction, of baby universe proliferation. This explains, in a rather parsimonious manner, what otherwise seems to be an impenetrable mystery—the odd and improbable bio-friendliness of the laws and constants of physics. If intelligent life is, in effect, the reproductive organ of the universe, then it is entirely logical and predictable that the laws and constants of nature should be rigged in favor of the emergence of ever more capable intelligence. Indeed, the existence of such a propensity is a falsifiable retrodiction of the hypothesis.

I find this vision of our cosmic role to be tremendously inspiring and empowering. Not only are we essential elements in the ecology of the universe, but your Selfish Biocosm hypothesis gives us a shaping and participatory role in cosmic evolution. Instead of being passive passengers on a cosmic journey, it seems you're suggesting that we (and other forms of life) have the potential to direct that journey to a much larger extent than we previously thought possible.

Many people have told me that they find my two books—*BIOCOSM* and *The Intelligent Universe*—to be profoundly optimistic. That comment always warms my heart. Martin Luther King once said something that I really agree with. He said, "The arc of the universe is long, but it bends toward justice." I would add that the long arc of the universe also bends toward progress (both technological and cultural), toward cooperation, toward interdependence, and toward a profound respect for all life and intelligence, both here on Earth and wherever else it may exist in the vast cosmos.

The essence of my cosmological vision is that we inhabit a cosmos that is a kind of ecosystem-in-waiting—a universe custom-made for the purpose of yielding life and ever-ascending intelligence. Central to this idea is the notion that every creature and every intelligent entity—great and small, biological and post-biological—plays some indefinable role in an awesome process by which intelligence gains hegemony over inanimate nature. This notion implies that every living thing and every post-biological form of intelligence is linked together in a joint endeavor of vast scope and indefinable duration. We soldier on together—bacteria, people, extraterrestrials (if they exist), and hyper-intelligent computers—pressing forward, against all odds and the implacable foe that is entropy, toward a distant future we can only faintly imagine. We are the builders, we are the ancestors, we are the co-creators of that vast cosmic life and mind of the future. But it is together, in a spirit of cooperation and kinship, that we journey hopefully toward our distant destination.

That's why I am an optimist.

Amazing. It's a incredibly powerful vision that you're offering about the universe and our cosmic role and destiny in it. Thank you for sharing it here.

Chapter 5

The Quantum Universe: An Interview With Fred Alan Wolf

Photons in two places at once, electrons tunneling through solid matter, particles traveling backward through time, Schrodinger's cat, quantum entanglement...the list of intriguing results and enigma from quantum physics goes on and on. For more than a hundred years, physicists have been puzzled, fascinated, frustrated, and amazed by the unexpected results that quantum physics predicts about the nature of the world we live in. But as physicist Richard Feynman famously said, "...the paradox is only a conflict between reality and your feeling of what reality ought to be." Perhaps the reality is that the universe is much stranger than we think...

Dr. Fred Alan Wolf is a physicist, author, and lecturer who specializes in the relationship between the new physics and consciousness. He received his PhD in theoretical physics in 1963 from UCLA where he researched high-atmospheric particle behavior following nuclear explosions. He has since conducted and contributed to research in quantum physics, psychology, physiology, and consciousness studies. He has taught at the University of Paris, the Hebrew University of Jerusalem, the University of London, Birkbeck College, and most recently, San Diego State University.

A dynamic and engaging speaker, Dr. Wolf has taught and lectured around the world explaining the mysteries of quantum physics and consciousness in a way accessible to diverse audiences. Sometimes known as "Dr. Quantum," he has appeared on many radio and television shows and documentaries, including *What the Bleep Do We Know!?*, *Dalai Lama Renaissance*, the PBS series *Closer to Truth*, and many others. He frequently consults as a technical physicist for the media and industry.

He is the author of more than 14 books, cds, and many technical and popular-level papers and articles. His books include *Taking the Quantum Leap* (which won the National Book Award), *Mind and the New Physics*, *The Dreaming Universe*, and the *Yoga of Time Travel*.

Stephan Martin: You've spent your life researching, writing about, and teaching quantum physics, which has revealed some very strange things about the world we live in. Can you share with us some things you've discovered about the universe that aren't generally well-known and appreciated?

Fred Alan Wolf: There are some interesting things that have come to light in quantum physics during the past hundred years or so. To give an example, one thing we've discovered is that when you're trying to represent the way an object such as a particle moves, you have to represent it in terms of waves. This is one of the first paradoxes that quantum physics puts into the mix: even though a particle seems to have a definite position and a definite location in space and time, when it's not being observed, it acts very strangely, like a field of waves spread out over all space and time out to infinity. I know this sounds crazy, but that's how all particles behave!

Another bizarre effect shows up when you try to combine quantum theory with Einstein's theory of relativity. Einstein's theory of relativity says that nothing can go faster than the speed of light—no particle, no wave, no physical process at all. Now when you try to combine relativity with quantum physics, particles turn out to have both positive and negative energies. Since we've never observed particles with negative energy and we're not even sure what that means, let's assume that particles can't have negative energy and see what emerges from our theory with this restriction.

What emerges is quantum field theory, anti-matter, and particles that can go backward in time! All of these things have been experimentally verified. So by trying to restrict our theories about the universe so that things make more sense, what emerges is something even more amazing and seemingly more nonsensical. You see, if you only allow particles with positive energy in your theory then you must also allow particles to go faster than light. But faster-than-light particles are really weird: they're called tachyons and they have very strange properties.

For example, we assume that two events in our universe that someone observes simultaneously will be seen to happen in a particular order, and say that A follows B by an observer moving to the left of the first observer. But accordingly relativity, someone who is moving to the right of the first observer to you would see the whole sequence happening in reverse order: B happening before A. It's as if time is going forward for one, but backward for another. So what we find with relativity is that there is no universal time order for events that some could observe simultaneously: observers moving at different speeds don't necessarily agree on the order that such things happen. Now when you combine both quantum physics and relativity, you get the prediction that not everything has to travel slower than light—some particles can actually travel faster than light, and this shows up as I said above, as if they were traveling backward in time. A particle going backward in time acts like anti-matter, going forward in time, but with the opposite charge. So what we call anti-matter may simply be particles of the same mass and charge going faster than light!

Suddenly, by putting a few restrictions on our theories to try to find out what kind of universe we live in, all of Pandora's Box bursts open, and all this remarkable fantastic craziness comes out! I think this is really the universe at play.

Physics is really a set of rules that physicists have come up as restrictions on the way nature has to behave, and whenever they try to restrict it, instead of calming things down and making things more possible, sometimes very impossible or very amazing counter-intuitive things come popping out.

It sounds as though the universe does not want to be put into a box.

I would say that is a very strong statement and one that is definitely true. The universe does not exist in a box, and any arguments made that try to restrict it to a box turn out to be false!

There are many examples today of where physicists still fall into this trap of thinking the universe is a box. For example, everybody says that there was a Big Bang, and since the law of entropy predicts that things will degrade and run down over time, the universe must have started out in a state of high order.

But that's rubbish! It's an argument based upon a closed box system. If the universe were in a closed box that would be true, but it's not in a closed box.

I think the whole argument has got its tail on its head. I don't think the universe started out in a state of high order—it started out in a state of extreme chaos! That's what everything starting out with an explosion like the Big Bang means to me—it starts with chaos, and then becomes more ordered over time. The majority of physicists don't look at it that way, and I don't agree with them. How do you explain atoms appearing? How do you explain stars, planets, solar systems, and highly ordered galaxies emerging? If you exploded a box with all the elements in it, how long would you have to wait before the box turned into Fred Alan Wolf? It just doesn't happen in a box universe, so there must be something else going on.

That something else isn't usually taken into account in physics, something which is called intelligence, or the universal Mind. The concept of these things in physics is simply not looked at, because it's too difficult to deal with, it's too subjective. One physicist named Hugh Everett III tried to make a theory out of this in the 1950s, but at the time it was severely put down by other physicists and led him into a severe depression. But these days his ideas about parallel universes have re-emerged, and it's the big theory today.

I think that consciousness and Mind are very much a part of quantum physics and that this universal mind has an ordering effect on the cosmic. It's not necessary to have things only going from past into future, but there may also be another field going from future into past, which is ordering the present. When God speaks, He doesn't speak from the present, He speaks from the future.

Is Mind or consciousness the ordering principle you're talking about here?

Yes. There must be, in my opinion, an ordering principle for the universe, because what Mind does is to take chaos and turn it into order. That's what the mind does—it orders the universe. It's Mind's only function, really.

Many interpretations of quantum mechanics strongly suggest that Mind or consciousness is an inseparable part of the universe.

I think it's definitely something that must be included. There must be some way in which a spectrum of possibilities gets whittled down into a simple number of actual events. From a plethora to a single number, from the many to the one, it's not something that goes in the direction of chaos, but it goes in the direction of order. Order is the whittling down from all possibilities into one.

And consciousness is the central ordering element that allows this whittling down from a multitude of possibilities to a single event to happen. Now you've also written about there being only one Mind in the universe. We may think we have individual minds, but are all these reflections of this single Mind?

Yes, and that's something that's very difficult to explain to people. People ask me constantly what the one Mind is and I find it very challenging to explain because it's something that is very foreign to us. Explaining unity is the most difficult thing anybody can do, because unity is something that is indescribable: you need duality to explain unity. That's what makes it so difficult.

There are some good arguments from quantum physics which suggest that there has to be one Mind in the universe in order that multiple observers could have common and similar experiences. Individual minds, or the appearance of what appear to be individual minds, can be explained as projections from this one Mind. There cannot be a separate compartment somewhere issuing statements that my mind is separate from yours. My brain may be separate from yours, but my mind isn't.

Yet if we are all facets of a single Mind, we continue to act as separate entities. For example, we each apparently have free will, or at least we would like to think so.

If there are individuals acting in a way that appears to be free will, does that contradict there being only one Mind? I don't think it does. That may simply be how the Mind works. A brain has individual neurons and one neuron is not doing the same thing as another, so I don't see why the Mind reflecting and bouncing around within individual brains cannot have unique signatures in which people are doing unique things.

Now a large majority of people on the planet do not behave as if they had individual minds. They are what is called brain-washed, whether by their leaders or the media, so it's something we should all be aware of, whatever culture we live in.

One thing you've written and spoken about is how training the mind or developing some sort of focused intention can have a dramatic effect, not only in terms of our thinking, but maybe in shaping reality itself. In the quantum world, for example, intention seems to change the evolution of a quantum state.

Yes, what's been demonstrated in a number of experiments is that there is something equivalent to what I would call intent acting in the world. Experiments show that by making selective observations in a certain way, we can steer the evolution of a system in a direction, which by its own devices it would not go.

I often use the example of the quantum-watched pot, referring to the saying, "A watched pot never boils." If there are quantum atoms that are bathed in radio energy, and they're observed while bathing in that radio energy, then it's possible to observe them in such a way that they never get a chance to absorb any of that energy. So you can alter the formation of the absorption spectrum of a group of atoms simply by watching them. This has been demonstrated a number of times with beryllium at the National Institute of Standards and Technology in Colorado.

Now of course when you're doing experiments like this, we're dealing with very small numbers of atoms under specific conditions. To extend these results into human behavior might be too big a jump, but I think it provides a good lesson in learning how to learn from our experience. For example, if we're learning to do a task, vigilant observation of ourselves may reveal things we're doing wrong so we won't do them again. In this way we're able to modify our behavior through our intent.

Whether or not people can shape their own reality, it's still empowering for people to hear that their intention and attention can make a difference in their lives. Since we touched on parallel universes briefly earlier, and because you've written a book about them, I wonder if you could say more about the way in which quantum physics suggests their existence.

The big reason this idea came into being was to try to restrict, or box in, our thinking about quantum physics by getting the observer out of the way. Everybody knew that by observing these experiments and making measurements, the researchers were affecting the outcome, but they didn't know what to make of that.

The old way of thinking was that scientists were isolated, separate, and objective observers of nature peering into their experiments to see what was happening, but they didn't expect that this looking in was changing the results they were getting! Once they discovered that by observing the experiments they were affecting things, they didn't know how to understand that. Nothing is more disturbing than going from the many to the one by observation, with no clear mechanism why it would go to one particular state over another, and why the observer in these experiments would make any difference at all. This is very upsetting to anyone trying to find an ordered understanding of the way the universe works. Parallel universes were invented in order to get rid of the observer, since scientists really wanted to eliminate them from our experiments and go back to the way things were before we knew anything about atoms or quantum physics.

Let's warm up to parallel universes with a slightly different example. Think about a quantum system, which can be in one of two states. Let's make it very simple, like a quantum coin, with heads or tails as the only possibilities. In the normal world when you flip a coin, it lands either heads or tails, and whether we observe it or don't observe it doesn't matter—it's always going to land showing one or the other. In the quantum world, that's not the case. Until it's observed, it's both heads and tails showing at the same time! And if an observer comes along in the quantum world and makes an observation, say they call it "heads or tails," what happens is that the world is split into two parallel worlds, one where the observer sees heads and one where the observer sees tails. Both outcomes exist simultaneously, each one containing their own form of the observer and coin together.

So now we have one observer being split into two, each one in a different parallel universe seeing a different outcome for the coin toss. And if more and more observers come in and make observations of the coin, they will unanimously agree on the results of the coin toss. Everybody in one world says, "Ah! The coin is heads. It is obvious that we agree we see heads!" In the other world they're doing the same thing, and without knowing it these two worlds have become so split apart that it's virtually impossible to bring them back together again and find an equal relationship between them. So the result of making many observations of the same system is to split it more definitely toward one or another outcome. This is a theory called decoherence in quantum physics.

You see, before many observations are made, all the different possibilities for the outcome are fuzzy and they can add up or "interfere" together to make a new possibility. For example, another observer could come in, look at that coin in a slightly different way, and find an entirely new outcome for the coin toss, such as the coin standing on edge, neither heads nor tails. But many observers together will start to agree on a single outcome of a coin toss and the system will become more definite and distinct.

The whole idea of parallel worlds came in as an attempt to make the observer something like a coin, something that was an inseparable part of the system and not something from the outside, observing "objectively" and independently. So if every observer was like a coin, then with each coin toss they will be split into one observer that sees "heads" and another observer that sees "tails," each existing in their own parallel universe where they saw that particular outcome. Now an observer can be many things: a human, a computer that records observations, or even a combination of neurons in a brain.

Well, what does all this say about consciousness and how it affects a quantum system? It turns out that it doesn't seem to have any bearing one way or the other on the nature of consciousness, because as far as the observer is concerned, who sees heads or tails, the world has just spontaneously changed from a whole spectrum of possibilities to just one when the observation was made. So as far as he's concerned, he's come to the same conclusion he would have come to if the other parallel world didn't exist.

So this is where the parallel worlds idea is essentially the same as the idea that consciousness collapses the wave-function, or that the so-called observer affects reality. They all turn out to be equivalent, and so people have tried to think of clever ways in which to test to see if these parallel worlds are still there. In all attempts where they've tried to do this, they were, but these have been in very simplified experiments. So that's where we are right now. The idea of parallel worlds doesn't seem to give any new insights into the relationship of Mind to the universe, because in each world the Mind has entered into the universe unequivocally and irreversibly, and there's no way to get it to separate itself.

So are all these parallel universes coexistent with our own, and is Mind the unifying factor among them all?

The parallel worlds view doesn't help us to understand anything more about whether the Mind is unifying no non-unifying. One thing I do see related to this has to do with the seemingly solid nature of physical reality. Why are things so solid, reaffirming, and robust in the physical world?

When you see something very definitely in front of you, say a ball on a table, it's the overlap of many different quantum states spread over a very small range of variations. Another way of looking at it is that it's an overlap of a vast number of parallel worlds in which I'm seeing essentially the same thing with very small variations between each world. Now if I don't pay attention to these variations or attempt to differentiate them they tend to overlap, and the overlap becomes like a glue—it makes the world more tangible and real to me.

Does that mean that there's a consensus in terms of what the world is? Does this consensus make the world the way that it is?

Yes, it means that consensus plays a very important part in shaping the world. The implications of what that means are very interesting, and people are doing research into this. Dean Radin, for example, has been looking at the events around September 11 and whether a large number of people were dreaming about the events during that time. Did the fact that maybe one million people saw this outcome in their dreams cause it to happen, or is it just a correlation? In these kinds of situations cause and effect can become intertwined, but in this case I think it's correlation rather than causative.

But if our beliefs are influencing reality in even a very small way, what might happen, for example, if we all stop believing in the solidity of matter? Could that shift something in a big way in the physical world?

If everyone simply says they don't believe in it, then it's not going to change anything. The fact is you still believe in it deep down, and it's very hard for you to get to a place in your own consciousness where you don't believe it. One way of doing it is to take LSD. If the whole world was on LSD I don't know what would happen. Because on LSD the world doesn't seem to be very strong; it doesn't seem to be as glued together as it might otherwise appear to be under normal consciousness. So I don't know what would happen, but it's a good question.

It's a fascinating possibility to speculate about though! Going back to the idea of correlation versus causation, and how things are ordered in time, you've written a number of books about time travel. If time is more fluid than we generally think, can the future in some way influence the present and the past? What kind of universe do we live in that time has directionality in some cases but not in others?

Well, it's a tricky business to talk about things going backward in time, and even more so to try to explain the effects that would result from it. But to begin with, we need to look at the way that we have come to the conclusion that cause and effect move the world, the belief that what I do now will affect what will happen in the future. There's some basis for the broader perspective that events happening in the future can influence or cause what's happening now.

The research I'm referring to was done by Benjamin Libet and others at the University of California San Francisco Medical School in the 1970s. They were investigating neural activity in the brain, looking at how triggering specific areas of the brain would create certain sensations in the body and how long it took for those sensations to register consciously. For example, if somebody pinches your toe, when do you feel the pinch? Naturally you would expect that if somebody pinches your toe it's going to take a little while for that signal to reach your brain. And until it reaches your brain you're not going to feel anything. What Libet found is that there seemed to be a delay between when the brain received the signal and when it registered it in consciousness as a sensation. This seemed to make sense, since the brain needed a little time to integrate the arriving signals to form a conscious response.

But what amazed Libet is that people were responding to the stimuli as soon as the signal reached the brain, before the sensation was registering in consciousness. In other words, their brain was responding to signals a full half-second or so before his subjects were even aware of them! How is this possible? Well, Libet decided to test this in subsequent experiments, and applied additional stimuli to the person after the initial stimulus signal had reached the brain, but before it was conscious. Incredibly, he found that the way people were responding before the additional stimulus was applied depended on how it was applied after. So this would indicate in some kind of strange way that what happened after was affecting what a person was experiencing before!

When he published these results, he was widely attacked by the medical community, because this clearly doesn't make sense if you only believe in a universe where time can go in only one direction, from the past to the future. People have proposed lots of alternative theories about how this can happen, but to date no one has been able to explain these results adequately. These results have been confirmed in a number of later studies performed by others, so it's not a fluke or a problem with his methodology.

There are other indications we have that what happens in the future seems to affect what we can perceive in the now. So we're in a situation where some kind of reverse form of causality actually exists—the future does seem to affect the present in very definite and measurable ways. We don't experience things as going into the future and then coming back to the now, but we either have the experience of something or we don't experience it, and then something happens later. But if that thing didn't happen later, we don't experience it, whereas if it does happen later we do.

Do you think this is what happens when people have intuitions or hunches?

I think it has a lot to do with that. Dean Radin's work also shines a lot of light on this. He's been looking at presentiment, and has found that people are able to sense whether something is going to happen before it happens. They may not sense it as a conscious thought, but they will sense it in terms of heightened skin resistance or some other physiological response, which would indicate their awareness of it.

So time may work in a way that may actually be very different than what we usually think.

Well, that's the conclusion. A distinguished physicist, Roger Penrose, wrote about this in his book *The Emperor's New Mind*, and I think a lot of other physicists were very unhappy with him for mentioning this. This is normal though, since as I said before, the job of physicists is to try to restrict nature, not to find ways to augment it.

And yet when they try to restrict it they inadvertently open up this whole new box of mysteries! Now, you've also written a book about the spiritual universe, so in closing, could you say something about how you see the relationship between science and spirituality with respect to studying the universe?

They're complementary, which means that one way we have of dealing with our experience of the universe is through love, feeling, hope, intent, fear, emotions, faith, or other responses, which cannot be put into a mathematical formula. The other way is to try to create mathematical forms that relate cause and effect, so that we can predict and control our environment and ourselves. But both approaches are complementary to each other, since they are both asking questions that arise from the same basic mystery: "Why did that happen?" and "Where do I come from?"

So in a sense we need both of these complementary perspectives to get the full picture of what we're talking about with the universe.

As Einstein said, "Physics without faith is lame; faith without physics is blind." The best I can say to you is that in spite of all of our efforts and in spite of all of our faith and all of our prayers, in spite of all our scientific reasoning, the universe is still a mystery. And we haven't come to the end of that mystery by any means. In fact the universe has recently become even more mysterious, now with the current observations of the universe's expansion accelerating, and with ingredients like dark energy or dark matter thrown into the cake batter. Some of us suspect that these new discoveries may be related to consciousness in some yet unknown way.

And consciousness is also a mystery that may be deepening as well.

Yes, and I don't think we're ever going to explain consciousness, because in order to deal with consciousness fully, we have to be fully conscious. We can't deal with consciousness from an unconscious perspective, because we don't really know what it is. We're always in it.

Exactly, like a fish in water.

Chapter 6

The Challenge of Psi: An Interview With Dean Radin

C an our thoughts affect the world around us? Does intention play a role in shaping the world we see and experience? For nearly four centuries scientists and philosophers have debated the relationship among Mind, body, and the material world. Mainstream contemporary science generally holds that the universe is composed entirely of matter, with mind as an emergent phenomenon of the brain. However, intriguing results from both quantum physics and parapsychology suggest that there may be more at work here than meets the eye. What kind of universe might we live in if our minds and conscious experience are not confined to our private individual brains, but play an interactive role in the world we live in? Is there good scientific evidence that this could be true, and if so, what might this mean for our theories about the universe?

For more than three decades, Dean Radin has been at the forefront of a group of scientists who take the claims of psychic and parapsychological experiences very seriously. Currently senior scientist at the Institute of Noetic

Sciences (IONS), he began his career as a concert violinist, then shifted to electrical engineering, graduating magna cum laude with a bachelors degree from the University of Massachusetts, Amherst. He later earned a masters in electrical engineering and a PhD in psychology from the University of Illinois, Champaign-Urbana. For the first decade after graduation he worked at AT&T Bell Laboratories and GTE Laboratories, conducting research and development on advanced telecommunications devices and systems.

For the past two decades he has focused exclusively on consciousness research, holding appointments and research positions at Princeton University, University of Edinburgh, University of Nevada, and three Silicon Valley think-tanks, including SRI International, where he worked on a classified program investigating psychic phenomena for the U.S. government.

The author or coauthor of more than 200 technical and popular articles and a dozen book chapters, Dr. Radin has published several books, including the bestselling *The Conscious Universe* (HarperOne, 1997) and *Entangled Minds* (Simon & Schuster, 2006). Motivated by an intuitive sense that the universe is far more mysterious and powerful than we generally accept, his work has continually challenged prevailing scientific worldviews while holding those who claim paranormal abilities and experiences to rigorous and stringent standards.

Stephan Martin: Your work in psi has covered a large part of the spectrum of research in this field and has led to some remarkable results. Can you say something about the most remarkable things that you have discovered about the universe through this research?

Dean Radin: I guess the primary thing is how much this research domain has helped to reveal how much there is left to learn about ourselves and the universe.

Are there specific insights or discoveries that have really challenged our ideas about the universe?

Well, the evidence strongly suggests that precognition exists. And if precognition exists, then we don't have a very good understanding of time. Time is essential to how we experience the everyday world, and if we don't even understand that, then basically all bets are off.

If I think too deeply about what's left to learn about the universe, the depths of ignorance we are faced with can put me into a kind of mental paralysis. One way to think about this problem is to estimate the percentage of what we think we know about relative to all that is knowable. For the average person, they might think, well, maybe we know 10 percent or 20 percent, or if they don't think about these things very much, they may say we know 100 percent of everything that's knowable.

But the longer I've been in science, and not just studying psi phenomena, the more I think that we're actually real close to 0 percent. The more you know the more you realize what you don't know, so I think we have a long way to go.

The mystery seems to deepen the deeper you go into it. This is interesting, because a lot of our beliefs about science say that it's a very quantitative approach to studying the universe, that the universe is a defined quantity, and so we're uncovering fixed amounts of it bit by bit.

If you look at what we think we understand, from the perspective of relatively recent primates that have developed a modest degree of self-reflective awareness, then what we've uncovered is a tiny piece of the whole pie. We are impressed by our fancy machines and our mathematics and all the rest of our technological toys, but our level of genuine understanding is still extremely primitive.

It seems that the more we discover, the more difficult the questions become. It may be that at some point we begin to bump up against a limitation of our own ability to understand things, and at that point we may require something like a global mind or some other sort of cognition enhancement in order to be able to ask the next level of questions.

It's interesting that we may need a global mind at some point to understand the universe more fully. Do you think that even now we might be bumping up against the edges of our own human capacity to understand the universe?

I think so. I've been thinking about this in terms of what we think we know about psi phenomena. We know just the barest inkling about it, much less what it means about the universe.

I wonder if one of the barriers to understanding the universe more comprehensively is that there may be assumptions being made about the universe that may not be fundamentally true. For example, the idea in much of neuroscience that consciousness is an epiphenomenon of the brain, as opposed to the research that you and others have conducted with psi that suggests that consciousness may be actually fundamental to reality, that it may be an aspect of the universe itself. So it may not simply be a difference of approach, but the fundamental assumptions between approaches might be in question.

Right. Even if there isn't a mainstream consensus within science, there are shared ideas that are mechanistic, materialistic, and reductionistic. But I think most physicists will agree that everything in the universe is connected if for no other reason than through gravity. It's difficult to create models of the universe that are too inclusive or holistic, because basic epistemologies in science are reductionistic, and reductionism is antithetical to holism.

I think a lot of scientists would agree in principle that it would be great to develop something like nested holistic models that showed interactions between matter and its environment all the way from the subatomic world out to the ends of the universe, but we don't know how to do that just yet, or even if it's useful to think about things in that way.

I think what we see happening in neuroscience is that people assume we can understand the brain completely adequately through classical physics. If that's so, then it leads to a certain line of assumptions about what's possible.

Under thoese assumptions, ESP is simply not possible, because it doesn't fit with the classical physics worldview. But if ESP is real, then something major needs to be revised. You need some other form of physics to explain it, whether it's quantum physics or whatever else is after quantum physics. But as soon as we begin to go there, it challenges all sorts of deeply held assumptions. The kinds of changes we're talking about would affect all of the sciences, from physics upward, and most scientists don't like that very much, so they don't think about it.

It's a lot of work to rework things from the foundations.

Right, and for my colleagues who feel threatened by such an idea it doesn't mean that what's being done now is wrong—it means it's simply not comprehensive. It's not as comprehensive as it might be if a larger understanding of what they've been specializing in is developed, which is what the whole history of science has been about. It's about taking something and getting a more expanded view of it. But scientists are human, of course, and humans don't like change (except perhaps in politics, and even then only as words to rally around).

It's the ongoing process of enlarging the context within which we're working, at the same time learning more and more about what it is that we're actually involved with here. So it's not that the mechanistic reductionist view of things is false, it's simply not complete in its current form.

Right. It's a method that is useful within a certain scope of phenomena, with epistemological assumptions that are useful within boundaries that match what we think of as common sense.

Except that science has repeatedly shown that common sense actually isn't very good at describing reality. Very few scientists (at least this was true when I went to school) have had any training in epistemology or ontology or the philosophical tools for understanding how we know what we know. It wasn't considered necessary, because we were taking an engineering approach to deconstructing the world using tools that seemed to work well enough, and that's all you needed to know at the time.

I think it's still the case. There aren't that many scientists who spend time worrying about whether their epistemology is adequate. Maybe in philosophy, but not in the sciences.

Right. It's not thought to be relevant.

Yes, and maybe it's only relevant at the leading edge where anomalous data starts to require a new epistemology or ontology because of the nature of what the data is implying. So, ESP is controversial and anomalous because it doesn't fit with the methods that people are being taught as adequate. Part of the resistance comes about because no one likes to think that what they're doing is inadequate.

In some ways trying to explain how things work while assuming that they're all independent of each other is like building a house of cards. One day you get this novel idea and say, "Ooh, I'll take this card and I'll move it like this," but everything else changes as a result of that. It turns out that you're dealing with a house of cards, where all of the cards are actually reflections of one single card, like in a hall of mirrors. But initially you didn't know that they're all connected.

So again we have this epistemological issue where we usually assume in any kind of experiment that there is some degree of control and separability among the variables, whether they are objects, tasks, people, and so on.... And yet the nature of psi phenomena suggests that separability at deep levels of reality really is an illusion. There is no separability. And if there's no separability, then how do you study anything? That's the puzzle.

Yes, the context, instead of being the background for the experiment, is deeply integrated into the experiment itself.

Yes. Instead of assuming that the foreground is not very deeply connected with the background, you find it's all background! The foreground is an illusion, analogous to one of those Magic Eye posters, where something pops out if you look at it in the right way, but it's "really" completely flat. From that perspective, everything that we see, including things that appear to be solid, are illusionary objects popping out like a Magic Eye in some background for which we have no name yet.

Unfortunately, I don't know of any other way of even talking or thinking about these things other than what begins to sound like mystical language. So I think that the mystics were probably on to something. Their experience tells us something about the actual nature of the world, which seems to be some unnameable substance of some type, and we project everything on to it. In the worst case, it becomes like the movie, *The Matrix*, in the sense that if you could see through the illusion, you could do anything. You could manipulate it in any way that you wanted. But since you're embedded within the same medium as everyone else, maybe you can only do that when no one else is looking.

I haven't gone much deeper into being able to describe it in these terms, but that type of reality is something that is suggested again and again by psi experiments. Fortunately, the effects we see are stable enough so that if we repeat them again and again we can begin to see systematic effects, which gives us the sense that we're dealing with lawful phenomena and not capricious accidents. But the repeatability might have more to do with the fact that we're relatively stable observers rather than the fact that the underlying medium is intrinsically stable.

This stability within the wide range of variable outcomes from these kinds of experiments is something you've discovered only through meta-analysis of large amounts of data.

That's right. Meta-analysis wouldn't work if there wasn't some degree of stability in the thing that we're looking at. So it may be, as I said, that the source of stability is us, and not the phenomenon itself, and maybe there's even no phenomenon separate from us. It's all caused by us in some way. I don't like to talk this way because it sounds too mystical…but that's where I'm led by the data.

Part of the new worldview that seems to be arising out of experiments such as yours is that Mind, or consciousness, or whatever that is, seems to be the underlying substance of reality.

I'm not sure I want to push it that far, but from a philosophical point of view I would consider myself a pan-psychist in the sense that I think that there is consciousness going all the way down. But the question is, all the way down to what? To electrons and below? What exactly *is* an electron? We don't actually even know what an electron is!

But there does seems to be something in all of this about relationships among things, things that have no names. If you keep asking the annoying "why" question, you will bottom-out at some point and get stuck. We just don't know yet how to answer most of the really fundamental questions. In fact we probably don't even know the right questions to ask.

It seems like these kinds of experiments seem to demonstrate that intention may actually have a part in shaping reality. Whether collectively or as individuals, do our intentions affect or shape reality?

It looks that way, at least to a small degree from what we can see in a lab. The question here is whether there are measurable, unmediated effects of intention. I think that there are, based on the evidence, but I think we don't really understand the limitations on what we're seeing just yet. Mostly the effects of intention that we're seeing are small statistical effects in a wide variety of systems. Sometimes you see huge effects that are difficult to repeat, but statistically these are effects very likely to be real.

Are these large effects the ones based on collective intention experiments such as the Global Consciousness Project?

No, they're mostly based on individual intention, either under extremely high motivation conditions or with extremely unusual people, or in unusual contexts...things of that sort.

Very large-scale experiments like the Global Consciousness Project are showing results that are not much bigger than what you see with an individual. It's just that there have been fewer of these big experiments, and they've been more specifically planned and defined. Now even though we're not getting incredibly huge effects as a result of global consciousness and intention, we are still getting interesting, repeatable results. I want to put it into context that what we see is not that different from what we see if we ask an individual to spend a lot of time and effort specifically focusing on a given object.

What is different about the GCP is that the events selected tend to attract not just a lot of people, but people who are intently focused. And the results we see from the experiment has made me appreciate more why experiments involving intention or attention should focus on meditators. We need people who have learned how to place their full attention or intention in a very stable way on a given object for a length of time.

So, has the quality of attention or intention been the deciding factor in these experiments?

It's not *the* deciding variable, but I do think it's a significant component.

So, experienced meditators, or highly focused people such as athletes, perform better than the average person.

Right. Anybody who has some kind of mental discipline that allows them to consistently focus on a single object or goal.

So it makes me wonder, are there significant effects from our intentions happening all the time, but we're simply not aware of them because of the background noise of our minds?

Oh yeah, I'm sure there are. These effects have to be occurring all the time, since there's nothing magical that happens in the laboratory that evokes something that wasn't there before. I think they're even expressed in everyday life all the time, but people don't think of them as psychic events. They think of "psychic" as major life events, like crisis telepathy events, or crisis apparition events—big things that they tend to remember. They don't remember picking up the phone and knowing who is calling, or getting a gut feeling that turned out to be true, and so on. There are lots of everyday synchronicities that I think are variations of psi effects, the same kind of mental interconnectivity with the rest of the universe that people sometimes pay attention to, but most of the time they don't.

This shouldn't be too surprising, because most of the time we don't pay much attention to anything. We run on automatic pilot most of the time. If you take a look at the cars on the highway outside the window right now, how much attention is the average person paying to their driving? I'm sure it's 5 percent of what's actually going on in their heads. They're mostly thinking about something else or talking on the phone. So, if 5 percent of our attention is on what's happening, and 95 percent is on plans and other things, it's no wonder that people don't pay much attention to psi, because that's in the background too.

Another factor might be that people are not generally taught that psi actually exists—that it's something that they can pay attention to.

Most of the surveys show that the majority of people do believe in it, but they may not think that they have it here and now, all the time, unless they've had many personal experiences with it.

If people didn't believe in psi, then you wouldn't see constant references to these experiences in books, movies, and television. People respond well to psi as portrayed in the media because they have an intuitive sense that this is real for them at some level. A TV show like *Heroes* or *Lost* is juicy, because people feel that that there's some possibility it is real. If they felt like it was beyond the bounds of what's possible, then they wouldn't resonate with it, and the show wouldn't be very popular.

Now a skeptic would say, "Well, it's just wish-fulfillment," and I'm sure for some people that's the case. But I think in the majority of cases people will privately confide they have had some kind of psychic experience or they know someone they trust that has had one. I've found that when I've spoken to anyone long enough, including some very well-known skeptics, they will admit having had experiences of this type. But they might interpret it in different ways. A skeptic will feel too much cognitive dissonance and say, "Well, it must have been coincidence," or it must have been this or that ordinary effect. But from an experiential point of view, the experiences are universal.

I wonder if our worldview plays a factor here, given that our current cultural worldview is largely based on a separation and materialism, and so therefore psi can't exist.

That is probably true to some extent, but anthropologists have gone to indigenous societies that don't hold that worldview—they hold a more holistic worldview, and you don't necessarily see stronger psi. You might among a subset of the people who are Shamans or people who would be the equivalent of a Shaman, but not so much among the average person.

In this society we don't have the equivalent of Shamans, so we call the Psychic Friends Network, or something like that instead. My guess is that for people who are deeply connected with the universe in that particular way, it's a talent, and a relatively rare one. In this society it's probably the same as in any indigenous society, roughly between a tenth of a percent to 1 percent of the population. That's pretty small. So you might have one in a hundred or one in a thousand people who can consciously feel this kind of connection, which means that most people are not feeling it, at least not consciously.

So if we live in a universe where psi exists, and we don't really know what psychic phenomena are or what they mean, then in a sense maybe it's easier to say what the universe is not instead of what it is. For example, it's not just matter, at least in the current way we understand matter.

Well, that's a criticism of all the results in psi experiments, where psi is defined by what it isn't. If you do a telepathy experiment and you show that there is a statistical increase in the amount of information apparently moved from one person to another person, then the psi effect is what happens after you go through the two dozen explanations for what you know it isn't. And so the thing that is left over, which is the residue, or the absence of other explanations, becomes the explanation. Many of my colleagues say that this is a serious problem, because psi is defined in negative terms.

But I say that's not really true, because you can also make a positive definition for psi. For example, psi is the direct acquisition of knowledge anywhere in space or time. That said, what these experiments are really telling us is that the common-sense feeling of objects being separate is actually an illusion, in which case, we're not really getting information from somewhere else. We're simply becoming aware of something that is always present, here and now.

Again, I'm starting to sound like a meditation teacher, but that's the direction that it's leading...that the universe is in your head and your head is the universe, and you have access to information anywhere at any time. And your ability to perceive this is completely dependent on how you allocate your attention.

If you focus your attention and cut through all the distractions and see the world for the way it really is, then you discover a worldview that fits pretty well with that of many of the world's spiritual traditions, namely that there's a single holistic hunk of stuff.

From a perceptual point of view psi and this spiritual view are perfectly compatible. I can see Jupiter because I'm not really separate from Jupiter at some level that I can directly experience. At the everyday level of awareness,

Jupiter and I are obviously very separate, except for maybe gravitational influences. But at another level we're not so separate. It's this other level that requires a different way of perceiving the world, and that's where psi phenomena first starts to come about. How you translate intention into all this is still unknown.

My suspicion is that if you can perceive the world such that everything you feel or see reflects the interconnectivity of it all, then it would be like a passive incoming perceptual information flow. But if you could reverse your participation by pushing information outward, then the world itself would change. It may only change at a subtle level that may not be immediately apparent at the level of the eye, but that's why we use sensitive instruments to see these effects.

But to change the world in big ways, such that I could think of this bottle falling over and then actually see that happen immediately, might require a much, much larger degree of "information push" than I'm capable of. So, maybe the electrons in the bottle actually do move every time I think about it, but to get something that looks like a conventional force to levitate a bottle...I can't do that...yet.

Perhaps it's a question of energy versus attention. There may not be enough energy flowing at the moment to produce a significant force.

I don't think it's energy flow per se. I think it's more like information, or subtle modulation of existing energies. At the levels that we're talking about there's nothing clearly identifiable as energy or matter or space or time. There's just relationships. One of the great advancements of science in the 20th century was the realization that a relationship is a thing. In the 19th century and prior the most important things in the universe were objects.

But in the 20th century the idea arose that objects can be defined by the relationships between them, and so the relationship became more important than the object. If you carry this idea into the subatomic realm then there are no particles there—only relationships. And if that's the level that you're working at, then everything is information, because that's essentially what relationships are.

At a deeper level, information may literally create the world. How this deeper level couples with the everyday world, we don't know yet, but I imagine that it may have something to do with redefining the relationships that are the threads in the fabric of reality.

Could it be a new set of physical laws that we're simply not aware of?

Well, I think the physical laws that we are aware of are all relationships anyway. We cast them into mathematical terms and we make up names like *electrons* and so on because they show a certain degree of lawful regularity. But I imagine that once we gain a better idea of the informational nature of these relationships, then something like levitation might well be possible. Whoever, or whatever, is doing the levitation would need to tweak some aspect of information that describes the physical laws and make them work slightly differently in that area of space.

They've been able to change their relationship to those laws.

The idea that everything is relational is not even very controversial from a fundamental physics point of view. But the real game changer is nonlocality. The full impact of this startling discovery, which came out of quantum physics, has yet to penetrate most of science, even though we're talking about effects that have been discussed for nearly 80 years, and demonstrated as fact for almost 30 years. Nonlocality is just so far from common sense that most people either don't believe it, or they just don't think about it much.

For example, I was at a conference in Portugal recently talking to a neuroscientist. I said something like, "Well, we know that nonlocality exists and that psi phenomena are at least compatible with the idea of nonlocality—it might not explain it, but it is consistent." And he said, "Yeah, but we don't need nonlocality or to think in quantum terms in order to explain what is going on in the neurosciences." I said, "Really? The brain is a quantum object. Any physicist would agree with that. Action in the brain is occurring at the level of ions and below, which is at the quantum scale, in which case we have to think of it as a quantum object." He didn't like that at all, because one of the implications of a quantum brain is that you are no longer dealing with individual particles of matter in the head. Rather, you're describing a substance that has both particle-like and wave-like aspects. In its wavelike mode, it reaches out to infinity, and not only that, it goes out to infinity faster than the speed of light. So what we call gray "matter" in the brain is made of neurons, but it is also something that extends to the edges of the universe and plays fast and loose with concepts like time and space. This is not a popular idea in the neurosciences, because it requires a radical change in epistemological assumptions used in the neurosciences, which is basically that of reverse engineering.

I was really struck by the language and the methods that are used in neuroscience to understand the nature of the brain, because they are almost exactly what an electrical engineer would do when asked to reverse engineer a black box. It's the same basic approach: You figure out what's inside the black box by the way it behaves when you poke it in certain ways, and then you start mucking about with the components and the circuits, and see how the behavior changes, and eventually you come up with a model about what's going on in there.

You can learn a lot through reverse engineering, but if you're trying to reverse engineer something like a radio, even if you finally understand that the signals it receives are turned into music by special electrical circuits, that tells you nothing about the source of the music.

And what the experiments from psi seem to show is that we need to understand the mind to understand the universe, because at some level they're interconnected.

I'm not sure how many scientists think about the whole universe, other than those whose job it is to think about cosmology and astrophysics and so on. It's just too large a concept to even try to grasp. The reason why I think about it sometimes is because I'm led to the conclusion that if it's possible for things to appear to be isolated or separated, but they're really not, then I don't know where to place the boundaries. And if there are no boundaries, then we must be connected to everything.

Unfortunately, once you get to this holistic notion, which is similar to Bohm's idea of an implicate order, then it's easy to get stuck, because once again it's too big of a problem to study. At least within cosmology you can have models that describe how the universe would evolve if it started this way or that, so you can at least grasp it mathematically.

But you don't know how to grasp a model of interconnectivity where at some level the mind is connected with everything else. It makes my head hurt to try to imagine that. Another thing that makes my head hurt is to ignore the problem. And then there's the idea that we're able to perceive through time. Precognition also makes my head hurt.

Yes, if space and time don't exist the way we think they do, then what are they?

The thing is, they don't fundamentally exist and yet they're not an illusion either. At least not in the sense of it all being a solipsistic illusion. There's something there, but it's not like anything that we're used to in terms of stuff that our eyes and hands are used to feeling and seeing in everyday terms. So it's quite curious. It's as though we are in a virtual reality and there is something else there, some kind of Wizard of Oz behind the scenes who is actually making things happen. That has a certain appeal to it, because we can sort of imagine a story that goes along with it, but I always get frustrated because even the most sophisticated stories are still just stories.

We're just at the very beginning of understanding these things. If you look at this from a historical perspective, we're just barely getting to the point of developing ways of thinking beyond ourselves and beyond common sense. And so 5,000 years from now, I can easily imagine a similar interview taking place in which my counterpart will finally admit, after professing on all sorts of semi-miraculous topics, "Well, now that we know all this, now we realize that we really don't understand much of anything at all."

We're dealing with a very complex puzzle, a puzzle about the nature of reality and our role in it. I think exploring this puzzle is exciting and personally meaningful, but I believe the value of this work goes far beyond academic interest. Gaining a better understanding of who and what we are, and what we may be capable of, is becoming an increasingly vital component of the future course of history. What humanity becomes depends on who we think we are.

Part 2

The View From Spirit

If science is based on the systematic explanation of the universe, then perhaps the spiritual and mystical traditions of the world are based on the direct experience of it. The discovery of the common ground between the two is one of the most exciting dialogues taking place today. For our purposes here, I propose a rough categorization of "the spiritual" into religion and mysticism. The former is the organized body of traditions, rituals, and perspectives that seeks to explain the relationship between the human and the divine. Mysticism is the inner core of these traditions that seeks union and direct experience with the divine.

In this sense, the mystic shares much in common with the scientist in that each is seeking a deeper understanding and appreciation of the universe through direct engagement with reality. Science attempts to explore the physical outer universe using the quantitative techniques of the mind and the tools of the laboratory. Mysticism investigates the inner dimensions of reality using the qualitative approaches of the heart through direct (unmediated by past conditioning) perception. One seeks the truth about the natural world; the other the truth about oneself. Mysticism and science can be seen then as different but complementary approaches to understanding the whole of the universe. Mysticism picks up the investigation of inner reality where science leaves off, and science explores the outer universe that is largely neglected by mysticism.

That the universe seems to have both an interior as well as an exterior is remarkable enough. The tremendous body of literature from the world's spiritual traditions describe the inner world as vast, diverse, and as rich as the outer universe that teems with galaxies, planets, and life. In the sacred texts of the Upanishads of the Hindu tradition, we find the following description of the inner reality: "Smaller than a grain of rice, smaller than a grain of barley, smaller than a mustard seed, smaller than a grain of millet, smaller even than the kernel of a grain of a millet is the Self. This is the Self dwelling in my heart, greater than the earth, greater than the sky, greater than all the worlds."[3]

In many spiritual traditions this inner reality is experienced as not only coexistent with the universe of stars and galaxies, but also as the larger context and source out of which all phenomena arise. Lao Tzu, in the Taoist tradition, refers to this when he claims, "Though [the Tao] is uncreated itself, it creates all things," and "Worlds and particles, bodies and beings, time and space: All are transient expressions of the Tao."[4]

These examples are a testament to the richness of the inner cosmos that mystics have explored from diverse vantage points throughout the ages. The interior universe is not only vast, but the terrain also looks somewhat different from the perspective of each mystical tradition. One spiritual path may see the universe as the embodiment of love and compassion, while to another reality it appears as a sea of consciousness and light; yet both will agree that the ultimate nature of everything is a mysterious unity. The various spiritual traditions and perspectives are then like separate and distinct paths climbing the same mountain. Each can describe the peak and its cloud-shrouded heights from its own unique terrain, yet all agree on the unity of the mountain.

Both the inner and outer universes seem to need a multiplicity of perspectives for a more complete picture of the whole. Yet how are the inner and outer perspectives related? If the universe is a fundamental unity, which science in many cases assumes and mysticism commonly claims, then why do the inner and outer universe look and feel so different? How can the universe be boundless and infinite on the inside, yet seemingly measurable and definable on the outside? What does it mean to say that the universe may be bigger on the inside than the outside?

The relationships between unity and multiplicity, physical and spiritual, and inner and outer, are what make the dialogues between scientists and mystics so fascinating. Beyond the philosophical, understanding these relationships may have some very practical applications as well. For example, results from quantum physics suggest that the presence of a conscious, subjective observer is an integral part of the experiment, and so without a more complete understanding of the nature of consciousness and the role of subjective experience in the cosmos, we may not fully understand these enigmatic data. Of the spiritual traditions, Tibetan Buddhism has such a comprehensive and systematically organized map of the human mind and states of consciousness that contemporary neuroscientists are now approaching Tibetan lamas for insights into some of the most persistent questions of their field. The synthesis of the common ground between science and religion continues lead to new revelations and insights that will benefit both in the future.

Yet there is a third perspective that needs to be included here, one which precedes both the scientific and the classical mystical understandings of the universe, and this is the indigenous perspective. The indigenous view is arguably the original or primordial human view of the universe. Its perspective has its roots in the living soil of the earth, and has never experienced the split of the scientific and religious viewpoints that occurred in Western culture. My conversations included indigenous elders in the spirit section rather than the cultural, because their cultures represent perspectives and ways of living on the earth that arise from their spiritual experience. For indigenous peoples, humans, nature, spirituality, and the universe are inextricably interconnected, so that no aspect of their cultures can be understood independently. Their traditions represent a unifying perspective that is unique from other spiritual traditions, and yet fully aligned with the common view of the universe as a single interconnected whole.

As we will discover in these dialogues, native peoples are not so much oriented toward the methodological investigation of reality, so common in science and mysticism, as they are in the deep alignment with and celebration of existence. Ritual is used to return to alignment and harmony because, at the heart of things, humans, spirituality, nature, and the universe are all one for these peoples. Ritual is to the indigenous practitioner what meditation is to the mystic and the experiment is to the scientist: a window through which the universe reveals its deeper nature.

As I explored the ideas in this section with spiritual practitioners of different traditions and cultures, I began to notice similarities and commonalities. Although the ideas they expressed embraced a wide variety of topics, metaphors, and ways of perceiving, I noticed that each holds an abiding and unshakable trust in the universe. Their natural sincerity and generosity of spirit, and their shared sense of relaxation and confidence in reality are qualities uncommon in our culture today.

Many of them rest in a larger perspective that fully accepts all of life's chaos, turmoil, and travail as part of yet one more wave of existence to ride. As the Reverend Michael Dowd says here, "The main thing that has driven creativity and transformation for billions of years is chaos, breakdowns, and bad news." Even when everything falls apart, life goes on, and it is this trust in and celebration of the process of life itself that I found refreshing.

The other common element that struck me among these men and women of spirit was the profound sense of gratitude they all shared, an attitude of waking up in the morning and saying, "Thank you, Universe." This stance seemed so natural and unaffected that I was frequently moved to re-evaluate my own life, momentarily losing the myriad of questions I had about the universe as I settled into the completeness of the present moment.

Indigenous elders, in addition to the sense of trust that all the spiritual practitioners shared, also seemed particularly at home when talking about their relationship to the cosmos. I suspect this is partly because they have never separated themselves from the natural world, and so they do not have to struggle to return or reconnect to it as many Westerners do. Native cultures have also never elevated themselves above the rest of the cosmos, feeling a natural kinship with all things and moving in their environment with a grace and ease that suggests a deep belongingness to the world.

As we will see in this section, the spiritual, mystical, and indigenous perspectives all have much to offer the world toward a more complete and satisfying view of the universe. We begin with a conversation with the Reverend Michael Dowd, whose embrace of both evolution and spirituality recasts each in a more inclusive and sacred light. Next we talk with Hameed Ali and Karen Johnson, founding teachers of the Diamond Approach, a contemporary spiritual perspective, on the relationship between spirit and matter, as well as the need for direct spiritual experience in understanding the universe in a personally relevant way. With Lama Palden Drolma we explore the universe as seen through Tibetan Buddhism, as well as the role of the sacred feminine in spirituality and culture.

We then open to indigenous views, speaking with Native American author and activist Gabriel Horn on relationship, sacred purpose, and the Great Mystery. African elder and priestess Luisah Teish shares the wisdom of Africa and the role of the ancestors in returning to balance with the universe. We end this section with a rare interview with Peruvian healer Eda Zavala on the indigenous universe of the Amazonian peoples and their profound relationship with the world.

Chapter 7

The Great Story of Our Time: An Interview With Reverend Michael Dowd

Think science and religion are irreconcilable? Think again. The Reverend Michael Dowd is an "evolutionary evangelist" who is rapidly becoming one of the leading voices in the synthesis of science and religion in America today. Dowd is the author of the controversial best-selling book *Thank God for Evolution: How the Marriage of Science and Religion Will Transform Your Life and Our World*, which is being praised by a host of Nobel laureates and religious leaders alike. He and his wife, noted science writer Connie Barlow, have worked for many years to promote a sacred story of the universe that brings together the wisdom, wonder, and awe of traditional religious movements with the evidence-based, collective intelligence of modern science.

Dowd graduated with top honors from Evangel University in Springfield, Missouri, where he received a BA in Biblical Studies and Philosophy. He also graduated with honors from Eastern Baptist Theological Seminary (now Palmer Seminary) in Philadelphia, Pennsylvania where he earned a Master of Divinity degree. Rev. Dowd served as a United Church of Christ minister for nine years, pastoring churches in Massachusetts, Ohio, and Michigan. His 1991 book, *EarthSpirit: A Handbook for Nurturing an Ecological Christianity* (Twenty-Third Publications) was one of the first attempts to look appreciatively at biblical Christianity from the perspective of a modern cosmology.

In 1995 Rev. Dowd began working with Jewish, Catholic, Protestant, and Evangelical leaders across America on social and environmental issues, as religious organizer for the Washington D.C.–based National Environmental Trust. From 1997 to 2000 he headed the first government-funded program designed to produce large-scale voluntary citizen behavior change along stewardship lines in the United States: The Portland Sustainable Lifestyle Campaign. In 2000 and 2001 he served as campaign manager of Global Action Plan's EcoTeam and Livable Neighborhood Programs in Rockland County, New York, working with urban communities to foster more earth-friendly lifestyles and healthier, friendlier, and safer neighborhoods.

Since April 2002, Michael and Connie have permanently traveled the continent sharing their inspiring view of evolution in churches, schools, and living rooms across North America. Their vision of a sustainable, life-giving, empowering universe that bridges longstanding divides between "my God," "your God," and "no God," and between "my religion" and "your facts," has won them many fans and supporters that include religious leaders from every denomination and some of the world's most esteemed scientists.

Michael and I talked in their Dodge Sprinter in the parking lot of his next speaking engagement. The van, which they affectionately call "Angel," is painted white, with the side of it prominently displaying a Jesus fish and Darwin fish kissing, with red hearts bubbling up out of their union—an apt image for the viewpoint of the topics we were soon to explore.

Stephan Martin: Many people these days are struggling to reconcile their religious beliefs with the results and methods of science, yet you've found a way to overcome this seeming conflict. How does your understanding of the universe bridge the faith-reason divide?

Michael Dowd: Well, it helps to start with understanding the nature of symbolic language. All words are symbols that point to something beyond what they can ever nail down in any ultimate sense. If you imagine before there was human language, we related like other animals. Prior to language, we didn't have a word for Reality, we just experienced It. We didn't even speak of "the universe" until a few hundred years ago. In fact, the Stoic Greeks referred to Reality as a whole as "Cosmos"—a proper name, an I-Thou relationship. Not *the* cosmos, but Cosmos, a living being that they were a part of. People living 10,000 years ago would have said "The Goddess," which was how most cultures then, as best we can tell, personified Ultimacy.

Now about 5,000 years ago, writing and the plow were invented. Plows require male strength, so as a result of writing and the plow the major metaphors for Ultimate Reality began to shift from feminine to masculine. Gods replace goddesses. Then, about 500 years ago, when mechanical clocks were invented, we began to using clock-like analogies, and imagined Reality (the universe) as like a giant mechanism, with God as the otherworldly clockmaker. So you can see how our words and metaphors for Ultimacy have evolved and shifted with the times.

Today, we don't merely believe, we *know* that as a whole is creative in a nested, emergent sense: subatomic particles within atoms within molecules within cells within organisms, and so on…. No matter what kind of religious or non-religious group I speak to, nobody debates this nested nature of creativity. God, from this perspective, or the Goddess, Allah, Great Spirit, or any other divine name, is nothing less than a sacred, proper name—a personification of that ultimate Creative Reality that includes yet transcends everything. In other words, God is the one and only Reality that is not a subset of anything larger or more comprehensive. God is a meaningful, sacred name for the largest nesting doll, to use that analogy, although you'd have to imagine the largest nesting doll being infinite in all directions to get the sense of what I'm trying to point to.

Because we humans are a subset of the whole, and can't get outside the whole to examine it, we have to use analogies and metaphors to describe the nature of Ultimacy, the nature of "The Whole." Kind of like the blind men and the elephant, however, people living in different parts of the world would have encountered aspects of reality—different plants, animals, terrain, and climate—

and thus would have naturally used different analogies and metaphors to try to describe the nature of Ultimacy.

You see, birth, life, death, the cycles and rhythms of nature, the elemental forces of the universe—these are *undeniably* real. Like it or not, we humans have always been in an inescapable relationship with a reality that we could neither fully predict nor control. And given the nature of our brains, there's one thing that people in every culture and throughout history have instinctually done: we've used metaphors and analogies to understand and relate to that which is unavoidably, undeniably real, and/or mysterious. We can't *not* do this. Consciously or unconsciously, we will *always* interpret via metaphors.

Thus, all images and concepts of God are more or less meaningful interpretations and personifications of Undeniable Reality, or Unavoidable Mystery. And it didn't take a genius to figure out that if you trust, or have faith, in what is ultimately inescapable, your life works better than if you judge or resist what is Real. This is not theological rocket science.

Whenever any story, any culture, or any scriptural passage claims "God said this..." or "God did that...," what follows is necessarily a meaningful interpretation of some individual or group's inner or outer experience. It is never a measurable fact. In other words, had CNN or ABC News been there to record the moment of divine revelation, there would have been nothing out of the ordinary (nothing miraculous) to report on the evening news—nothing other than what was coming out of someone's mouth, or pen, or whatever folks wrote with back then. If we fail to understand this, we belittle God and will surely miss what Reality is revealing today. And we mock God if we imagine that a truly divine communicator would have spoken to humanity as a whole more clearly through goat herders and fisherman in the distant past, via their dreams and intuitions, than through cumulative evidence discovered by the global community of scientists alive today. After all, if the worldwide, self-correcting scientific endeavor is anything, it is the pursuit of collective intelligence and a cultural system designed to hold people accountable for their factual statements—their truth claims.

As I discuss at length in Part II of my book *Thank God for Evolution* ("Reality is Speaking"), facts are God's native tongue. In the same way that Reality is always speaking to us individually through our feelings, circumstances, and relationships (that is, through the facts of our experience), empirical evidence is how Reality (God) speaks to us collectively. Few things are more important, it seems to me, than appreciating this and acting on it at all levels of society; the sooner the better.

I'm still not exactly clear on how you see God relating to the universe.

The word *universe* is what I call "day language," the language of our normal, everyday discourse. Words like *God*, *Allah*, or *Goddess* are what I refer to as "night-language," the language of metaphors, poetry, and vibrant, meaningful images. But all these terms are pointing to the same fundamental reality: that fecund realm of Ultimate Reality and no-thing-ness (nothingness) out of which everything emerges and which sustains and holds everything together. So it's natural that different cultures would have relationalized, or personified Reality differently. That's why there are so many different stories and images of God all over the world.

For me the universe is a proper name so it's not *the* universe but Universe.

I understand that you prefer speaking of "Universe" as a proper name (with a capital U), as opposed to "the universe" (with a little u); why is that?

Yes, it's like the difference between Earth (proper name) and *the* earth. We never speak of *the* venus, *the* mars, or *the* jupiter—it's always Venus, Mars, Jupiter—proper names—indeed, mythic names! *Earth* too is a proper name. We relate to this planet differently if we think "the earth," little "e," and imagine that it's a bunch of resources for us to use for our benefit, than if we relate to it as Earth, or Gaia, or some other mythic, sacred name.

The question "What is Universe?" describes the known aspects of the universe, what we can measure, what we can test, what we can hypothesize about—the physical laws, the patterns that we see that have consistency and regularity, but it also includes the whole realm of what we can't measure, what we can't know for sure, because we're part of an enormous, stupendous whole.

A Christian interviewer once asked me on a talk show, "Are you saying that God is the universe? God is more than the universe!" and I said, "The Universe is more than the universe!" Stephen Hawking wrote a book called *The Universe in a Nutshell,* which is a deceptive title. Because in his own book he mentions that physicists agree that 23 percent of the universe is dark matter and 73 percent is dark energy, neither of which we know anything about. That means that everything we know about the universe is only 4 percent of what the universe actually is! I tell people that his book *The Universe in a Nutshell* sold 22 million copies in 17 languages. How many people do you think would have bought it, had he titled his book "The Four Percent of the Universe That We Know About in a Nutshell"? [laughs] Probably very few!

So in a real, scientific sense, the universe is more than the universe! That is, we use this word *universe* as a catch-all for everything, for the whole of everything, or Reality. Yet it's only a word, a term that can seduce us into thinking that nature is an *it* to be exploited for our benefit, rather than a *Thou* to be related to in a mutually enriching way.

When I say that nature is "a Thou to be related to," then the question becomes how do we relate to this measurable and nonmeasurable Reality in which we live and move and have our being? What I often remind people is to think about every meaningful relationship that they've had with anything in their life. All our meaningful relationships are with he's, she's, and living its. If we have a meaningful relationship with some non-living it, like a boat or a car, chances are we've given it a name! [laughs]

Here we're sitting having this conversation in our van, which we've named "Angel," and this little GPS system here on the dashboard is the voice of Angel. And I'm here to tell you: Angel is a trustworthy guide! [laughs]

So we've made this non-living "it" more meaningful and added more joy in our lives by naming it. People have always had a meaningful relationship with the Whole of Reality, in part because they have invariably personified or relationalized it as a Thou. This is one of the ways that we're able to bridge the science/religion divide. Those who fail to realize that God is *always* a personification of Reality, measurable and nonmeasurable, miss everything.

So in that sense, naming actually establishes the relationship and defines our role in that relationship. I see the difference between saying *"the* universe," which tends to separate me from it, and "Universe," proper name, which honors It as our source. To continue our dialogue about science and religion, we have this idea from science that the universe is not only more than what we can say it is, but also that it's changing, dynamic, and evolving. You often speak about recognizing the story and message that's embedded in and being expressed by the universe, and you sometimes call yourself an evolutionary evangelist. I wonder if you can say more about the evolutionary nature of the universe and how you see this as good news, or gospel?

Sure. It's vitally important to understand what I call "the holy trajectory" or "sacred direction" of emergent complexity. When we *get* this, we see that the universe isn't merely a chaotic, chance, meaningless, purposeless, directionless process. Complexity has a direction. This is not saying that some otherworldly entity or intelligence outside the system has figured it all out or is pulling strings or making it happen in any particular way.

I'm simply saying that from the perspective of now, looking back, we see greater complexity, interdependence, and cooperation emerging at larger and wider scales throughout time. Few scientists alive today would argue with this understanding of evolutionary directionality. In fact, the last major scientist who even tried to take issue with this view of emergence was Stephen Jay Gould. But since he died in 2002, many others, such as Robert Wright, John Stewart, Richard Dawkins, Sean B. Carroll, Simon Conway Morris, Stuart Kauffman, Ursula Goodenough, Terrance Deacon, and Ray Kurzweil, to name just a few, have written popular books and articles on evolutionary emergence. This way of thinking about directionality is now widely accepted.

In addition to greater complexity, interdependence, and cooperation at larger and wider scales, we also see increasing evolvability. Life keeps getting better and better at evolving. Indeed, in us, life is now learning how it has evolved for billions of years. We are in the early stages of learning how to align ourselves with this process and will, in the decades to come, begin to consciously evolve, rather than just muddle through unconsciously.

This gives me hope. I'm deeply inspired by this. It's what wakes me up each morning excited to do all I can to cocreate a just and healthy world for our planet and its diverse and wonderous species. I see this sacred evolutionary view—this "Evolution Theology" perspective—inspiring people to cooperate across ethnic and religious differences. It can also inspires people to live with greater integrity, love, compassion, and generosity. It can help us bridge our differences and know that we've got dependable guidance that isn't merely from ancient texts, but through the entire range of sciences.

Science is revelatory; it reveals divine truth. Speaking religiously, one could say that God has been revealing Himself/Herself/Itself throughout the course of history. Understanding complexity's trajectory is vitally important, because it allows us to easily discern what "God's will" is: for us collectively to grow in compassion and cooperation, to grow in integrity, and to grow in our ability to align our programs, policies, and institutions with this sacred trajectory. When this happens, the self-interests of all the parts will be aligned with the well-being of the planet as a whole. That's the key. Our top priority must be getting ever better at aligning individual self-interest and group self-interest with planetary self-interest. When this is effectively done, individuals, corporations, and nation-states that benefit the larger common good will themselves benefit. The more good that they do, the more they'll benefit. Thus, they'll be incentivized to do as much good as possible. Individuals and groups that harm the common good will be taxed, penalized, or will suffer moral strictures. In this way, it will be in all of our self-interests to do the right, just, ecological thing. And it will also be in our self-interest to *not* do the unjust or un-ecological thing. And we learn this not from ancient religious texts, but from seeing the entire history of the universe as scripture—as divine guidance.

Another inspiring and hopeful thing is realizing that seeing ourselves and our world from an evolutionary perspective provides guidance to us as individuals regarding how to live lives of joy, happiness, bliss, fulfillment, and purpose, with relationships that thrive. This is something that we now have real knowledge about—not just beliefs about. We have measurable, empirical knowledge about how to do that.

Through science?

Yes, through science! Science is just another name for our best collective intelligence. Through evolutionary psychology, evolutionary neurobiology, and an evolutionary understanding of ethics and morality, we get fabulous guidance regarding living in fruitful, productive, on-purpose ways. Why do some individuals thrive while others don't? Why do some groups cooperate really well where others fail? We now have real knowledge about all this that was simply not available to our ancestors.

Another key piece is having a shared sacred story that allows us to understand the nature of sacrifice for the common good. That's why having a story that unites us across ethic and religious differences is so important. This is what Connie and I call the history of everyone and everything—the epic of evolution—"The Great Story."

Evolution Theology thus builds bridges, provides guidance, and restores realistic hope. It bridges head and heart, science and religion, faith and reason. It also bridges different religious traditions and helps us value religious differences. It also bridges family members—it helps humanists and evangelicals in the same family, for example, to find enough common ground to have a deep and meaningful conversation and things that really matter. For many people, this was simply not possible before.

Because the facts of science aren't widely disputed, there's common ground for a conversation to take place.

Right, and now we have language that functions as conceptual common ground, such as "public and private revelation," "day and night language," "facts as God's native tongue," and "createheism." These are perspectives that are providing enough common ground so that people from very different backgrounds can have nourishing conversations from the heart. So an evolutionary worldview builds bridges and provides guidance, both personally and collectively.

To use religious language, God's will is now obvious and universal. Obvious in the sense that it's right here in front of us and universal in the sense that

God's will for you, me, and our species is the same thing: live in deep integrity. When I say "God's will," I mean it is the *only* way that leads to a healthy future.

The third thing I would say about a sacred, science-based, deep-time perspective is that it restores realistic hope. I don't mean otherworldly hope, like Jesus the cosmic janitor coming to clean up the mess we've made, but a real, natural, this-world hope that is respectful of the traditional religious orientations and can ultimately usher them into a larger perspective.

For example, one of the things about a deep-time view of reality that gives me hope is the fact that the main thing that has driven creativity and transformation for billions of years has been chaos, breakdowns, and bad news. When I trust this process in my own life and in the world, I'm inspired to be in action without fear.

Such an understanding gives me the larger perspective to trust the chaos of my life, the challenges that I must deal with, and it also allows me to trust the turbulent transitions that we as a species are likely to experience in the next hundred years or so. When we look to the looming issues facing us: overpopulation, species extinction, global warming, the growing gap between the rich and the poor—many people feel overwhelmed. When I look at these things, through sacred deep-time eyes, I get excited. Because if we didn't have problems at this scale—problems that are undeniably and indisputably in need of our attention—we'd keep pushing off the changes that we need to make for another several hundred years.

Two hundred years from now people will look back at the difficult challenges that we and our children faced and they'll say, "Thank God they had to deal with those challenges!" because that's what will have forced us to evolve in healthy ways.

Yes, we made the choices we did in response to the difficulties we are now facing. It seems like another area where the Great Story provides guidance is looking through the whole history of the universe and seeing how these challenges have been overcome in the past. We're here because of all the obstacles that all the previous organisms had to overcome.

Precisely. And this is where an evolutionary perspective can become both personally and relationally transformative. When we understand our brain's creation story, for example—that is, how the brain with its embedded instincts evolved—we realize that practically all the things that we find frustrating about ourselves and each other served the survival and reproductive needs of our ancestors. In other words, we wouldn't be here without those very same traits in our lineage! For example, we all have our Lizard Legacy (our reptilian brain), our Furry li'l Mammal (our old mammalian brain), our Monkey Mind (the rational/verbal part of our brain), and our prefrontal lobes, what Connie and I playfully call our "Higher Porpoise"—the part of our brain concerned with goals, commitments, good judgment, and such—our higher purpose.

When we understand that traits such as self-centeredness, status-seeking, promiscuity, overeating, and craving foods that have lots of sugar, salt, or fat in them have been what's been needed in the past for us to have this conversation right now, we have access to a freedom that we've not known before.

The challenge now is that we live in a modern world that's cocreated through language, so we make promises and enter agreements, we say that we'll do this, and then our instincts lead us to do something different. When we can realize that these traits have served us in the past—when we can find gratitude for these traits—paradoxically, it makes it much easier to stay in integrity—partly because we're no longer judging ourselves for having these aspects of ourselves.

It's much easier for me to stay in integrity now that I know how my brain evolved, and understand why the challenging parts of myself, my "addictive nature" served my ancestors in the past. Understanding all this allows me not to judge myself *and* it helps me live in integrity now, partly by having a circle of support. Integrity is a team sport. Thanks to an evolutionary understanding of my instincts, I no longer find it challenging to be in integrity around things I used to struggle with. In my world, I call that "grace!"

You talk about evolutionary integrity in your book. Is this what you mean by it?

Yes, refer to it variously as "deep integrity," "big integrity," or "evolutionary integrity." In a Christian context, I talk about it as Christ-like integrity, and what I mean by this is the embodiment, the incarnation, of trust, authenticity, responsibility, and service. "Salvation" is found in a stance toward life that is open-hearted and open-handed, rather than one based on fear or arrogance. If you think you can have the peace that passes all understanding and freedom around your unchosen nature from the stance of arrogance and fear, you're kidding yourself. Trust and humility are essential.

One is aligned with reality when one is humble and recognizes that there's something larger than just one's ego at work. When we come from a place of arrogance or fear, we're often simply out of touch with reality. Not all kinds of fear, of course. I mean, if a tiger jumps out at you…

There's an evolutionary purpose for fear.

Absolutely. Another aspect of evolutionary integrity is responsibility. If you think you can have real joy and peace and serve some larger purpose by being irresponsible and blaming someone or something outside yourself for your life being the way it is, you're also out of touch with reality. The last aspect of deep integrity is serving some larger purpose than your own animal needs—to serve a larger whole, to be a blessing to another or to the world in some way.

These four—trust, authenticity, responsibility, and service—I see as the four essential components of deep integrity, of being aligned with Reality. In my book, I refer to this as the REALizing of traditional religious concepts—taking concepts we previously thought of as supernatural or other worldly and showing how they're measurably real, for everybody, everywhere. The REALizing of sin and salvation, for example, is recognizing that we're not just about a snake who tempted a woman long ago. Original sin is concerned with the fact that we all have an unchosen nature; we have inherited proclivites.

All of us have instincts that evolved in a world in which we no longer live. Our current context, for most of us, is not well-matched to our instincts. You wouldn't expect a bear or a crocodile or a skunk to go counter to its instincts very easily. Yet we are expected to go counter to our instincts all the time. I mean, as a high-testosterone male, my instincts are to mate it if it moves! [laughs] Yet if I act on my instincts, I destroy my marriage, I destroy my mission. My life goes down the tubes. So the question becomes: how can our instincts, our energies, our deep yearnings serve what is most important to us and what we're most committed to? That's what being in integrity is. To use religious language, that's what being "in Christ" is all about. And from a non-religious perspective, that's what it means to be aligned with Reality.

One could also say that following your instincts is going the way of evolution. I mean, why not give in to those impulses? It sounds like there's another instinct you're talking about, a higher instinct.

Well there is, and one of the things we've seen throughout cultural history and cultural evolution is that we keep finding ways of cooperating that supersede the needs and wants of any one individual. We've created larger scales of cooperation through beliefs, through moral codes, and through scripture, sacred stories, laws, constitutions, and so forth. If we are to move into a just, healthy, sustainable, life-giving future, then we have to recognize *how* life has created these greater spheres of complexity throughout time. We need to find ways to align our laws, our medicine, our politics, our economics, and our education with the way life really works, so that we can move into the future in a healthy way. To the degree that we ignore this direction of life, or think that our role is to dominate or oppress or use nature only for human benefit, then we're out of touch with Reality, and will suffer the consequences—and bring about a very real hell.

What do you see as the future for twenty-first century spirituality and its relationship to science? What's the direction these two fields are going?

Well, for me spirituality is not anything ethereal or other worldly. It's about right relationships with, and at, all nested levels, temporally and spatially. The opposite of spirituality would be wrong relationship, at some nested level. It's pursuing one's own self-interest at the expense of the larger or smaller spheres of our existence.

The main thing I see happening throughout the course of the next hundred years is that we will become ever more conscious of the process of evolution, as well as the necessity of aligning everything that we do with the process of evolution within and around us. And we will find ways of reorganizing our governmental and economic structures so that it is in the self-interest of individuals, corporations, and nations to do well for the larger common good.

It's also important (and exhilarating) to recognize that we really can have freedom around our unchosen nature. Once we know this, we can allow those energies to serve us and our loved ones, and our world, in profound ways.

Maybe we can even honor them as part of our evolutionary heritage, so that they can express themselves in healthy ways.

Yes, absolutely! That's exactly what I'm talking about. For many years, Alison, my first wife, and I, and our kids, celebrated every full and new moon with treats. I would only allow myself alcohol only on the full and new moons and the kids would only allow themselves chocolate or candy or whatever. We did this for seven or eight years in the late 1980s and early 1990s. What we were doing was honoring that part our instincts and nature to have feel-good substances that kick off the dopamine in our heads, while keeping it from getting out of hand. As we all know, it's easy to get addicted to those things. But of course, it doesn't have to be an either-or relationship, where we either binge or we have to stay away from them altogether.

Now, for myself, throughout the last decade and a half I've come to a different place. For me, now, having even a little bit of alcohol in my life is not what I want, because it simply takes too much energy to keep it to just a little. So from a purely pragmatic standpoint, I now avoid alcohol entirely. But I still occasionally do chocolate or caffeine in a ritualistic way.

It sounds as though you've brought yourself in right relationship with yourself, and also with life itself. You love your life as a result, and that's really a living testament to aligning yourself with reality in this way.

Yes, it is stunning to me to be in the place where I know I could die tonight and I have no unfinished business, no resentments, and no secrets. When I look to the past, I've cleaned up all the messes and I've apologized to all the people I've hurt (at least those I could remember and track down). When I look to the future, I have no fear—I have nothing but trust and faith. When I look to the present moment, I'm happy virtually all the time. I have heavenly joy—the peace that passes all understanding—every day. I'm with a marriage partner who is stunningly perfect for me, truly, in every way. By grace, I've gotten to the place of having no fear, no resentments, no regrets, no shame or guilt, and no unfinished business. All the people in my life whom I love know it. I've recently told them so. I personally don't know any more joyful place to be than this state of mind. And it has everything to do with having wholeheartedly embraced a sacred evolutionary perspective.

It sounds as though your life is one big celebration. Do you have any last thoughts to share on the blessings of evolution?

Everybody doesn't have to "get it," everybody doesn't have to evolve, everybody doesn't have to become like some enlightened guru or something. It takes just a few of us to change the system, and the fact that we're all different from each other is a good thing. The fact that we all have different strengths and weaknesses is a good thing, from an evolutionary perspective. It's kind of like a bioregion—the biodiversity is what makes it a healthy bioregion, and the same is true of consciousness. The key is finding people whose gifts and limitations are a good match for yours. I'm just eternally grateful to be alive today, doing this work, with Connie as my partner.

Chapter 8

The Spiritual Universe: An Interview With Hameed Ali and Karen Johnson

❝The universe is a multidimensional manifold where all dimensions intersect the dimension of knowledge at all their points. Hence, knowledge pervades the whole manifold, making it into a magical self-luminous holographic world of exquisite meaningful deep knowledge," writes A.H. Almaas in his book *Inner Journey Home* (Shambhala, 2004). We can know this directly, he suggests, because we are the universe itself and therefore participants in this field of knowledge and consciousness. Our capacity to know the universe directly through our own immediate experience is a radical idea for many of us accustomed to investigating the universe through telescopes, microscopes, and other scientific instruments. Yet it makes perfect sense if we can accept the idea that we are the universe itself, and therefore reflect some of the properties of the whole. Discover your own deeper nature, and you have found the deeper nature of the cosmos. For more than 30 years Hameed Ali, Karen Johnson, and their colleagues and students have been doing just this—using direct human experience as a window into the underlying nature of reality.

Hameed Ali and Karen Johnson are the originators and head spiritual teachers of the Diamond Approach, a contemporary path of spiritual realization. This approach combines traditional spiritual practices such as meditation and self-inquiry with the insights and developments of modern depth psychology, and emphasizes practice and self-realization in the midst of everyday life.

Hameed Ali was born in Kuwait in 1944 and came to the United States in 1963 to study physics. He stopped his studies just short of his doctorate, finding that science could not offer answers to the deeper questions he was asking about life and the universe at the time. He later earned a PhD in psychology, focusing on Reichian Therapy. For the past three decades he has been teaching and developing the Diamond Approach, which now has spiritual groups and teachers around the world. He is the author of more than 14 books on spirituality and spiritual psychology under the pen name A.H. Almaas, including *The Pearl Beyond Price*, *The Point of Existence*, *Inner Journey Home*, and most recently, *The Unfolding Now*.

Karen Johnson is a long-time friend and collaborator with Hameed Ali in the development of the Diamond Approach. Educated in the arts, dance, and psychology, and with an active interest in science, her primary passion is in the understanding of human nature and its place in the universe.

Stephan Martin: You've described the universe in your writings as a multidimensional manifold in which the physical dimension of the cosmos is coexistent with its spiritual ground, or Being. Can you say more about this and the relationship between these various dimensions? Why is the physical dimension so different from these other subtler spiritual dimensions?

Hameed Ali: It's a very subtle question, and I'm not sure there's an exact answer, as I have many questions about this myself. In the Diamond Approach, we find that reality discriminates itself into different dimensions that can all be experienced directly. These dimensions of existence are also co-emergent in that they all interpenetrate and are simultaneously present with each other and in our experience in each moment.

For example, the universe can be seen and experienced as composed of physical matter, but it can also be experienced as pure consciousness or as a boundless ocean of light and love, as many spiritual traditions and teachings have described it. It is simultaneously all of these and more, depending on which dimensions of experience and reality we are attuned to at the time.

Now when we recognize the existence of these other dimensions and see them as co-emergent and arising together in our experience, the physical actually doesn't appear physical in the way we usually think of it, but as one dimension of many, all arising out of the same spiritual ground. The physical universe is really not physical in terms of being separate from the spiritual, but it has certain properties that differentiate it from the other dimensions of existence.

The main property of the physical, from what I see, is that the forms in it are more stable and longer lasting than those of other dimensions, and also that physical objects or forms don't interpenetrate each other. Objects in the physical dimension interpenetrate with other dimensions, but not with each other. They can't go through each other.

Karen Johnson: They *can*, but they tend not to.

HA: Yes, that's right. Usually if you have two balls, they will bounce against each other and not interpenetrate. That's a characteristic unique to the physical dimension. Other dimensions don't have that limitation.

Now, what makes it that way…I don't know.

It seems that physical matter has a certain denseness or density, that these other dimensions don't have.

KJ: That's not actually true [laughs]. Science will tell you that physical matter is mostly empty space!

HA: In our opinion, that's not a valid discrimination, since there are other dimensions more dense than the physical. From the perspective of the deeper spiritual dimensions, the physical appears as ephemeral, and the spiritual dimension is much more dense and real. Physical matter is dense and opaque if we look at it only from the physical dimension.

KJ: If we take ourselves to be exclusively physical beings, then we're taking ourselves to be dense, and so we perceive the world from that perspective of density. But in fact the density is not inherently there—it's the mind that creates the denseness and opacity.

So the density is actually within ourselves, in our perception of things?

KJ: It's our limited perspective that causes us to perceive the physical as dense. Our ignorance of the deeper dimensions of existence creates what we perceive as the density of the physical world. When you perceive the physical from the real density of the spiritual ground, everything appears as if you could put your hand through it—it looks like a dream.

HA: That's why many spiritual teachings say that the world is like an illusion, like a dream. When you see it from its deeper dimensions it appears ephemeral, light, and transparent. This corresponds with physics theory that says that matter is mostly space. What we consider matter is just the interaction of forces according to physical laws, and this is what gives it its density and cohesion. But it's not really—it's only our perception of it.

KJ: This is why the inner nature of an electron is basically nothing, arising moment by moment from nowhere. This is what really happens! [laughs] Concepts such as nothingness and nowhere are very difficult to answer through conventional physics, but they can be experienced directly through our spiritual nature. For example, the nature of a singularity is an unknowable idea in physics. But your deeper spiritual nature can be experienced directly as a singularity, as a point with no dimension to it, but has infinite potential. In physics, something with no dimension is not measurable, and so we're at the limits of that paradigm.

When you recognize your deeper nature from your own direct experience, it can bring up paradoxes in our mind about the relationship between the physical and our true nature. So you have to come at it from both sides, the physical and the spiritual. I think science is fabulous—it explains all kinds of things, but only on the level of physics. Beyond that, it's restricted by the limits of its own thinking.

So it seems that many of the paradoxes of the relationship between the spiritual and physical world stem from confusion in our minds about what's truly real and what represents the deepest level of reality.

KJ: It's also our loss of connection to the deeper level of reality that causes us to perceive the world from a more superficial level, and so we believe the physical world to be fundamental in a way that it really isn't. Many people think that physical reality is real, and that the spiritual reality is somehow "other." A better way to approach things is to ask ourselves how we know what's real from our direct experience, and how does that relate to the spiritual?

I can see how this belief in the fundamental reality of physical objects prevents people from perceiving how everything is arising out of nothing from nowhere in each moment, as you said. I've found that many people have a hard time with the Big Bang theory because it suggests that the entire universe came out of essentially nothing.

HA: This brings us back to the earlier description of matter in physics as the interplay of forces. For example, the interactions of the four fundamental forces in physics are the basis for all matter, so the physical world can be described as the interaction of forces as much as anything else. But to think of it as forces already assumes a physical reductionist perspective. From the perspective of true nature and spiritual reality, there are no interactions between things and therefore there are no forces. The idea of objects and forces already implies a mind founded in the physical universe, in the ideas of separateness inherent in physical reductionism, and so the whole metaphysics of modern science is in question from a spiritual perspective.

Because there is fundamentally no separateness?

HA: Yes. From a spiritual perspective, nothing causes anything else—there's no cause and effect because everything is fundamentally a unity. That's the idea that Karen was talking about, how everything emerges out of a singular unity, out of nothing. When it is constantly emerging out of nothing, it is continually emerging in every moment in a different yet unified pattern. We can look at that pattern and conceptualize the different forces and objects that we find in physics, but it's not really how things are on a deeper level.

Results from quantum mechanics such as entanglement and nonlocality also begin to question a purely reductionist approach, particularly when objects that are widely separated can act as one system under certain conditions. Do you see these results from our theories of physics as expressions of this fundamental unity of reality?

HA: It could be. The way science is going it could connect the two at some point. There are already many people writing books about how science is proving spirituality, but I don't think it's there yet.

KJ: One of the difficulties I have with trying to make the connection between science and spirituality work is that things on both sides tend to get stretched beyond their natural limits to try to make something fit. Intuitively, it seems like they should fit, but another whole way of thinking has to happen on both sides before something emerges that is a single unified combination of the two. With the new paradigms emerging in science, many people are saying, "See, science proves spiritual experience," but they're making a stretch happen that doesn't necessarily fit scientific data with personal experience.

HA: When people find parallels between science and the spiritual, they assume that they are talking about the same truth. But parallel truths are not identities, and you cannot use similarities to prove each other.

KJ: The fact that these parallels exist is interesting in itself, and is telling us something about reality, but I don't know just yet what it means. The best thing from my perspective would be to allow our lack of knowledge about the connection between science and spirituality to be there, and to see what arises naturally from that, without an attempt to create a connection that's premature of actual direct knowing.

HA: I think many people jump to conclusions too soon. For example, people discover the entanglement of particles in quantum physics and they think that it's the same as spiritual nonlocality. If physics nonlocality is a reflection of spiritual nonlocality, then why doesn't it show up everywhere? Spiritual nonlocality is true everywhere for everything at every time, so why does it happen in physics only in limited circumstances and conditions? If at some point they find out in physics that nonlocality is true for everything all the time, then that would be an interesting discovery.

KJ: The gap in the middle between the two is much more interesting to me than the parallels between them. Why aren't things nonlocal in the physical world as they are in the spiritual realm?

HA: Following a question like that to its end might lead to the discovery of the secrets of matter. For example, why is the physical dimension of the universe different from its other dimensions? No one knows at the present time. Spiritual teachers don't know because they can't explain matter either. They know that its nature is the nature of everything and that it interacts and has physical properties, but I've never heard any explanation about why it has those properties.

There are theories or metaphysical systems that say that it's all gradations of consciousness, the same basic stuff of experience.

HA: Yes, but what gives it those properties? Why don't things interpenetrate physically? What makes it that way? Just as spiritual teachers don't understand the physical properties of matter in a complete way, theoretical physicists don't understand spirit—they can't explain it.

It sounds as though science and spirituality are two sides of the same coin, and yet it's still premature to know what the exact relationship is between them.

KJ: Yet we can know that they are two different aspects of the same phenomenon directly through our own experience. Spiritually, we can see that spirit is present in matter, that they're not two different things that you can separate from each other.

HA: The way I sometimes think of it is like the particle-wave complementarity in physics, where light can be seen as either as a particle or as a wave, but it is really both at once. If you look at the world from the particle view, you see matter. If you look at it from the wave view, you see spirit. They're both always there in the same sense, but it depends on how you look at them. That's one way to think about it, but remember it's a metaphor and not an explanation.

These may be questions for 22nd, 23rd, and 24th century physics. I'd like to return to something we touched upon earlier, which may relate our experiences of the physical universe with the spiritual. We can demonstrate through modern astronomy and cosmology that the universe seems to have had a beginning 14 billion years ago, and yet from what you said earlier, it can be seen to be arising in its entirety every moment. How can we reconcile these two? How can it be both 14 billion years old and yet arising fresh and completely new in every moment out of nothing?

HA: I don't see a problem with both being true at the same time. It's true that things are arising freshly in each moment, and so maybe things started arising freshly in each moment several billion years ago. Maybe before that, nothing was arising! So you could hypothesize that this process of arising had a beginning. Some teachings believe that, and some teachings don't. It's not a contradiction in my mind that both could be true.

If that's true, then are they both arising from the same source? Did the universe begin from the same source that it's arising from in each moment?

HA: The source that is nothing![laughs]

KJ: Yes, of course. How can you have more than one source? I think the question of time is what skews things for many people. Often, time is thought of as something that can be measured the way other things can, but that's more of a convenience and it's not actually true. When we experience our true nature directly, we're beyond time. Things arise every moment in a pattern that changes and evolves. When that pattern builds on itself, it brings life into it and more complex systems appear.

But all this doesn't take way from the fact that nothing exists underneath things. Since this arising began billions of years ago, we can see a progression in the pattern of existence that we call the evolution of the universe, but the source of it all continues to be the same source it's all arising from right now...and right now...and right now. Each moment the pattern is shifting and is slightly different.

So we can refer to that simply as a change in the unified pattern but not time as a separate distinct phenomenon.

KJ: I would call it real time, rather than some kind of linear time that projects from back then in the past through now and into the future. The now that's arising is always the same now, because there is only the now. I think where people get confused is when they think things began to evolve in the past and now they are old. For example, this chair was there what we think of as 10 minutes ago, but it's actually only here right now. "Ten minutes ago" never existed, except as something in our minds. The whole concept of time makes people think "Well, if that happened then, how can it be fresh now?"

Right, like it still exists somewhere in the past.

KJ: Yes, as if it's still there somewhere, but it's not, and that's the difficulty people have. The only reality is the present.

So the entire universe only exists in the present, as a singular unified field simply changing shape moment to moment?

HA: Yes, that's the perception. It's like a morphing.

KJ: It's like a changing unified pattern.

HA: Yes, and many of its changing patterns are described by physical laws. The discovery of physical laws is the recognition of patterns that are consistently arising. But they are still conceptualized in the modern view as resulting from objects and forces. The idea of separate objects and different forces breaks down when you see the universe as a unity.

So what is it that maintains the whole pattern moment to moment, if it's all arising out of nothing? Is there a universal memory that remembers the pattern each moment as it arises out of nothing? What maintains everything in between moments of arising?

HA: Actually, this has to do with the process of manifestation. I would not say that manifestation has a memory, but has instead an inherent order to it and a consistent pattern of appearance. The order does not require memory, but is self-organizing in an orderly way.

KJ: I think one way we can see this expressing itself is in nature. For example, when a plant grows, it doesn't go, "Let's see, we need a little more photosynthesis over here instead of here…" It just grows. But because of the complexity of the human mind we tend to think of everything as being dependant on mental operations. But when we're in touch with ourselves in a deeper way we feel a natural flow, and when we can really let go into that flow we feel that something in us comes forward spontaneously, a natural process that doesn't need us to reach in and "do it."

By letting go of our beliefs about how things are done we can begin to see how the universe actually functions. We can see how we ourselves unfold naturally when we simply open to what is. As we develop, that "isness" develops itself—we don't develop it. When we don't let go and don't interfere with our natural unfoldment, we get a direct taste of how the universe develops and grows. We don't have to be enlightened to experience this directly and know that this is true.

That's an important point that you mention here, that we can discover something both about ourselves and the universe at the same time, through our own direct experience.

KJ: Yes, and there's a good reason for this, since it is this larger reality that is living through us. So we never have our own separate life or our own separate evolution. When we're really open, we feel the universe coming through us and as us in a distinct and particular way through this unique individual consciousness in this moment. We see that it's not about "me" or "mine," but about opening to what's present wherever we are right now. When we do this, we can get a taste of the larger perspective since we are that.

So how can people know when they're aligned with this larger cosmic process? Can we hinder it? Can we facilitate it?

HA: The process of the development of the human soul is already an alignment with the cosmic process. Waking up is the awareness of this process, and so by waking up to our deeper nature, we are naturally aligning with this larger process. You see, the way we're thinking about and discussing things right now is really the scientific way of looking at truth. In the scientific way of thinking, we want to find truth in order to explain things.

The spiritual way of looking at truth is slightly different. Spiritually, you want to find the truth, because the truth liberates. When you find truth, you feel good and are uplifted and liberated, and so you love the truth as a result. In spirituality, explanation is not as important as liberation. Liberation is the indication that there is alignment with something larger. The more you sense that you're liberated the more you know that you're aligned.

KJ: Yet I have to say that liberation for me provides its own kind of explanations. Each time I have a new step into liberation, it actually explains many of the obstacles that came before it that I couldn't see from the other side. There's something very pleasurable and satisfying to me about understanding the larger scope of things, so that when I feel myself being liberated, I want to *know* what it is that's liberating me. For me, it's not just an explanation into the mechanics of how things work, but an explanation that allows me to have an intimate understanding of the mystery of the universe. It's beautiful to understand it simply for what it is, not just because it explains things.

HA: Scientists as well see beauty in discovery, and that's part of what scientists get excited about. But science is an explanation of the outer world, and not of oneself generally. If you can really explain yourself to yourself, then that's liberation. That's what psychology attempts to do, but it usually doesn't go far enough.

Do you think that's because personal experience is currently missing from science as part of the data?

HA: Science obviously doesn't include personal experience as part of its approach since the general view is that observation can happen more objectively through instruments than through humans. The importance of human consciousness in scientific exploration isn't generally acknowledged.

Yet behind every scientific instrument is a human consciousness.

HA: Right. Without the human consciousness there would be no instruments and nobody looking through them. But the orientation in science is currently such that it includes the objects of the universe but misses the subject. I don't really understand why it is that science doesn't question the nature of the subject that is behind all the observations. It would seem that the subject is the most important. Now I know how it developed with Descartes and all that, but still the observer needs to be there—you can't observe without the observer! So what is the nature of the observer? Including the observer might be the beginning of a bridge between science and spirituality.

Now with discovery of the central role of the observer in quantum physics we see that we cannot fully remove the subject from the scientific process, so it would seem that there's currently a call to bring the observer back in, to bring the subject back into science.

HA: True, but they still think that the qualities of the observer are not relevant, that the observer is yet another object, and not a consciousness.

Bringing the observer and the subject back into science seems to bring us back around to our earlier discussion of the relationship between science and spirituality.

KJ: I've played with a mind experiment at times that explores the relationship between the physical world and spirituality. I've noticed that the physical world is hard, and when I feel myself as separate from my deeper nature, I notice I feel hard as well. So I wonder if everyone on the planet saw the world from the perspective of its deeper nature, and they saw its ephemeralness, would it still be experienced as hard? Is this hardness the way the universe expresses its ego nature? It seems to have all the principles of an ego structure with hardness, rigidity, and resistance to change, etc.... In the same way, ego structure doesn't really exist fundamentally, but we feel it as hardness and inflexibility and all the things that we attribute to the physical universe.

But when we feel ourselves as beyond our ego and experience our deeper nature and its flow and so on, the physical world remains physically hard even though we perceive it differently from this deeper place. For example, even though it looks ephemeral, I'm still able to sit in a solid chair and walk around. But in this mind experiment, I wonder if everyone everywhere saw the ephemeral nature of the world, would it still have the same hardness and structure?

So I wonder why do these two experiences feel so different? Is it that matter isn't aware of its deeper nature in the same way just yet? Does the material world in some sense have to wake up to its spiritual nature, and do we as sentient beings need to be aware of it for it to awaken?

So is the universe in some sense waking up to itself?

KJ: Yes, the universe itself may have its own degree of unconsciousness that expresses itself through us and through matter by arranging it in certain ways. It's just like when we're unconscious, we arrange ourselves in certain ways that aren't true to who we really are. But if we go into whatever is there and investigate for ourselves, we always find our deeper nature.

So then will the denseness and rigidity that we perceive in matter then dissolve into its deeper nature when it is brought to consciousness?

KJ: Maybe it will become a more fluid and flexible world of light and spaciousness but still retain its physical form.

HA: Or perhaps matter will lose the particular physical properties that distinguish it from other dimensions of existence. For example, some Buddhist schools believe that the world is the way it is because of collective karma, and it will continue to be this way until all the collective karma is dissolved. But they don't say what the world will become when this happens.

So collective enlightenment will literally change the world!

HA: Yes, according to these teachings, if everybody's enlightened then that will change the actual character of the world. At the same time, they also say that there is endless time and endless beings to be enlightened, so it may not happen anytime soon.

KJ: The difference here is in thinking of matter from what we know of the soul in our perspective and how it can be rigid and inflexible when it is conditioned by ego. When we see through our ego-based conditioning, our soul opens up and we feel ourselves as light and ephemeral. We don't feel the heaviness and clunkiness of the body in the same way that we did previously.

When I think about physical laws and spiritual laws I know that they are the two sides of the same thing. Manifestation takes place on many levels and all of these interpenetrate each other. So if our personal experience is a window into the cosmic reality, then if we study and explore ego structure and how it develops and evolves then maybe we will understand something about the larger cosmic process of development.

HA: This also addresses what people call miracles. Miracles are basically a breakdown of physical laws. These do happen sometimes, which means it's possible for physical matter to not obey those laws in those instances.

Some people have talked about physical laws as "habits" of the universe, applicable most of the time, but not always.

HA: Yes, and it reminds me of Aurobindo's idea about death. His idea is that we die only because we believe we will die. In this case it's a collective belief, and not just based on the individual. So he says that if all animal life stops believing in death then there will be no more death. It's conjecture, but it's fun to think about.

Hameed, in some of your writing you have referred to what you call the cosmic pearl, where our collective spiritual nature and physical nature are becoming increasingly integrated throughout time into a harmonious whole, just as an ocean pearl integrates sand and secretions into itself over time. Do you see this as the larger view of what is happening, that throughout time the universe is becoming a cosmic pearl?

HA: That seems to be what we perceive to be happening. We see a process evolving in that direction, but it's a very slow process.

KJ: I wonder if we'll ever get past adolescence! [laughs]

HA: You could think of the universe as a hologram, where each part of it, each soul, each organism in the universe, is developing. The process of development is happening everywhere, so as human consciousness becomes more clearly seen, experienced, and integrated, it affects the whole. Soul actually pervades everything, including the human soul, so if you see it that way then it becomes natural to see that the whole thing is actually evolving.

So is there a particular role that humans have in this process of cosmic development, given our capacity for learning, self-reflection, and growth?

KJ: Our capacities give us a particular opportunity in this universal development, but we're also very careless with these capacities. If we look at the fraction of humanity that is doing real work on themselves, it's very small. We've liberated the mind in many ways in modern culture, but we haven't really liberated the heart or soul yet. We have a special position in nature in that through self-reflection and awareness we can be in touch with the truth in ourselves in a very deep way, but I think that we're also very slack in that responsibility. In a similar way we're being very slack with our technology and what it's doing to the Earth.

HA: What's special about the human being is that we have the potential for perceiving, experiencing, and living all the dimensions of reality. We don't see other beings having that same potential. There might be others who do, I wouldn't say that there aren't. Maybe there are other animals who do, or extraterrestrials or life elsewhere…who knows? We see that human beings at the very least have this capacity for experience, but I wouldn't say that it's necessarily limited to just human beings.

This capacity for growth, conscious evolution, and contribution to the whole seems to be unrecognized by many people, who don't seem to realize that their own work on themselves makes a difference in a larger field or perspective.

HA: Yes, it's like a mass of protoplasm, where certain locations in it become self-organized and more conscious and aware of their contribution. Even though this is happening in only a few locations, they're all the same being.

I wonder if all the parts of the protoplasm have to become conscious and more aware for the organism to evolve to a higher state. Is there a minimum critical mass that can change the whole?

HA: I don't know. For myself, I have never seen an indication of that, but it doesn't mean that there isn't. It's an optimistic idea, though.

Do you think this is true of liberation? If there are more liberated individuals in the world, does it make it easier for the rest of us to achieve liberation?

HA: Oh, yes. That's what most spiritual teachings believe. A liberated person has an immediate and direct influence on the larger field that we can perceive directly. The more conscious and open a person is, the more influence they have on the surrounding field.

KJ: It does seem that more and more people these days are encountering and getting sparked by spiritual ideas. Spiritual work has grown bigger and become more widespread, and the amount of spiritual information available to people these days is huge and increasing rapidly. While there are a lot of difficult challenges in the world right now there are also many opportunities for spiritual growth. It does seem as though there's a quickening.

HA: I think we can become optimistic when we think of quickening in the usual sense, of being positive and accelerating in that direction. The quickening can also take a negative turn as well. Overall I tend to be optimistic, but I'm aware of times in history when the quickening of events has been positive at times and negative at others, so who knows?

My observations around this have been somewhat paradoxical. Many times I have seen people have breakthrough experiences, much deeper than I expected, and yet at other times I've been disappointed in seeing that people really have not learned as much as I thought they had. So many times I can't tell, since I see different results at different times.

I wonder if it's the difference between having a deep experience, and then allowing that experience to change one's worldview.

KJ: Yes, it's often about integration and letting your deeper experience continue to inform your perspective. People tend to place spiritual experiences somewhere within their worldviews instead of the other way around. I think this is where people get caught up, with lots of ways to open up and have deep experiences, but not enough ways of learning how to use them fully and allow them to teach us.

In closing, is there anything that you two feel would be helpful for people to know about the universe and their role in it, beyond what we've covered already?

HA: Don't believe in any final conclusion about things. Always leave the question open…

KJ: …and dive into it headfirst! Keep an open mind, and remember that any spiritual experience is only the taste of what's possible, and you have to really be willing to immerse yourself in it to see it fully for what it is. I think the hope for humanity as well as for individual liberation is to not be satisfied with particular experiences, but to use experience itself to open up more and more to our deeper nature. This orientation, along with the recognition that there is no end or final conclusion, creates a momentum of unfoldment that will take us back home.

Chapter 9

The Buddhist Universe: An Interview With Lama Palden Drolma

The Buddhist universe is truly vast. Human experience occupies only a small part of the myriads of worlds, realms, and planes of existence that form the basis for Buddhist cosmology. Although the number of realms and worlds varies with the particular sect of Buddhism, all agree that the universe is a very big place. While scholars from different traditions continue to debate the ultimate nature of the world, whether there is a self or no-self, the nature of emptiness and form, and other paradoxes, all agree that our existence as humans in this particular time and place is a very precious opportunity for insight, growth, and realization. Many contemporary Buddhist teachers emphasize this last point, that whatever the ultimate nature of the universe, it is in the here and now that we discover the greatest treasure of existence: our own true nature. Lama Palden Drolma is one of those teachers, helping students navigate the many twists and turns of a complex universe in order eventually find their way back home.

One of the first Western female lamas authorized to teach in the Vajrayana Buddhist tradition, Lama Palden Drolma has been a student and teacher of Buddhism for more than 25 years. She is the founder and resident lama of the Sukhasiddhi Foundation in Marin County, California, where she works to make the teachings of Tibetan Buddhism available to all, and particularly for Westerners interested in spiritual practice in the midst of daily experience.

She completed the traditional Tibetan Buddhist three-year retreat in 1985 under Khabjé Kalu Rinpoché, and has since studied with many of the great Tibetan masters in all lineages. She has an abiding interest and focus in bringing the teachings of the deep wisdom of the dakinis and the sacred feminine to modern-day people. A practicing psychotherapist and the mother of two, she seeks to foster psycho-spiritual awareness in the midst of ordinary life, so that all of our daily experiences can be transformative vehicles for cultivating wisdom, compassion, and loving kindness wherever we are.

Stephan Martin: Let's begin by talking about the Buddhist vision of the universe according to your tradition.

Lama Palden: In the Vajrayana view, the essence of Buddhism is that the whole phenomenal world that appears is infinite. According to Mahayana scriptures, there are many, many universes, and there's intelligent life in many of those universes. It's vast, beyond our comprehension. And the essence of all of this is generally translated usually as Mind. Sometimes I translate it as awareness. You could also say it is consciousness; it is Mind in the sense that all we experience is directly related to our own karma, and our own stream of awareness.

In addition to our individual karma, we also have group karma, where we're thinking this [gestures to surrounding room] is all very solid and real, but it's actually all awareness. Due to the similarity in our group karma and the intensity of our own individual karma, things seem very solid, but it's actually not solid at all. It's appearance and emptiness unified, which is a Mahamudra Dzogchen point of view.

So do we perceive the phenomenal world as solid because of consensual belief?

Not because of consensual belief, but because we have made a fundamental split. We don't fully perceive our inward clarity of awareness, and so the outward clarity of what appears (or lack of clarity) is a projection of our own state of consciousness. Ultimately, it's all inseparable openness and awareness, whether internally or externally.

Now even though we all have our own experience, we perceive parts of reality to be the same because we all have this shared karma of having a human body and the karma to be in these situations. Within this karma and our living it out, there is consensual reality and that differs by culture.

The other thing related to what you were asking about the Vajrayana view is that the whole universe, everything that appears either internally or externally, is a teaching. The reality of what is, is not separate from how it symbolically teaches us.

Could you say more about that last point? What does it mean for the universe to be teaching?

If we open ourselves moment by moment to what is, and what is present in our experience, we find it is always teaching us.

In terms of providing opportunities for insight and learning?

Yes, and for directly realizing the truth of what is. Relative truth and ultimate truth is being pointed out continuously to us, if we can understand what it is saying. Sometimes we do get glimpses, through experiences in nature or elsewhere, of something that's being communicated to us. Similar to what Brian Swimme wrote about in a small book 10 or 15 years ago, where he says if you really look at the stars and you really *feel* the situation where there's this vastness above us, below us, and in every direction, it's going to put ourselves and our lives in a very different perspective than our usual limited viewpoint.

Sure, so in some sense that's the deeper truth or perspective that's trying to come through in that situation.

I think the way they would say it in Buddhism is that it's all groundlessness. For the ego, that's kind of scary, but the good news is that it's ultimate freedom. Who we really are is as vast as the cosmos.

We have a limited sense of our self, which is due to taking that vast awareness to be a separate self, and then projecting everything else as "other." Through this basic duality of ignorance and the subject-object split, we take our self to be this limited small self instead of inseparable from the vastness of all that is and realizing that it's all Mind.

A lot of physicists are starting to talk about "freedom at the foundations," the view that openness and freedom are the ultimate nature of the universe. That sounds similar to what you're saying.

Yes, there's been a lot of correlations that have come up in the past 20 or 30 years between physics and Buddhism. For example, in the Madhyamaka tradition of Nagarjuna and Chandrakirti, this table [points] has no inherent existence. If you took this table all apart, you could not find the "tableness," but nevertheless the table is there. So you can't say the table isn't there, but that it doesn't fundamentally exist as a "table" in the ultimate sense. Although the table doesn't fundamentally exist, they don't deny that it is still appearing, so this is why they call it "appearance-emptiness." From what little I understand, this is similar to the view of modern physics, where the table is there and clearly exists.

Is this related to the idea of interdependence, the idea that there's nothing that you can pull out of the universe and say, "this is a table?"

Right, because it's dependent on what *isn't* a table by contrast, which goes along with all the logical Madhyamaka arguments of interdependence and mutual dependence that prove emptiness. Now the way that interdependence is generally talked about is that we're all connected, that one thing leads to another, etc.…. This is important and these are all true, but this is not the deepest understanding of interdependence in Buddhism.

One related idea that Duane Elgin talks about is the idea of the living universe. In Mahamudra and Dzogchen, emptiness is said to be spontaneous presence, so that nothing in the universe can ever truly die. Awareness itself never dies, so this is where the idea comes in that there really is no life and death or birth and death. Since we are fundamentally this awareness, the physical can die, but the consciousness doesn't die.

Since everything that exists is ultimately this awareness, it's all alive in that sense.

This sounds very similar to what Duane Elgin talks about when he says the universe is alive in the broadest sense and also a living field of intelligence at the same time.

Actually, that is very closely connected with Mahamudra and Dzogchen in that this awareness that is the nature of everything is wisdom itself. But this takes discovery! We don't usually see this because we've so constricted our experience of awareness to that of a limited self, this collection of stuff that we feel and think we are—all the things that we negatively project onto the universe and the other "out there." The path in Buddhism is to release all that.

Have you noticed particular obstacles with Western students around this?

Yes, and this is where I feel that for Westerners, doing psychological work is usually essential for spiritual unfoldment. It's not that these traditional spiritual systems don't work, but that we have all this ego stuff in the way, so it's helpful to work through our psychological issues. For example, many of us are too afraid to feel the groundlessness, or we're too blocked to feel love and compassion. People get traumatized or hurt and become too vulnerable to open themselves up and actually feel a deep love for themselves or another.

Culturally, I think we're not as comfortable just resting in ourselves as they are in other cultures. In the Himalayas and India and elsewhere, they just hang and they're relaxed about things. [laughs] We're not so much. A lot of issues in the West come down to fear and the fact that we haven't been nourished by what is actually nourishing, so this is where psychological work can be very helpful. For example, opening to the vastness of the universe and really feeling that there's infinity underneath us and all around us in all directions—that brings up a lot of fear and groundlessness for people. Normally we're trying to ground our identities around our house or job or family, but actually all that is a limited construction about who we really are and what's really happening.

We don't usually see that these things are constructions.

No, we don't, and if we start to open in meditation or spiritual practice or by studying cosmology, and we really start to get it, we're not going to be able to open to that fully without working through our insecurity about groundlessness. I've seen that with people a lot.

Another barrier to opening to the bigger picture might be the belief that the universe is inhospitable or at least not friendly to us.

Yes, and from a Buddhist point of view, that's a projection. We think there's an other that needs to be defended against and we have had certain [negative] experiences and we project that outside of ourselves as karma, and so maybe the universe seems like it's hostile, but it's really our own mind displaying itself back to us.

From the perspective of the universe as a teacher, these could be opportunities for learning about both ourselves and the universe. On a related thread, does it seem to you that humanity as a whole is evolving?

I think so. I think the Earth and the human plane is a place where beings come to learn. It's not like we're all learning together and then we're all going to transcend and go to some other place or reach this utopia together. It's more like Grand Central Station, where we're each learning our individual lessons in the same place collectively.

The Buddhist point of view is that our lives on Earth are an incredible opportunity for growth and evolution. It's like the best possible situation for learning. We have suffering, we have joy, and we have these amazing faculties of the human being. It seems like in one sense humanity as a whole is evolving. For example, if you look at the history of philosophy and the development of science and the spread of human rights and similar things that weren't even talked about 4,000 years ago. That's evolutionary, I think. On the other hand, we're still really destroying each other.

Sometimes it seems as though things are progressing really slowly.

Yes, and the way I look at it is on a more individual level. There is such a wide spectrum of development in our species, my sense is that everyone is evolving on some level. It's highly individualized, even down to different parts of ourselves, which are more developed than other parts. Overall, I do think we're learning and developing and growing in a process.

And who knows? For example, the patriarchy got itself way out on a limb by developing in a certain way, and now it's gotten us to a place where we're in an environmental crisis. But maybe in the bigger picture, that had to happen. Maybe that was part of the evolution of our culture that we had to get ourselves way out on a limb. I also think that patriarchy was not an entirely male creation, since we've all been male and female in different lives, but it's more of a playing out of aspects of human consciousness.

Yes, the masculine and feminine aspects of our culture are different than male and female genders. Since this relates to the feminine aspect of your lineage, I wonder if you could say more about that.

Yes, I feel, along with many others, that a true feminine approach to the world has been dormant in our culture for at least a few thousand years. The masculine aspect of our culture is extremely good at creating forms, structures, and systems of philosophical and spiritual understanding, both academically in the mind and in the physical world.

While the masculine is oriented toward making distinctions in a certain sense, the feminine aspect is more about letting go into this vast openness. Instead of creating distinctions, the feminine is oriented toward feeling the inseparability of things. The feminine is less about structure and hierarchy and more about the lateral and the equality of all beings, more about the caring quality of interrelationship. It's also about formless wisdom, about how to dissolve into formlessness and realize that aspect of who we are.

I feel that in Vajrayana and Tibetan Buddhism in general we need to bring both those aspects of ourselves into full fruition. In Vajrayana the feminine is considered the wisdom aspect and the masculine is considered the aspect of skillful means. For example, there is the realization of compassion and then there's the creation of the form for compassion to manifest.

So is one more about realization and the other about acting in the world based on that realization?

Yes, it's more about benefiting beings based on the realization. It's somewhat different than Hinduism in that the feminine is the vast openness of awareness that is the wisdom, and the manifesting forth for the benefit of others is the masculine side. In the feminine wisdom compassion and unconditional love arise, and then the masculine aspect puts these into form.

Again, I think that dissolving and opening into the unknown is more the feminine. For example, in the birth process you just have to relax into it for the baby to come out. You have to learn to relax into something greater than yourself—you really can't control it! [laughs] The best laid plans of giving birth don't really help much, so you basically just have to let go...

...and trust the process.

Yes, and the more fear and control you have around it, the harder it is to give birth.

Which makes sense when we look at our culture, which is very masculine, and how much fear there is about just trusting the process.

Right, and I think there's a lot in the feminine wisdom that could help with that. In terms of Vajrayana and my feminine lineage, it's about cutting through class distinctions, racial distinctions, and all of that. In the awakened masculine perspective people feel that too, but it's really the feminine that cuts through all that and realizes that our essential nature is the same. This essential nature that is this vast openness isn't nothingness, but is cognizance. It's a cutting through conceptuality to experience the ultimate nature of things, which is considered to be beyond concepts and conceptual thinking.

I feel also that in the feminine there's an aspect of laterally sharing with each other, of collaboration, and the capacity to create holding and loving spaces for things. There's a tremendous amount of joy and delight from just expressing our love with each other.

It sounds like a wonderful world! [both laugh]

Now one of the principles of the feminine is harmony, so with my spiritual center I didn't want to create a place where everyone is closed off, shut down, or uptight. I mean, who wants that? So from the beginning I tried to encourage people to speak from their awareness itself and out of their ego in order to connect with each other on a common ground that was more true being and basic goodness. It was amazing that it actually worked, and as a result people take responsibility for their own stuff and so our sangha is very loving and full of tremendous joy.

It sounds as though they're starting from a place of commonality, rather than difference, and going from there.

I think people want to grow spiritually, and so taking responsibility is part of that. But also the feeling of people supporting each other is something that comes from the feminine.

Yes, collaboration instead of competition, as you said. In closing, I'd like to ask if there's anything further that you feel would be helpful for people to know, that they might not always recognize in their everyday lives.

One thing is that this entire existence is completely amazing. In the Western worldview we still think that if you can't see it, then it doesn't exist, and our culture is still very much immersed in that perspective. Yet if you think about it, it's a miracle already that we're on this planet, hurtling through space at an incredible speed, going around the sun and not falling off…and the whole thing is actually working!

The more we can open to the amazing miracle that we're a part of, the more we recognize that the nature of who we are and the nature of the universe are both wondrous and amazing. Everything is also obviously inherently intelligent with this tremendous brilliancy—otherwise how would this whole thing work? Where the faith and the trust comes in for me is seeing that everything is not only intelligent but also a wisdom process as well. That's also the nature of who are—we are this wisdom and compassion that's the ground of everything, and it's possible to realize that and embody it.

It sounds like a very inspiring view to end on. Thank you.

Chapter 10

Walking With the Earth: An Interview With Gabriel Horn

❝❝The first peace, which is the most important, is that which comes within the souls of people when they realize their relationship, their oneness, with the universe and all its powers, and when they realize that at the center of the universe dwells *Wakan-Tanka*, and that this center is really everywhere, it is within each of us."[5] Oglala Lakota healer and visionary Black Elk's words speak to the heart of the native vision of the universe: everything is relationship and all is sacred. The native healers, writers, and visionaries I spoke with about the universe all shared this sense of sacred relationship and humility in the face of the great mystery that underlies all things. The feeling of natural kinship with the world that came through these conversations with them deeply impressed me and I slowly began to realize how much has been lost by both contemporary and traditional peoples in the transition to modern industrialized culture.

Gabriel Horn (White Deer of Autumn) is a writer, speaker, activist, and associate professor of literature and creative writing at St. Petersburg College in western Florida. His books for adults include *Native Heart*, *Contemplations of a Primal Mind*, and *The Book of Ceremonies*. He has also written several books for children, including *Ceremony in the Circle of Life*, *The Great Change*, and the *Native People/Native Ways* series.

Horn has been active in teaching, preserving, and honoring American Indian philosophy, culture, and ways of living for more than four decades. He was active in the American Indian Movement (AIM) in the 1970s, when he helped establish The Heart of the Earth Survival School, and became the head teacher for The Red School House. He also served as the cultural arts director of the Minneapolis American Indian Center. His efforts were directed at helping Native American youth reconnect with and preserve their indigenous heritage and native ways of living. A tireless activist in the struggle against racial discrimination and injustice, Horn has led many efforts to revise Western historical views to include Native American accounts of historical events, and to insist that academic institutions of higher learning include American Indian literature in the curriculum of language arts departments, not relegate it to anthropology.

Throughout his life Horn has been passionate about teaching and sharing indigenous ways of relating to the environment, the Earth, and the Great Holy Mystery that is at the heart of Native American perspectives on the universe.

Stephan Martin: Perhaps we could start with you talking about your background and history, and how this has shaped your understanding and viewpoint of the universe.

Gabriel Horn: Like many people, I have mixed ancestry, but I was taught that an Indian does not come in parts and percents of blood; you either are Indian, or you are not. Blood runs the heart; the heart knows what it is. Mine is Indian. My beliefs are Indian. I am a member of the family of Nippawanock and Metacomet and Princess Red Wing of the Narraganset/Wampanoag tribe and nation. It is because of them that my Indian identity asserted itself in an intelligent way, and they are more or less responsible for much of what I have learned, although there were other elders and teachers for me all along the way.

And I'm still learning. At one point early in my life, after my youthful idealism about changing the world had come to a quick end, I felt very alone and lost. I felt like I couldn't make a contribution because I didn't know how or what to do. When I had broken down to my lowest, my uncle held me in his arms and he said, it's time for you to go for your vision. Even though I knew he was right and I went in the way he instructed me, I didn't receive the vision that would guide me on my way at that time, but I returned knowing one thing: through the fasting and self-reflection I learned that I had to deal with my anger. And until I released that anger that had been built up from childhood, I would not receive the vision about my purpose that I desired.

It was only later when I was a teacher in the AIM Survival Schools that I was really granted the vision of my life. From that point on I became aware of my purpose, my primary purpose as a man, and I knew, as I still know, that as long as I stay on that path, whatever happens to me and whatever I do on that path is okay, because I'm within the circle of my vision. But if I step out of that circle then I will have to take the consequences. So it was the vision that I was given that allowed me to probably live to be as old as I am now (61), because I've been in some tight situations along the way. If I ever lost sight of my vision, I quickly refocused on it, so that's what I attribute my survival to up until this moment. It was the vision my uncle told me to go on that gave me the understanding about my life that he knew I needed. Without it, I would have been lost.

Please keep in mind that everything that I'm sharing is what I have been taught and what makes sense to me from my experiences. I can't say that my views represent all indigenous peoples, but I think they make sense to most traditionally thinking native cultures. The vision enabled me to have a sense of purpose, and I have since learned that as men, we have to seek for and find that purpose, and if we don't find it, then we wander. But if we search for it, it comes. It can come in different ways to different people, and I found it my way because that's how I was instructed to do it, but that doesn't mean it can't come in a different way to other people. It also didn't come the first time I searched for it, but at a different time. I have been taught we have to be open for it and when we are ready, it will come.

Everything that I'm talking about is connected to the universe because we are each connected to the universe. And when I say "we are each connected," remember it's what I was taught, and I'm not assuming that you believe this or that, but it's what I was taught. We're connected to everything in the universe, and so everything we do is an aspect of the universe.

You talk about the need to seek for and ask for guidance about your purpose in life. This seems to imply a particular relationship with the universe, where guidance, support, and inspiration from the universe is a part of this relationship.

Yes, exactly—the universe is a part of me and I am a part of it. It's not something removed from me. And from what I understand, it's only through sacrifice that this understanding can come. In other words, from what I have learned, we can't come to that understanding by being greedy or self-centered or self-absorbed. It has to come from self-sacrifice. That's where fasting and the commitment to do good come in. But it's not about asking a higher power, but knowing for myself that I am a part of the universe and seeking that part within myself, to connect to it, for my purpose.

And from what you're speaking about, it's an interrelationship, one based on reciprocity and exchange.

Yes, it's an interrelationship, which is where the term "All My Relations" comes from. We're related to everything. So that's how I look at life. I look at the fish and the trees and the animals and even the insects and everything is related to me and the stars and the sun and the moon—I have a relationship to all of them.

It seems like they are all in some way expressing their role or place in the universe, and speaking to your role as well through your relationship to them.

Exactly. They each have a purpose, and they know their purpose innately. An ant knows its purpose, maybe not with its head, but it knows. So yes, that's what we seek as men, from what I understand. If we don't focus on a positive purpose, in a spiritual way, then we can become dangerous because we have the power to destroy and so that's what we do with our lives.

Well it's interesting that, as humans, we need to seek our purpose. It seems as though it's somehow given to fish and animals and all the beings around us.

Yes, that's right. And from what I have been taught, women, whether they choose to or not, are born with the innate ability to give birth, which gives them a purpose. We as men don't have that innate purpose, and so we have to search for and find ours. Even though a woman can find other things in her life for purpose, she still has that innate purpose with which she was born. But as men, we're not born with a purpose in the same way, so we're the ones that have to openly seek it. That's what I was taught and that's what I've learned.

Yes, I see. Now given the different purposes of men and women, do you see a particular role of the human in the universe? Are there particular teachings from indigenous cultures about the role of the human in the cosmos?

Well, I would think it's primarily to live in harmony with our environment. I can't think of a greater purpose. I think as we evolve, maybe we become more spirit than human, more spirit than physical, and maybe that's part of our larger purpose. But I think to find the balance in our lives, living in harmony within our world, that's a great purpose in itself.

Yes, so much of our modern world has gone away from that and has lost its balance in terms of harmony with our environment and the natural world.

Well the Western European American view, which could also include China these days, has a civilized mentality that allows a person to think that they're separate from nature. I'm saying things in this way because this is my understanding. I think that what has happened is that Western culture and religion has created a God that looks like them and has emotions like them—like men, not women, but men. Because of this, they allow themselves to think that men, who look like they do, are superior because the First Cause of the universe looks like they do. With that sense of superiority, they're then unable to recognize their relationship with other life forms, and so they become alienated. It's in their minds they do that. They're still a part of nature, but they've separated themselves in their minds and in their hearts.

This has enabled them to use all other life forms for their own benefit, and because they believe their God gave them permission to do this, they believe they can go anywhere they want and feel justified to do whatever they want. They can't even look at women as being equal either, because the First Cause to them was a man or man-being. So as their sense of superiority grows, they begin to separate from nature even more, and so they're able to take more than their share and more than they need. It's not about taking only what you need anymore, it's about what they want, and they're entitled to do this because they've used their religion to enable them and give them permission to do this.

Because they have this permission, they can kill animals for sport, they can kill each other and other humans en masse, and they can exploit the natural resources of Mother Earth. The Earth is no longer a living being for them, and so they can drop atomic bombs and do what they want because they have separated themselves from the Earth in their minds. The idea of killing an animal for any reason other than for absolute necessity is unimaginable.

We saw in the news the other day that they cut down an 80-year-old tree, decorated it, and put it in Rockefeller Center in New York. They cut this tree down, to decorate it for their purpose, for their entertainment, to symbolize the time of year when they consume. Then when they turned on the lights, they say energy for the lights of the tree come from solar panels. That's good, but they don't take the next step. Yes, it's good that the lights are powered by solar panels, but you just killed this incredible being. What message are you sending to your children and to the world by doing this, for no reason other than for decoration? It's this kind of mentality that can shoot wolves from planes, like they do in Alaska, for bounty. We look at that, I look at that, my wife looks at that, our children look at that, our people at one time all looked at that as murder. It's murder because those are our relatives and they're being killed for no purpose other than for sport and greed.

Recognizing this means living in this land and seeing my country not as some abstract concept of democracy, but as the streams and the lakes and the trees and the animals. This is the country that we're loyal to because this is what we love. We love our country because our country is the Earth and is the rivers and the fish and all living things.

The Western world hasn't evolved spiritually, because most of its technology still produces toxic wastes as a byproduct. Until humans evolve spiritually, they can't have a clean technology. Maybe that's what the Earth is teaching now with the environmental crisis. Maybe the Earth is saying: you're either going to learn to live in harmony with the environment or I will have to shake you off to take care of myself. The Western mentality has spread all over the world now, and is spreading like a cancer. Everywhere it goes, it gobbles up the beautiful places like a cancer gobbles up the good cells of the body. So I don't see civilization in its current form as a good thing. If you're going to respect life, you're going to respect all life. You can't say, "Well, I'm going to respect some life and not other life." So if they don't recognize the tree as a living being, then they're not getting it.

When we're talking about the concept of the great mystery, we're saying that we're part of everything in an unimaginable, indefinable totality. In the different tribal languages that I've encountered, the best translation of the universe is as a great mystery, because it's not definable. Even to call it "spirit" is something we have no business doing, because we're putting a definition on something we have no idea about, because we don't know the mystery. Science isn't going to learn about the mystery the way they're seeking it, because they're using technology to do it. Even the phrase "Big Bang," the most accepted scientific theory about the origin of the universe, is rooted in technology. Think about using a phrase like "Big Bang" to describe the idea that everything was one, and from that one, everything came. Now compare this with a Zuni Creation account, which says, "In the Beginning of Newness...throughout the great space of the ages, Awonawilona (the Mystery, the All-Container) solely had being...save everywhere black darkness and void desolation.... Then the All-Container conceived within its own being and thought outward into space...." You see? Indigenous people embellished the First Cause of Creation rather than describing it into something so hard and so callous as a "Big Bang." Do you hear the difference?

The name "Big Bang" sounds more like something coming from technology, like an explosion, rather than something growing organically.

It's using the word *it* in the way we talk about animals in a zoo. When you go to a zoo and watch people with their children, they'll say, "Oh look at that rhinoceros, isn't *it* big?" What English does as a language is it objectifies the universe, it makes everything into an "it." It allows a child to use the word *it* to describe a living being at the same time that child is learning "it" in phrases like "take out the trash, *it* needs to be taken out tonight" and "look at that eagle, isn't *it* beautiful?" It's that objectification that is learned so young, when they don't see these other forms as being living relatives to themselves, so they objectify everything and everything becomes dead.

So it's no wonder by the time they're adults, their whole world is based on separation.

What I'd like to think I'm doing with my life is giving people a glimpse through a porthole into another way of looking at the universe and the Earth. This other way of looking at and living within the universe is very old. I was taught that this way of living came with our DNA, and somewhere along the way, we had a split and some people went one way and some people went another way. One way connected us and kept us connected and the other way disconnected us. But we have a choice.

My hope is that a more natural way of living in harmony within the universe is still in our DNA. One thing that you shared with me that gives me hope is that there is this primal, this original understanding of the Earth and the cosmos and our relationship to it.

We all come from tribes, don't we? Long ago, didn't we all connect to being tribal peoples? When you read the Hopi and different tribal accounts of creation, you get the understanding that there were previous worlds to this one and that there was emergence from one world to the next and that the emergence of human beings in whatever way they did were those human beings who remained connected, who were still addressing the Moon and the Sun and the Earth, who are still sending out those vibrations and are placing signs that are there for us to see. They were the ones to successfully emerge from each previous world. And maybe now there is an emergence of new human beings, not just of one race or one tribe, but those of us who are seeking to live in peace, who are seeking to find harmony in the way we live on the Earth. But I don't think it's about skin color or eye color. It's about how we look at the world and how we live.

Is there any advice or guidance that you can offer to people seeking to live in a harmonious way, who are hoping to live in a way that is not separated from nature and the universe?

We don't have to go anywhere—it's all right here. This is the Holy Land. The way to know how to live is right here, and has always been right here. We need to look around where we are and we need to respect this land and see it as the Holy Land. I only say "it" because I'm talking about it in English, but this Earth as a mother deserves our respect. The indigenous peoples all over the world deserve our respect. I know that some people will respect these native peoples and their traditions, but I don't know if Americans will in a national sense. But our loyalty should not be to a flag, but to the Earth and the future generations. Our patriotism needs to be to the land to protect the land and the waters and the life forms that live with us.

In the face of the predator-like energy that sucks the life out of everything it encounters, we each need to do what we can to find our purpose, our niche, and to keep going just like our ancestors did, so that we can receive the wisdom that they have passed on to us.

Many people, even some Indians, believe that God and the Great Mystery is the same thing. They're not. The Pipe and the bible come from different philosophies and are different concepts. From what I understand from the old ones that have gone on, it is the Great Mystery that makes us Indian, and once we lose touch with that concept, with the idea that we're interrelated with all things, we cease to be Indian. I've gotten in trouble for saying these kinds of things in the past, but this is what I've been taught.

I was taught, as was my wife who speaks Lakota, that we have no concept of forgiveness. Native languages, in general, didn't even have a word for "forgive." To forgive is to absolve of responsibility, and we did not do that. If you committed an act that hurt somebody or if you did something that hurt other life forms, you had to learn from that and you had to accept responsibility for doing that. You could try to make retribution, you could try to do what you could to balance that off in your life, but the idea of asking for forgiveness is a big convenience that comes from Western religion and civilization. It's pretty convenient if you think you can do anything you want and then get it forgiven, no matter how bad or how selfish your actions.

As Indians, we had purification ceremonies and ways to purify ourselves because we do toxify ourselves along the way, especially when we're young or irresponsible. But the idea is we learn from those mistakes and then we cleanse ourselves and we fast and we clear our bodies out so our spirits are more able to grow. But just as we assume responsibility for our freedom, we also assume responsibility for our mistakes. I think this is really important because I think the concept of forgiveness without responsibility is a real flaw in Western civilization and in Western religions.

It's an easy out. It's a way of avoiding responsibility, and as you said, the recognition that we are interrelated and that comes with a responsibility, that our actions have effects.

Well did you ever hear of the seventh generation?

Sure.

In what we do, and especially in decisions that we make about the environment, we have to think of how that's going to affect seven generations from now. We have to ask, how is this going to affect them? What an incredible concept.

Princess Redwing, she said to me once, "Gabriel, it would shame a man to be eating in his home with his family while the family at the lodge next to him was going hungry. It would shame him to do that." That's the concept of tribalness, of community, of caring for one another. That's the wisdom that's here, and that's what we need to go back to before we can go forward. This is what we've lost.

I was reading in the news recently that science is saying that the largest known object in the universe is called the "cosmic web." They have taken pictures through these telescopes in space of the interconnectedness of the universe, and yet they still think of it as an object. If the scientists had only asked, if only they had listened to the ancient peoples before them who have known about the cosmic web the whole time, they wouldn't have had to use the dirty technology they've used to find these things out. That's what is sad. Every time they put one of those ships up there they are putting a hole in the sky, in the ozone, in the part of the sky that protects us. And every time they send one of those ships out there they glorify this. So we have a very different way of looking at things, and these two ways are very different from each other.

Do you see any way that these two can be brought together—Native American cosmology and the scientific cosmology of Western culture?

I only can see it happening if what science is discovering through their dirty technology is what the indigenous people in their wisdom already knew through spirituality, through a spiritual understanding. But the arrogance in exploring the mystery with their current dirty technology is not going to find that understanding, but is destroying the world as we know it, so I don't see them coming together right now.

It's also about how we use language. When we talk about these things, we can use language that is more appropriate.

I know some people have different concepts of God, but I think the connotation of God is still of an anthropomorphic man-like being, and no matter what one's concept, as long as they use that term they're taking all that baggage with them. When we say *the Great Mystery*, there's nothing implied there, there's no ego implied there about knowing something that is unknowable in that way.

When you use the phrase *Great Mystery* you're talking about something which is everything.

Yes, it's the sum total of all things that ever were and will ever be and everything is a part of it. That is the big difference. It isn't removed from us. In my earlier life, I'd been exposed to Catholicism and I'll never forget the day my Uncle Nip and I were outside looking at the stars, and I still had this idea that there was some entity up there that was specifically looking out for me. Even though I was calling myself an Indian, I still had this concept. My uncle said to me, "You're going to have to let go of that, if you're going to be Indian. You're going to have to let go of the idea that there is a being up there with a finger going "I'm going to help Gabriel" or "I'm going to put this in Gabriel's way" or "I'm going to do this for Gabriel." That was a turning point in my life because I realized what he'd just told me right there and I had to let it go and

I was afraid to let it go. I was afraid, like anybody who was raised that way would be, to let it go. But as I let it go other understandings came.

We always believe that the Earth will continue because she's billions of years old. Civilized man certainly won't, but she'll continue. And I was told that if the Earth decides that it's time for you to go, don't worry about it. If it's time, it's time. And if you go with everything else, that's okay because it's the Earth's time. These days I have children, so I'm hoping that they will continue. But that's the hope they carry.

You've written about the importance of reverence, ceremony, and ritual in our relationship to the universe. Can you say more about this?

I think the most important thing I've learned is to have gratitude. In every ceremony, I was taught to go into it with gratitude and respect. I think when you enter a ceremonial state of consciousness you embrace everything with gratitude. I was taught that when we say "thank you" we say it to the beings themselves. We say "Thank you, Grandmother Moon. Thank you, Tree. Thank you, Deer. Thank you, Wolf. Thank you, Waters." We don't thank something or someone else for them, but we say thank you to them directly. Going to the water and saying thank you to the water is so important because we're mostly water. Not just saying "I'm grateful for the water," but going to the water directly and saying "thank you." That's interrelatedness.

Everything we do, or at least what I did when I started walking this road, is to start dropping your ego all along the way. What's important, I think, is letting go of that ego. We also have to stay connected to the natural cycles. The more we disconnect from the cycle of the seasons, the less natural we become. I can ask my students when the next holiday is, when winter break begins, when their next class is, and when their job starts after class, and they can tell me. But if you ask them when the next full moon is, they haven't got a clue. With Christmas coming, how many people are going to think of the solstice? It's like this civilization has connected to artificial time, to man-made time, and disconnected from natural time.

I try to help my students see that. I know we have to live within this civilized framework where we have class that starts at 8:50 or 9:50 or when-ever, but that doesn't mean that I'm separated from the new moon, the full moons, and the phases of the moon or the turning of the season's cycles. We have to stay connected to that, because I think that too reminds us of our interrelationship, to our connection with the universe. The concept of time teaches us that we're connected to the universe through cycles.

I think this understanding of connection and cycles is something that needs to come into the way we teach our children about the universe.

And you don't have to be Indian to do that. Our people are tribal peoples whether they came from Asia or Africa or Europe or Ireland or wherever. It's about reconnecting to the part of us that is primal, the part of us that is ancient, the part of us that was in our original instruction, in our DNA. There was a sign that we used to have at Heart of the Earth when you walked into the school (a crowded apartment in the Indian Housing Projects), and it said: "If we do not survive as a people following the instruction and purpose of our creation then we must ask ourselves, what is the purpose of survival?"

The purpose, as we taught in the survival school, is to live in balance and harmony. We have always struggled with our human frailties and our human flaws, but we had societies that evolved to not nurture those flaws. It's a struggle to live that way. It's not easy.

Strange things are happening these days. The Mayan, who are keepers of time, and from what I've learned are the most respected in the field of time cycles, say that 2012 is the end of a great cycle. It's like the end of a season, and my hope is that with the beginning of the next cycle there is the emergence of people who simply want to live in peace and in harmony.

Are there any last pieces of wisdom or guidance you'd like to share?

I've been labeled and regarded as radical, even militant, for the ideas that I've been sharing. But I am willing to fight for what I believe, and that to me is the concept of militancy, to stand up and say, "Stop it, I'm not gonna let you do this anymore." That to me is the idea of a warrior. I don't know if people are going to get what I've been saying, but I know that I celebrate the life of the fish and the birds and the trees and the human beings who love and feel grateful for all these beings. I celebrate the sky and the moon and the sun, and so I have to keep my focus on that and remind myself to be grateful. In this way I can counteract the feelings of negativity and anger that can creep up. The best way to counteract negativity is to say "thank you" and keep showing your appreciation and maybe show a little kindness and generosity.

In closing, I would like to say thank you for everything that you've shared.

Thank you as well for allowing this interview. I don't know if you realize how special you are for doing something like this. And you have my support.

Chapter 11

Living in the Great Mystery: An Interview With Luisah Teish

T he wisdom of Africa is as great and wide as the continent itself. As the birthplace of humans on the Earth, it might be considered to be the origin point for all subsequent cosmologies, cosmogonies, and ways of interacting with the universe and the natural world. In a sense, all of our current views on the universe can trace their ancestry and lineage back to the primordial knowledge of the cosmos that originated in Africa. The knowledge and deep wisdom of how to live in harmony with a multifaceted and ever-changing cosmos is what Dagara elder Malidoma Somé has called "indigenous spiritual technology," the set of practices, rituals, and belief systems that have evolved throughout countless generations of living in the diverse and occasionally harsh African environment. This spiritual technology, he suggests, is based on an African cosmic consciousness that does not differentiate the spiritual from the mundane, the ritual from the practical, or the individual from the community or the environment.

Since its beginnings in Africa, this lineage of cosmic wisdom has expanded and diversified, until it now reaches all around the world. Through its dispersion across the Atlantic, it has now come to the United States, where it has reached Dr. Luisah Teish. Dr. Teish is an initiated elder (Iyanifa) in the Ifa/Orisha tradition of the West African Diaspora, and holds a chieftaincy title (Yeye'woro) from the Fatunmise Compound in Ile Ife, Nigeria. She is currently the chair of the World Orisha Congress Committee on Women's Issues. She is also a devotee of Damballah Hwedo, the Haitian Rainbow Serpent, under the guidance of Moma Lola.

In 1969 she received initiation into to the Fahamme Temple of Amun-Ra in St. Louis, Missouri, and later went on to study indigenous Native North and South American traditions (including the Caribbean). She has conducted workshops on Black and Native American culture at Medicine Wheels under the directions of Sun Bear's tribal elders. In 1993 she was awarded a PhD in Spiritual Therapeutics from Open International University's School of Complementary Medicine in Colombo, Sri Lanka.

Teish holds an Inter-Faith minister's license from the International Institute of Integral Human Sciences. She designs and conducts weddings, naming ceremonies, memorials, and a host of seasonal celebrations. Teish designed a Rites of Passage program for the Institute of Noetic Sciences, and is the director of the Full Faze Passage Council, a multi-racial, multi-cultural network of artists, consultants, and spiritual advisors experienced in events design and production.

Teish is also a writer, storyteller, and creative projects consultant. She is the author of *Jambalaya: The Natural Woman's Book of Personal Charms and Practical Rituals*, *Carnival of the Spirit*, and *Jump Up: Good Times Throughout the Season with Celebrations from Around the World*.

She is the Olori (director) of Ile Orunmila Oshun and the School of Ancient Mysteries/Sacred Arts Center in Oakland, California. She has taught at the University of Creation Spirituality, Naropa Oakland, John F. Kennedy University, The Institute for Transpersonal Psychology, and New College of California.

Stephan Martin: Can you say something about your background and history and how they relate to your understanding of the universe?

Luisah Teish: My name is Luisah Teish and I am among other things an Orisha priestess and a devotee of Oshun, the Yoruba Goddess of love, art, and sensuality. I grew up in New Orleans in the segregated South in a spirit-infused world where all of nature was alive and my elders talked to me through story and proverb. I grew up around a lot of mystery, and so having had that kind of upbringing put me on the search for answers to certain questions that a young child would have in such a mysterious atmosphere.

I would see women in my community do something that was different from what the women on television were doing and so I would ask them, "Why do you do that?" and they would say, "Because that's what the old folks say." I went and asked Mama Ludie, who was older than my mama, and she said, "Because that's what the old folks say." Then I went and asked somebody who was even older than her, and they said, "That's what the old folks say." I began to understand that "the old folks" were somebody much more than the older people in the community, and asking this question eventually led me to the study of cultural history that developed into a bigger study of African American culture, and then after much questioning I finally landed in the lap of African cosmology.

In our view, the world is a covered calabash. There is a rainbow serpent named Damballah Hwedo who contains all the colors of the rainbow and He arches the entire sky. His wife Aida runs under the water, and with their tails in each other's mouths, they together sew the whole calabash together. We're inside that calabash and so we share the same horizon with all other beings.

What some would have called an animistic point of view was pretty much second nature to me growing up in this kind of culture. We watched the behavior of birds and paid a lot of attention to what plants did. Everything around us was explained through story. So my childhood perspective matured into a feeling—not just a belief—but a feeling-sense that the universe is somehow an intelligence and a power that is both receptive and responsive. It's not a dead mechanical thing. As people of African descent, we have given personality to everything and often put flesh on it so it is easier for us to deal with, but we still understand that we are dealing with a bigger thing than ourselves.

The Great Mystery is all that is invisible that will never be known to us, and yet the great wonder is that we can still relate to it. To make relating easier, we break it down into mythological beings who reflect our collective experience, understanding, and relationships to the forces of nature. For example, when I talk about Damballah Hwedo the rainbow serpent I am talking about all the colors of the rainbow and about the full spectrum of possibilities of existence. I am talking about the collective memory of the Ancestors going all the way back to Fanta, our mitochondrial mother, and I am saying that I am a cell in the body of that continuance and that I have a relationship with it.

Stephan Martin: Can you talk more about that relationship with the universe and what that's like?

It's difficult these days to open a spiritual conversation about the universe without feeling like there's some necessity to respond to the recent craze with books like *The Secret* and things like the Law of Attraction. You know what I'm sayin'? So I'm gonna say this right quick. It's true that the Law of Attraction is at work in the cosmos, but it's been blown way out of proportion. The idea that the whole universe is just waiting to do whatever I want it to do is total bullshit.

There is such a thing as universal law and we are all subject to that law, but what we want to do is put ourselves in accord with universal law as it unfolds itself. I don't command the universe! I interact with it, I co-create with it, and I petition it, but I don't always like the arrangements She makes, you know what I'm sayin'? I think that we've forgotten the collective agreement that we've made as human beings between ourselves and the universe. I've made an agreement to place myself in the natural order with prescriptions around my relationship to other beings. For example, while I can see myself as a caretaker of those plants over there, I am not superior to them in any way. When I put myself in the right relationship with them I am capable of communicating with and receiving assistance from them, but if I get that, then I also owe them. So it's a reciprocal relationship.

Destiny, chance, and choice are also part of the universe. In my own belief, every person came here to be somebody, to do something, and to have certain experiences. Now before I took a body and was at one with the universe we talked about this assignment of mine (me and the universe, right?), but then in the birth process I forgot some of it because I got dizzy working on coming into being, you know? [laughs] Then when I got here, into the outer world, I had chance encounters with other beings who had other contracts and other pieces of information, and sometimes there was a nice exchange and I learned something or taught something, and sometimes the exchange only helped me to further forget who I was intended to be. So I have to do rituals and prayers and stuff to get me back on track with my original purpose and destiny, and so before it's all over my hope is that I will come to a point where I return and reconnect solidly with that great energy that is the universe. The way that I currently reconnect with the universe is as a priestess of the Goddess Oshun. Oshun is the power of attraction in the universe. She's the reason why two atoms hold together to create a molecule, okay?

So she's also responsible for gravity and all other kinds of attraction?

Yes, there it is. She is also all the sweet water on the face of the Earth. She is the muse who entices us to create art, the pull of attraction that makes us want to make love. This view comes from a specific area and group of people in Nigeria along the Oshun River. All kinds of miracles happen in this sacred river: barren women go and bathe in it and they conceive children; people who were in disharmony go in and come out wanting peace. In this view love and attraction are seen as healing modalities. Now, as a child of Oshun, I would say that I was born with a commitment that gave me a predisposition toward healing and the creation of beauty. And I knew this when I came into this life, but I was born into a world that said, "Hmmmm, you better not do that or you can't do that," so there's been a struggle between my pre-birth commitment and the world. But when initiation for a particular deity occurs, then we say that the full power of one's contract is reawakened, so now I know who I am and what I'm supposed to do.

Because we are a people who practice ancestor reverence, we feel that the thoughts, the feelings, and the actions of a person are like pockets of energy—they are never destroyed, but just transmuted from one dimension to another. So from this viewpoint, we will say something like "If Luisah Teish, the priestess of Oshun, does enough healing and creates enough beauty in her lifetime, then coming generations will speak of her as a revered ancestor, as one whose work and intelligence remains intact and can be called upon in need." In this same way, I call upon the spirit of various people who have lived before me, who have manifested that part of the spirit energy of the universe.

The fact that I am an initiated priestess of Oshun, I have a name that implies that the Love Goddess gives me my character. So if what I do is great enough that I am remembered way beyond leaving this body, if what I do has enough of an impact on the collective, and if what I do adds to the understanding of that part of the universe that we are allowed to wonder about, then somewhere in the distant future, the mythology will say, "Long, long ago, in that twenty-first century, there lived an Oshun named Teish and she did these wonderful things," then my life's story folds into the rainbow. So that's the romantic point of view! [laughs]

Now the reason me and the universe lock horns sometimes is because it is my experience that there is a tendency in the universe toward economy and efficiency that I find myself sometimes resisting. I can sit here and say, "I really wish I had an alpaca sweater." Or I'd love to blow a horn and have a three-day vacation." And I invoke for these three things, but what happens is that there's a knock on the door and there's a goat standing there with three horns on its head askin' for me and offering me a ride! You know what I'm sayin'? It's like wait a minute! I asked for these things and the universe delivered them this way! [laughs]

It also feels to me that the interconnectedness that I want to celebrate collectively is often thrust upon me in ways I don't expect and so I get upset, to which the universe says, "Well, wait a minute. Didn't you say you wanted kinship?"

I want kinship with *you*. I've invited *you* in here. Sometimes the Universe sends somebody else knockin' on my door and I go, "Where did you come from?" That kind of thing, you know what I'm sayin'? We find ourselves embroiled in other people's life lessons, right? The only thing you have to understand—that I have to understand—when these kinds of things happen is that to that other person I'm an "other person" too! [laughs] So, the universe has that larger perspective, whereas I'm looking more often from my immediate point of view.

The universe has a sense of humor that I don't always appreciate, but I do know that we are all different cells in the body of the universe, and that everyone you encounter comes either to learn something from you or to teach you something. Some people come to teach you what *not* to do and what *not* to be, if you know what I mean.

Now I'm painfully aware that everything I'm saying is colored by my limited understanding and expression of a finite being trying to talk about the Infinite, and I can only talk about what's perceivable to me and others on my level of existence. There are other pockets of energy existing in the universe who are much more intelligent than we are with better comprehension and better expression. Malidoma Somé, the African teacher from Burkina Faso, says that the stones are actually smarter than we are, and in Yoruba the traditional deity of the herbs is envisioned as a man with one eye, one arm, and one leg, who can see more, do more, and dance better than the rest of us. So, the plants are smarter than we are, and they know more about the universe than we do.

They've been around much longer than we have.

Yes, we're the newcomers! We're the baby playing with her toes in the midst of this amazing, amazing universe. Now having said all that, sometimes I feel as if there are these artistic directors behind the scenes who have us performing and improvising this Great Drama with only a few guidelines for the scenario and no rehearsals.

The message that I've been receiving for some time is that we are now coming upon a time in the world when a greater awareness of our relationship to the Infinite is being revealed to us, so that we can each improve on who we are becoming as part of it. The fact that science and spirituality are now beginning to embrace each other is amazing in itself and has great potential. The fact that people are doing less of "us and them" and more of "we" is revolutionary.

But it is an awareness of our relationship to Earth and to the sacredness of it is what's going to save us all in the end. That the Earth is sacred is a very old point of view that western culture has gotten away from and that we are now just returning to with a new knowledge. I think that this new consciousness, awareness, and concern for the Earth is the Universe giving us a few more pieces of something that will help us save ourselves and to reconnect to it. At least, that's the way I'm lookin' at it these days. We've gone so far off the deep end that we have to move back toward harmony because a great balance is what the universe is about.

Remember a poem by Lawrence Ferlinghetti called "Unfair Arguments With Existence?" When I have unfair arguments with the universe—and believe me I do—there are days when I am very, very accusatory and say, "You could have done better in the creation of the human. This mess is your fault!" [laughs] But then there are also times, when I look at the big picture and let myself imagine that we are each a grain of sand in an amazing galaxy of stars in a vast universe, it brings a different perspective.

The other question I think is important is whether or not the systematic intelligence that we are calling the universe is truly benevolent. I think the old way of thinking was, "There's something out there really controlling everything, being benevolent when it feels like it, and being malevolent when it feels like it." But I think that view is now changing to the recognition that It not only has consciousness, but that It interacts with us and that we're continuing It through our lives and actions.

Is there anything else you'd like to share about your perspective and the indigenous worldview?

What I really, really truly believe is that everything seems to be round to me. I don't see a lot of squares. So I think that as humans we need to stand in a big circle and have a representative of each culture and subgroup stand in the center and have everyone listen to the message that the universe has given to each one of us that we all need to hear. The Native Americans have taught us a lot about Earth stewardship, and we need to listen to them. The children teach us about trust and joy, and we need to listen to that too. I think that we are now being directed toward standin' in that circle, looking to see the piece that each one of us has to make the circle whole.

The other thing I wanted to say—when I talk about me and the universe arguing and going head to head—is that there are certain stages in having the kind of relationship with the universe that I'm talking about. I seem like I'm always the one who is asking for guidance, to remind me of my contract, and to show me what I'm supposed to be doing.

Well, the first level of guidance is simple instruction—you know, just go do this. That's fine, because if you say to me, "Walk across the room," I can stand up, put one foot in front of the other, and walk across the room, okay? The problem is that often times, information on "why" is given on a need-to-know basis. See, I want to know what's over on the other side of the room before I get there, right?

But often times here's what happens. I get up. I go into my meditation room. I say my morning opening, and then I say, "What's up for me today?" And what comes back is, "Do what I tell you to do today and then get up and do what I tell you to do tomorrow—okay?" You know, it's like c'mon baby, give me something![laughs]

And so if I'm stumbling along with my day-to-day guidance, sometimes I encounter what I call "spiritual entrapment." While walking across the room I look down all of a sudden and there are alligators nibbling at my feet [laughs], and no matter which direction I turn, I can't run, so I'm trapped. And because I'm trapped I now have to learn how to fly—the only way I can get out of this situation is to do something completely different and rise up and fly away.

The situation I really don't like—what I *really* don't like—is guidance by obstruction, where I've said to the universe, "Yeah, I really want to go across the room to over there," and I start walking over there and something comes and slaps me, spins me around, and I see the other side of the room, and I say, "Oh yeah, that's where I'm supposed to go." I don't like that kind of guidance at all. So, I have been trying to sweet talk, bribe, cajole the universe into clear, simple instruction with a long-range plan—printed and signed. May I have one of them? You know what I'm saying?! [laughs]

I think we'd all like one of them! [laughs]

We'd all like one of them, but She's not having it. She's not having it at all! When I ask for one of those things what comes back is a giant scream. So, it's a mystery. If you ask me what the universe is, right now I'd have to say it's a Great Mystery that is revealing Itself to us and through us in day-by-day increments. That's the best I can say right now.

Chapter 12

The Macrocosm and the Microcosm: An Interview With Eda Zavala

Eda Zavala Lopez is a curandera, a visionary healer descended from an ancestral lineage of healers of the Wari (Huari) Civilization, in the Central region of the Andes in Peru. She is also a sociologist and anthropologist who has researched feminine shamanism in the Amazon, and currently works with indigenous communities to help them to preserve their pristine forest and ancestral territories. Eda has made it her life's work to be the connection between the modern world and the sacred knowledge of the Amazonian plant medicine. Her commitment to protecting the traditional use of plant medicines of the Peruvian Amazon has brought her worldwide recognition.

For the past 20 years, she has lived in the Amazonian rainforest practicing the traditional healing ways of her ancestors. She and her brother Javier Zavala are the founders of Hampichicuy, a healing center in the Peruvian rainforest dedicated to the practice and research of traditional Amazonian medicine.

Stephan Martin: Could you tell us something about your background, your people, and how you came to be a Curandera (healer)?

Eda Zavala: My roots come from the Wari Civilization, before the Incas. The Wari were a very religious and philosophical group of people that dominated a great part of the central area of the Andes and very close to the Amazon. They were a very wise people, very connected to the cosmos, and I am certain that my knowledge about medicinal plants and my knowledge about other forms of connection with the universe comes from my ancestors. They live in my DNA, and so my knowledge is very ancient. My practice is a natural learning process and I try to maintain faithful to the teachings of my masters, so when I learn things in this way, I don't need to study. I just know by applying my intuition, my knowledge comes up instinctively, and so I know.

I am a mix of indigenous and Western cultures, because I grew up in the city and attended the university where I studied sociology and anthropology. At the university I learned another type of knowledge and I was fascinated with this other world where I was taught Cartesian logic, abstract thinking, and the power of knowledge. But the calling of the traditional world, the ancient knowledge in my DNA, was stronger and more potent than that of my intellect, and so I decided to work with the indigenous communities of the Amazon to show them how powerful their own wisdom is.

I wanted to work with indigenous people and learn about their wisdom, and share the other form of knowledge that I had learned at the university, especially to the young people. Many of these communities now are moving within a culturally and economically complex process, where they are forced to abandon their traditions and to adopt a Western model of development, without any possibility of integration. After many years I am able to better understand and manage this complexity. The university gave me the tools, but the great majority of brothers and sisters do not have access to them. I feel like a bridge connecting two worlds, the traditional and modern ways of thinking, where I can move and express freely, learn, and share the two types of knowledge in a non-conflicting and complementary way. This power of understanding and fine sensibility was given to me by my medicinal plants and the teachings of my masters.

What is the role of the healer in your culture?

The healer has a very important role in our culture. In our tradition, the world, the planet, human beings, animals, and plants are all intimately connected. We believe that every living being has a spirit and that spirit represents an energy. This energy is alive, it keeps moving and renewing itself, re-establishing itself, and transforming itself. This energy has always been in harmony with the rest of the living world, with the planet and its natural resources.

Traditionally the spiritual leader had the most important role within the community. He had the capacity to organize his people and establish them in a territory in order to use the natural resources of that area in a balanced way. When it was time to move the people to another place in order to allow nature to renew and enrich itself, it was the healer who would make this decision. And in this way the spiritual leaders knew when it was time to move, to organize, to develop, and to reproduce.

The healers are very good observers of the forests and often travel up into the mountains and deep into the jungle, through the forest to undertake spiritual retreats, hunt, or to collect medicinal plants. They drink different medicinal plants to be strong and to prepare themselves to cure people, and this leads them to find their own way of deeply and intimately connecting with nature.

So they had a very crucial and fundamental role in the community that was much more than a political role. In addition, the healer would initiate every person into their role in the community. For example, this child will become a hunter, this child will become a fisherman, this woman is going to bear so many children, and this other woman is going to become a healer. So there was a harmonious balance between productive activities and human activities, between nature and human beings.

Presently there are many communities that are losing this connection, because the old spiritual leaders are dying out. They are disappearing and there aren't any youth to teach and to transmit this cultural heritage so that they can take their places. The youth are moving out of their communities in search of economic opportunities so they can cease being socially and financially isolated. So when the elders die, parts of this invaluable wisdom that keeps an equilibrium in our relationship with nature, die as well. When the spiritual leaders disappear, part of this wisdom disappears and the world enters a more unbalanced state. When this happens, we lose the possibility of connecting with that ancient knowledge and wisdom, and ignorance overtakes and overshadows everything.

The whole world is losing from it—it is not only we who are losing our ancient vision and our respect for nature. The indigenous people are being forced to believe that modern society represents the best for all people. Personally, I am very concerned about globalization, because I believe that if people lose their traditions, they lose their spirit, and so they lose the possibility of connecting intuitively, instinctively, spiritually and mentally with the universe.

The modern world teaches us many things and demands so much from our minds, but it keeps us totally disengaged from our other senses, such as listening, and feeling, and without these senses we lose so much of our essence. So for me it is very important that traditional wisdom is kept alive, fresh, and present in our everyday life. I am a human being with mental and spiritual abilities just like anyone else, but the *difference* is that I am conscious of all my senses and my spirit, and not only my brain, but conscious of my intuition, which is the most important to preserve in our culture. It is not about outside knowledge, but about inner wisdom.

There is now a new movement of foreign people from the United States, France, Spain, or Chile, visiting the Amazon, and they have a great interest in learning from us. But they forget something very important: indigenous knowledge is humility and not a possession. They go back to their home country after two or three months saying "I'm a Shaman," and the majority profit from our medicine and appropriate our wisdom. Such behavior is pure arrogance. Where is the respect for our culture and acknowledgement of intellectual property of the indigenous people? There is so much ego and opportunism in this attitude. The true healers have known medicinal plants all their lives. We do not obtain our knowledge in a year, or three months. It is our way of life.

So what are these foreigners missing? What is it that they do not understand in coming to acquire this knowledge?

They are lacking humility and respect. The modern world is obsessed with two things: the ego and power. Why do they bother to learn indigenous wisdom? To help others or to become better human beings? Or to profit themselves in the name of the Indians? The true sages, the true teachers, are humble, compassionate, open-minded, and are not interested in accumulation of power, money, material things, status, or to be anyone "important."

We are not Shamans. We are healers. There's a great difference. "Shaman" is a category that was used by Western anthropologists with respect to ancient Mongolia. We Curanderos are people who first of all are indigenous, who are descendents from a direct lineage of healers. Our heritage, our knowledge, comes from centuries ago, and is transmitted through our blood, through our DNA. A Curandero is not just anybody. To be a healer is to have a gift.

A healer is one who knows the medicinal properties and who communicates with the spirits of the plants, understands the message of the birds when they sing, deciphers dreams and the weather, connects with the universe, sees inside a man's soul, and cures organic and emotional illnesses of men, women, children, the young, and the old. It is another kind of knowledge, of communication; it is another kind of bonding. It is a much more subtle language, more delicate, more invisible, and intuitive.

This learning and communication is intuitive, because you learn directly from the plants, from the stars, from nature itself.

Our knowledge comes directly from nature, from the plants, from the universe, from earth's energy, from an inner connection to all of them. It is this natural and instinctive connection that allows us to see the inside and not just the surface. I can see you inside. I can see through you. This is the power of our ancestral knowledge, the power of our plant medicine.

When people say "I'm a Shaman," It is pure arrogance, pure ego. When you go deep into the Amazon, go up into the mountains, you don't find the elders claiming "Oh look at me, I'm a healer, I'm the best, follow me." It is the people who acknowledge them, who identify them as their traditional doctors, and who respect them. They are simple people, very natural and humble. The ego does not exist in our culture. This is the big difference between being a Shaman and being a Curandero. Not just anybody can be a Curandero, but anybody can be a Shaman.

Does this humility come from recognizing that you are not the source of the healing?

It is the Creator, Mother Earth, the spirits, the pure energy of the universe that comes and teaches us the knowledge that we later share. It is not yours or mine. There is no sense of possession or property; it comes to you and you interpret it and later transfer it through healing—it does not belong to you. It is a gift that you receive and practice without personal ambitions.

How do Curanderos see the universe? How do the sacred medicine and plants of the Amazon help us to see the deeper universe?

When we talk about nature, we don't just refer to the planet Earth. We're talking about a cosmic nature. A stellar and a more universal nature, and it was through the use of these medicinal plants centuries ago, like sacred instruments, that the healers or Curanderos could connect themselves, men or women, with a much more comprehensive universal wisdom. There are no limits between space and time, between the stars and the Earth. The sacred medicine brings us just to visit the cosmos and recognize it. Our spirit frees itself and we travel through the interior and exterior of the universe, and it does not work in the time or space established by logic.

We first see the universe as inside ourselves. Each one of us represents a microcosm of our being that is inside of us, is our essence, and that small microcosm that exists within each one of us is represented outside of us on a universal scale. We are part of something that is huge and beautiful that is in the constellations, in the solar system, and space.

In the indigenous way of thinking each living organism is an organic, biological, and spiritual complex that has its own reason for existing and is intimately connected to other living beings. All of them possess a spirit and are able to communicate among themselves—the birds with mammals, the plants with humans, the toads with the rain, the sun with the moon, the wind with fire, the sky with the earth. All of them possess their own energy and are interconnected, expand, and reproduce. All living beings and celestial bodies are in permanent communication. It is very complex to try to categorize, measure, or quantify them in terms of Western ways of thinking, but this is how it is and we believe in it. It is demonstrated by the history and mythology of our people, and it is applied nowadays by our healers and arouses the curiosity of scientists.

When we drink the sacred medicine, the different chemical properties of selective plants work and awake a cosmic connection inside us, and produce a special reaction in our psyche. Anyone can connect to it when taking the right medicine and travel at different levels. This opens your mind and first connects your microcosm inside and then connects you with the greater cosmos.

Scientists call this "an altered state of mind by ingestion of hallucinogenic plants that have DMT." It is very important to clarify that our sacred plants are not hallucinogens; they are visionary, because they offer us the possibility of seeing our interior and of visualizing our own existence to better understand it. We don't hallucinate things; we become conscious of ourselves. When this happens our small energy bonds with the greater energy. For us, all this energy has life that harmonizes and integrates. We call that energy *spirit*, and all of us have it—great spirits, small spirits, and medium spirits—and everyone is spinning around within this little microcosm and the great cosmos. Once we begin to recognize the cosmos within us, we can connect with the greater cosmos directly. It is really very simple and very natural.

Are humans special in that we are connected to the universe in this way, with a microcosm inside us that connects to the macrocosm? Is that particular to humans?

No. Humans are not at all special. That is the problem with the Western culture—it believes that humans are the center of the universe. Our culture considers that animals and plants, lakes and rivers, mountains and volcanoes, have their own microcosmos. Everything, including human beings, has its own microcosmos, and it is all interconnected to form a great constellation in this enormous universe.

There's nothing complicated about this. Each living being contains a microcosm that is interconnected and integrated with the outside universe. Everything is alive and everything is energy that moves in this great life and cosmos, always in motion, always moving from one source to the next. There are no single or separate objects in nature. Energy is in constant circulation throughout everything, a powerful energy that is always moving to maintain a dynamic balance everywhere and in every living organism.

We do not have to think about this with our minds to know this is true. Birds, monkeys, trees, stars, the moon, and planet Earth are deeply connected and in communication with the universe naturally, and we are as well, whether we know it or not.

You have worked with many scientists and anthropologists who are interested in studying awareness and the indigenous view of nature. What do you tell them?

First of all, that there is no logical explanation for that which is a fact or a phenomenon in the life of the planet or the universe. Something that I find interesting about the citizens of the Western world, whether or not they are scientists, when it comes to an event or a phenomenon, including emotions and effects, is that they always say, "I think," whereas on the other hand we say, "I feel, I intuit, I perceive." It is an issue of semantics in the construction of language, or in the thinking structure. The cosmos is not solely a quantitative measure, cold and precise. Nature is not just a measure that is explained through a concept.

However, in many people's minds the function of planet Earth, nature, and the cosmos must be demonstrated in purely scientific terms in order for them to accept and validate them. This is not so for our native people; there are other types of explanations, and other way of perceiving things. We do not seek order or the measure of things, we seek harmony between that which exists above and below us, inside and outside of what is around us; we seek the energy that moves within everything, and we find it in our visions, in our dreams, through our instincts and intuition. We do not need to divide things in order to explain and understand life, stars, and the cosmos. And of course in our own explanation of things and phenomena, it is not about faith or religion, and anthropologists call us animists.

For example, when researchers or scientists have asked me how the spirit is connected to everything, I tell them that without that energy there is no connection with the great cosmos. Then they start performing tests, or create theories to explain these facts, and they discover that indeed there is a universal consciousness and an energy that is in constant movement in the cosmos, that exists whether they try to influence it or not. And "to better understand us" they take the plant medicine several times. After a long process of understanding and opening up, they start to have a personal understanding of how life's mysteries, nature, and the cosmos really exist and work without any scientific explanation that can prove it. They start to experience and understand the microcosmos personally, and find it amazing how for many centuries the indigenous people have been visiting places far away in space and know about the cosmos, and have been "riding" for so long without having to prove anything.

In your teachings, humans need to be in balance on the inside for them to live in harmony with nature and the universe. Can you say more about how people can do this?

It takes commitment. Many people ignore and are disrespectful to nature; they don't have any interest in understanding how things work and how to live a more balanced way with nature, and look for the cosmos to receive responses to their many questions. Politicians, for example, mining corporations, oil corporations, electronics corporations, and media corporations have their own interests, and they play many different roles in the name of science, of progress and development, but they are only creating conflict, which separates and divides us as human beings, and the only reason is money. As an indigenous woman, and a healer from the Amazon Rainforest in South America that I represent, constantly traveling between two worlds, I see a profound egoism and no desire to change anything. If they don't change, there is nothing we can do, and the planet Earth, our blue planet, is on the brink of total destruction, and some human groups are accelerating it.

So it is very complicated to distinguish between all these different interests and created conflicts. How can we all find a common understanding and perspective in this life, at this time? I see the only hope for the world now as being love, respect, humility, tolerance, and recognition of each other's being. We need to understand and accept each other's views and not worry about competing or about who is right or wrong.

We also each have to learn and find our inner balance and connection within ourselves. Last Saturday during the ceremony, no one had any judgments about themselves or others because they were connected to themselves from within. There was utter respect, love, and appreciation for themselves and each other. We need to express more of that. We need to practice it more often, every day, and spread that energy between friends, family, children, youth, elders, men, and women.

Things are moving very fast. Governments, politics, wars, and power are moving at a much faster rate now than in the past. For example, large, powerful corporations in the United States, Europe, China, and Japan are generally more concerned with making money than with the needs and possible positive contributions of the Amazon, of the people in the cities, of the indigenous populations in the world, and of the living beings of the planet. Most people in the cities are generally ignorant and don't know anything different; they don't make any difference, so they consume the goods of these corporations daily and are eating really badly. So, they get diabetes, cancer, and obesity as the result of a vicious cycle of a life out of balance.

The wisdom of ancient civilizations seems to have been forgotten. The modern human lifestyle has lost interest in the lessons of the ancestors and the connection to nature. People need to change their mindset and start making different choices that are not always the easy route in life. Our youth need to recover from the wars and negativity that they see around them and to begin having hope, dreams, and visions again.

The good news is there are people out there who are trying to help and create better societies. They want humans to survive on this planet, and so they are trying to preserve natural resources and change their ways of living. We need to remember that the universe is not an object or a collection of objects—it is all interconnected energy and flow, so whatever change we can make will have a qualitative difference.

Part 3

The View From Culture

Our culture is currently in the midst of tremendous transformation. Economical, social, political, cultural, and ecological systems are dissolving, reorganizing, and restructuring as corporations, organizations, and communities attempt to adapt to the rapidly shifting global landscape of these turbulent times. Most would agree that the world is changing more rapidly now than at any previous time in recorded history. Old approaches to solving our current crises seem ineffectual at best, and at worst are increasing the damage, adding accelerants to the firestorm of change engulfing us. The situation for many seems chaotic, discouraging, and disorienting, and some leaders and scholars are questioning the very future of human civilization on the planet.[6]

Yet in the midst of this great confusion and turmoil, I and my guests see something remarkable happening. Around the world, a new movement is being born, rising from the grass roots; people from all cultures and walks of life are seeking and discerning original ideas, creative ways of living, and integrative solutions to our global problems. People I talk to are discovering new sources of guidance, connection, and community that reach beyond the limiting political, cultural, and economic borders and structures of the past. In the face of a disorderly and seemingly intractable situation, these people are part of an enormous groundswell of hope, a feeling of something shifting worldwide, the excitement of new forms being born, things not yet seen, but distinctly sensed along the edges.

At the forefront of this shift are the cultural creatives: the thinkers, educators, and communicators who are not only developing hopeful new ideas and sustainable ways of living, but are currently living and actively promoting these ideas in our culture today. Sociologists Paul Ray and Sherry Ruth Anderson suggest that more than 50 million people in America alone are part of a growing movement that seeks to integrate the wisdom of the past with the needs of the present in moving toward a just and ecologically sustainable future.[7] The ideas that these women and men are bringing into the culture are the cutting edge of innovation and inspiration, as they synthesize results from contemporary science with the insights of the world's spiritual and cultural traditions into a truly global and cosmic perspective.

Brian Swimme suggests in the View from Science section that in order to face the daunting challenges present in the world today, we need to "reimagine in a radical way what it means to be human." In this section we meet some of the remarkable individuals who are doing just that. They are among the most incisive thinkers, scholars, and change-agents of our time, men and women who are looking beyond the limitations of our current cultural thinking to see the untapped potential of humanity. These individuals are bringing together the "big view" of the universe with radically new ideas of what it means to be human, combining the cosmic and the individual in personally and culturally transformative ways. The perspective emerging is that we are each the microcosmic expression of a creative universe, vast and evolutionary, the roots of which reach back to the beginning of space and time, intertwining our lives with those of the stars, the Earth, and all living beings as fellow companions and collaborators on an immensely shared journey. "Think Cosmically, Act Locally" could well be the slogan of this emerging twenty-first century perspective.

Conversations with these women and men suggest that cosmology, ecology, and humanity can all become integrated in a new perspective as our culture learns to apply the accumulated knowledge and deep wisdom of the human species toward a sustainable future that supports all. Seeking an alternative to the sense of existential separation from the Earth and cosmos that may lie at the heart of our ecological and economic crises, many of these cultural creatives find that we have the potential to see ourselves as co-creators with the universe, fully embedded in the rich and meaningful cosmic unfoldment taking place within and around us. This perspective holds us, not as handmaidens or puppets of evolution, but as fully empowered participants in its dramatic development, agents of a cosmic process that collaborates with the universe to create beauty, sustainability, and goodness for all beings.

Evolutionary futurist and author Barbara Marx Hubbard expresses this new perspective in describing how awareness of our evolutionary role can not only lead to the fulfillment of the human potential, but can also be a tremendous source of energy, creativity, and inspiration for us as individuals. Visionary and social activist Duane Elgin describes the inspiring and radical transformations that can happen when we begin to see ourselves as part of a living, intelligent, and conscious universe.

Religious scholar Christopher Bache introduces us to the expanded evolutionary perspective that arises when we begin to embrace reincarnation on a cosmic scale into our ideas about the universe. With astronaut Edgar Mitchell we see how awareness and knowing are fundamental to the cosmos and how much of the depth, breadth, and potential of the universe we have yet to explore. Mathematician and consciousness researcher Peter Russell brings together consciousness, light, and the acceleration of evolution as we explore the implications of this emerging new paradigm. We close with a conversation with cultural historian and scholar Richard Tarnas on the insights that astrology and the archetypal perspective can bring in awakening us as engaged participants in a vast cosmic drama.

Chapter 13

We Are Becoming the Future: An Interview With Barbara Marx Hubbard

❝We are process, not reality," exclaims anthropologist Loren Eiseley, writing about the ultimate nature of the human. The discoveries of Lyell, Darwin, Hubble, and others would seem to support this—we are the living embodiment of an ever-evolving universe.

Like a wave continuously cresting from its origin, the universe has been engaged in an uninterrupted process of evolutionary change that has surged from its beginning through atoms, molecules, stars, planets, cells, and now lately, humans. Of course, evolution does not end with humans, starfish, pine trees, or any of the life that surrounds us, and shows no signs of slowing down whatsoever. In fact, if the latest research is correct, evolution may even be accelerating (at least here on Earth), with evolutionary leaps and changes taking place all around us every day. After all, we ourselves change many times throughout the course of a lifetime, if not each day. "Yet where is it all going?" you may ask. What's the next step in the direction of evolution, and what if evolution itself is evolving as part of this ongoing cosmic process?

Enter Dr. Barbara Marx Hubbard.

More than nearly anyone else, Barbara Marx Hubbard has taken the idea of the evolution of humanity to its limits, having written and lectured extensively on the topic of conscious evolution and the future of humanity since she helped found the field more than 40 years ago. A well-known author, speaker, social innovator, and visionary, she worked closely with Abraham Maslow, Dr. Jonas Salk, and others in the 1960s, seeking answers to the global question "What is the next step for the future good?" In 1970 she co-founded the Committee for the Future in Washington D.C. and co-produced a series of 25 SYNCON (SYNergistic Convergence) conferences, interdisciplinary events that brought together diverse groups to match capacities and resources to find globally based solutions to systemic problems.

A gifted social innovator and community networker, she developed the innovative Theater for the Future, a multimedia story of creation that places humanity as an integral part of evolution and explores the potential that might be realized when everything we know we can do works. In the 1980s she was one of the original directors of the Center for Soviet American Dialogue and served as a citizen diplomat. She has also helped found many future-oriented organizations, including the World Future Society, New Dimensions Radio, Global Family, Women of Vision in Action, The Foundation for the Future, and the Association for Global New Thought.

She received her BA, *cum laude*, in political science from Bryn Mawr College, and studied at La Sorbonne and L'Ecole des Sciences Politiques in Paris during her junior year. She was later awarded the first ever doctorate in Conscious Evolution from the Emerson Institute.

Her books include *Conscious Evolution: Awakening the Power of Our Social Potential*; *The Hunger of Eve: One Woman's Odyssey Toward the Future*; *Emergence: The Shift from Ego to Essence*; *The Evolutionary Journey: Your Guide to a Positive Future*; and *Revelation: A Message of Hope for the New Millennium*.

She is currently president and executive director of the Foundation for Conscious Evolution, and is now producing a seven-part documentary series entitled "Humanity Ascending: A New Way through Together." She is also currently involved in a number of global educational initiatives designed to provide developmental templates for people to take the next step in world-wide human evolution.

A warm, gracious, and eloquent communicator, Dr. Hubbard and I explored the many implications, recognizing ourselves to be co-creators with the process of evolution.

Stephan Martin: One idea that is central to your work is that cosmic evolution is becoming conscious of itself in human beings, creating the possibility for conscious evolution. Can you say more about that? What does it mean for the universe and evolution to become aware of its own development and capacities?

Barbara Marx Hubbard: That is such a great question. It's clear to me that for billions of years evolution has been manifesting enormous creativity and intelligence in generating systems of awesome complexity. On planet Earth, it has been generating life, animal life, human life, self-consciousness, and then all of our cultural extensions of human consciousness. It seems to me that only in recent times, perhaps when we first discovered the cosmic background radiation signature of the original flaring forth, that we became imbued with the awareness that the universe has been and is now evolving.

Although these ideas had been inherent in some of our philosophies, they had never been scientifically understood, and as Brian Swimme says, the study of this "birth narrative" or this cosmogenesis is one of the greatest scientific discoveries of all time.

As we began to become aware that the universe is evolving we also began to see that we are part of that universal process of evolution. Now around 1945, when we began to make the first atomic bombs, we began to realize that we could, by understanding nature through science, affect our own evolution and even destroy all life on Earth. That understanding led to the insight that the universe has not only been evolving, but that we're part of it and that we can affect evolution through our actions. Everything we do, from making nuclear weapons to having babies and growing the kinds of food we eat, directs our evolution in some way. Then of course we began to understand DNA and realized that we could affect the design of life itself, and this has led to all the extraordinary genetic technologies of the past 50 years.

So what I think has happened is that through human intelligence and our awareness of our own participation in universal evolution, evolution itself began to move in a very slight way toward conscious choice. In an extreme example, our conscious choice could render ourselves extinct, or we might consciously choose to become co-evolving with nature. Some people see an implicate order and deeper intelligence in nature that expresses a progressive intention toward higher complexity and greater consciousness. When I began to see that for myself, I recognized that we are an embodiment of the whole story of creation—our atoms, our molecules, our brain, is a resume of the whole universal story. As we become conscious that we are affecting evolution, then we recognize that we are evolution becoming conscious of itself.

It's in this regard that I and many others feel that the advent of the next stage of evolution is as important as the advent of life itself. Whatever evolution is—we are that. So instead of putting evolution as something we are witnessing outside ourselves, evolution is what we are expressing, and the subjective aspect of that expression is our impulse to create, transform, and survive, both as a society and as a species. Scientifically and technologically we have the capacity to either destroy all life or to evolve life beyond the current human condition, toward what I think of as the universal species. So conscious evolution for me is the evolution of evolution from unconscious to conscious choice through human beings.

It's such a big and empowering idea, and so new for our culture.

It's really new, and I think it's new because it's actually the first time that any species has had this awareness on planet Earth. We don't know about elsewhere in the universe at this point.

Because it's such a new and radical idea, I think it's hard for people to take in that they have this capacity for evolution and that they actually are evolution in the process of evolving.

It is hard, and a quote by James Martin, from his book *The Meaning of the 21st Century* comes to mind: "Evolution on earth has been in nature's hands. Now suddenly it is largely in human hands. The extreme slowness of nature-based evolution makes it almost unnoticeable alongside human-based evolution. As we automate some of the processes of evolution the rates of change will become phenomenal. This change from nature-based to human-based evolution is by far the largest change to occur since the first single-celled life appeared. Its consequences will be enormous. And when it happens on a planet, it is dangerous. The creatures that take evolution into their own hands have no experience in the game."

This insight gives me compassion for the fact that we really don't know what we're doing. How could we? We used to think that God was in charge or the king or the priest or the pope, and it turns out that they don't know what they're doing either! [laughs] So the authorities of the past are fading from relevance, and the authority of consciously evolving humans is nascent.

I'm really struck by the idea here that in the end it's all up to us. What do we do with that?

You know I feel that it's not a neutral universe, but a generative one. The universe generates—and this is from Teilhard de Chardin—higher consciousness, greater freedom, and more complex order. So when you and I are sitting here having this conversation we are the universe in person exploring, and that exploration is evolving our capacity to be conscious *of* evolution and conscious *as* evolution.

I'm beginning to see that everything important that we do is real-time evolution. We are evolution evolving through this conversation. You are evolution, and I am evolution, and we've decided to have this conversation together, and I would say that evolution is doing very well in this moment as a result! [laughs]

I don't think it's only up to us as if we are in a vacuum, as the existentialists used to think, with no meaning in the universe except what we give it. I remember feeling really depressed when I read that. Then I read Teilhard and I felt that the universe has a propensity toward higher consciousness and greater freedom…and so do I! I recognized that I was implicit in this process of universal evolution, rather than a separate person making decisions entirely on my own. In a way I became an expression of universal evolution in person.

Right, and that takes it to a different level of evolution, because it seems as though we are talking about evolution as something beyond the mechanism of DNA. That there's something else here operating beyond the biological level, something else that's evolving.

Well of course we're aware of cultural evolution and that we're affecting our own biology and ecology and so forth, but I think conscious evolution is more than that. It took 14 billion years to get a species on this planet aware of evolution and the fact that it could evolve and co-operate with it. From the point of view of design, I think this is a major triumph for evolution. I'm not speaking of an external deity here, but of the generative genius of evolution in coming up with a species capable of participation in evolution at this level. It's really a great labor of love to get this far. I look at the universe as a developmental process and Earth as a subsystem of that process, with the deepest code of that to create more conscious life.

This idea of co-evolving, co-operating, and co-creating with nature is such a powerful concept. You also write about the possibility of humanity at some point co-creating with Spirit as well, as an unrealized potential. Is this something that you see is coming about now?

I do, and I think we're becoming a universal species as we speak. When you combine the spiritual, social, and technological capacities that we have, the kind of life we're giving birth to is beyond all the creatures and the conditions extant now. It may even be beyond carbon-based life for all we know. There are quite a few people that are trying to find a name for this species that is the fusion of the biological, electronic, and technological in a new way, but I call it the universal human.

You see, my intuition is that the innate tendency toward greater complexity, consciousness, and freedom, combined with high technology, is going to create a species capable of residing on the Earth and in the solar system, but of eventually transcending its Earth womb. The universe may well be filled with life like this, but we're still too young as a species to know.

It's not just at the level of radio waves and telescopes, but at the level of higher consciousness and mass resonance that we would be able to penetrate the higher dimensions of reality at the universal level. I think that this universal species is being born in many of us now, and perhaps as several species. Why should speciation stop with a furry biped with an eternal spirit? Why would it stop now?

As many people have pointed out, we are not at the endpoint of evolution.

Certainly not! It's not like we're at an endpoint and we can say "Oh look, we've finally arrived." We're still a very immature species, and we may not make it—a lot of species don't. If we do make it, I don't think we're going to stay as a self-centered, self-conscious human who's planet-bound. I think we're going to become universal. Every now and then I allow myself to become a universal human, and I meditate on all the extended capacities a universal human has: I have extended intelligence, extended environment, and extended lifespan. Through the Internet I am connected to the entire global intelligence. I imagine myself as a living consciousness of the noosphere, and when I do that I can feel that I'm no longer what I was. I was born in 1929 you see, and that was really before the advent of conscious evolution.

You've really gone through this whole transition in our culture.

My generation is the last to have lived through it before any of this was known. As a woman who lived through the 1950s and 1960s and been a wife and mother I feel like I and others like me are carriers of this new code.

It's like you are midwives for the birth of this new universal human.

We are, and it's born in us and through us. We are what we are giving birth to. And the more it happens as you, the more you can midwife it happening as others. That's the real meaning of being an elder, to help that process happen for others.

Could you talk about some of the other characteristics of the universal human that people might be beginning to see in their own lives and experience?

What's happening now is that the awareness of a global reality and a global crisis that is breaking down our planetary life-support systems is awakening in people what I call evolutionary consciousness. It's the recognition for people that they have an effect, not only on their individual lives, but also on the lives of their community and their world. The greatest personal effect is the stimulation of creativity and the yearning for joining that creativity with others to express the vast potential that seems to lie within us. We are each carriers of such tremendous potential, and when we join together with others and their potentials toward the birth of this global universal humanity, then new reservoirs of creativity are being tapped in us. Many of us feel that way.

It's almost as though these wellsprings of cosmic creativity become activated.

That's right, and Brian Swimme speaks so eloquently about the creative generative capacity of universal evolution. Since we are evolution in person here, our generative capacity at a time when the planet is in a crisis of the emergence is making a quantum leap. Every day I feel more creative, and I'm supposedly aging and dying! [laughs] For me it's going the other way, and I've coined a word for post-menopausal women: regeno-pause.

I feel that when a woman is no longer producing eggs she begins to be attracted to giving birth to her full potential self and its expression in the world. When this happens, she's turned on by creativity in the same way that she was turned on by procreativity. It's amazing that our bodies can give birth to a child and that we can nurse and nurture a new life simply because our bodies know how to do it. We don't know how to do it, but our bodies do. My sense is that when we start giving birth to our life's passion and purpose then the authentic feminine self knows what to do even if we don't think we do with our minds. This is true of men as well, but there's something very special about women because our bodies are designed for the radical generation of new life.

When a woman lives for a long time past her childbearing years she starts to get "vocationally aroused" by the expression of her life's purpose in the world, then I think she's evolving the species. We didn't used to live this long before, without having to be a grandmother for huge families. I call her the evolutionary woman, and she is seeking partnership with evolutionary men and others in order to give birth to herself and the world.

This is what you've spoken about as "supra-sexuality."

It is, and I think the drive for self-evolution and self-expression is just as strong as self-reproduction and self-preservation. It's an emergent drive comparable to self-reproduction, and it expresses itself through creativity to join not your genes together, but instead your genius. It's like what we're doing in this conversation. You obviously have a deep interest and background in this field. I love this conversation, because it happens to also be an expression of my own genius.

Yes, and I can feel that my own creativity is being activated by our conversation now, and so together our mutual creativity is building.

Yes, that's supra-sex right now. The universe is enjoying itself right now! [laughs] If there wasn't enjoyment in creativity in the past, then there wouldn't be so many babies who grew up to be so creative. I think the world will continue to evolve more through supra-sexual creativity than through guilt and fear.

Yes, it's certainly more pleasurable.

Yes. Guilt, fear, control, and power domination are increasingly frustrating. Look at what's happened to the United States, trying to control and dominate other peoples around the world. Look at our inability to control it, and how it engenders the very same crises that we were supposedly trying to oppose.

Now crisis is vital to evolution for newness to emerge, and failure is important to prevent the repeat of past mistakes. We are currently in the midst of a transition from a system based on power and control to a system that is inherently emergent and creative. I think this shift needs to be made through the synergistic convergence of the creative and emergent aspects happening in our culture right now. We need to connect the positive elements in a creative and nonlinear way through novel interactions, just like we are doing in this conversation.

Hopefully those who are inspired by reading this interview will have their own conversations and be lit up to inspire others. Creativity seems to be much more contagious than guilt or fear.

I've coined the phrase "telerotic" to describe this process. It's the combination of the words "telos" and "eros," and it means to fall in love with the fulfillment of the potential of the whole. I've always been attracted to emergent possibilities, the telos inherent in evolution toward higher consciousness and greater complexity.

So telerotic for me means to fall in love with the universe becoming more complex, more aware, and more self-aware. I'm attracted to that in my self that is going toward higher consciousness and greater freedom, and I'm attracted to that in other human beings as well. Eros has a life of its own. It draws us to unite with each other to create at a sexual level, but the universe itself is fundamentally erotic. Atoms, molecules, and cells all unite with each other as part of this universal erotic process.

Now the natural movement is from erotic to telerotic, but when it's frustrated or blocked it goes toward neurotic. Neurotic is when you have this erotic drive, but it's frustrated, so you go into violence, substance abuse, pornography, and depression, and all of these are at least partially due to suppressed creativity. When I turn on the TV these days, I see so much of this frustrated creativity and very little emergence of novelty.

Now I've sought out people with emergent creativity my whole life, so I know that it's widespread in the world today. But if I didn't know all these creative people who are out there and working for a better world, I wouldn't know this was happening from watching the news and reading the newspaper— I wouldn't have a clue based on the media!

I think that having these kinds of conversations can evoke this emergent creativity in us, even if we don't have the framework that this is the nature of the universe.

I found that since my vocation is as a communicator and storyteller, when I speak with people about this, often they will have tears in their eyes and tell me "I've always known this." But they didn't hear it before from their culture. It's one reason why people love to listen to Brian Swimme. He's radiant and he is the universe personified and telling its own story. He obviously loves those billions of galaxies and exploding supernovas deeply. You yourself must have this telerotic attraction for universal evolution to be doing this project.

I do, and for me it's the process of discovery. As an astronomer and as a trained scientist I love research because it's always uncovering something that's new.

Yes, and humans have certainly been curious about the process of discovery for hundreds of thousands of years, yet your awareness, your consciousness that you are evolving through doing this project is new!

It strikes me as similar to something you've written about as "vocational arousal." Could you talk about that and how it relates to our finding our role in the universe?

I think that individual vocation is part of the design of creation. When you get turned on to something, it's not just to any old thing, but you have a very specific role to play in universal evolution. The more a person has a strong vocation, the more they find themselves to be part of a larger design. I feel my vocation is not just a personal profession.

In vocational arousal you're aroused not only toward something specific to your life's purpose, but other people also become excited by what you're excited about, which in turn arouses you to further levels of excitement in a feedback loop of relationship. When this happens, you're more expressive of who you truly are, and the other is more expressive of who they truly are and out of this vocational arousal comes co-creation.

Yes, creating together something new that didn't exist before.

Out of sexual arousal comes procreation and the birth of a new being. Out of supra-sexual co-creative vocational arousal comes a very specific creative joining. It doesn't happen just any old way. You see, this is a very specific joining that we're involved with here because you have a very specific interest that you've cultivated with your knowledge, and I have a very specific interest that I have cultivated with mine, so this is very specific fusion of genius that is coming together here. We're involved in a kind of meta-love story through our mutual vocational arousal.

And what we're co-creating here is something that's very unique, something that hasn't existed before. I wonder if you could give some advice to those people who are still looking for their vocational arousal.

One's best clue is anything that attracts you, even if it doesn't initially seem important. If you follow that attraction, then you begin to discover more, and particularly if you read a book or meet a person or hear about something that attracts you, then go for it as much as you can.

For example, I was attracted to Abraham Maslow's writing when I was in my early 30s, so I managed to call him up and have lunch with him. I did something that might not be easy to do, but I followed the attraction. I began to follow more and more of the attraction and I would get feedback, and find out where the attraction was strongest and more genuine. You follow the attraction according to what's emergent most strongly in yourself, and when you find something that fulfills your own expression more fully and your capacity to serve more deeply, then you go more that way! I would say that path will lead you to your vocation.

Brian Swimme talks about the process of allurement, where we're drawn or attracted to certain things, and this sounds similar to what you're describing.

Yes, it is, and I love the word *allurement* to describe this process. Sometimes I also think of it like a mother who falls in love with her unborn child. I'm a mother of five children, and when I've been pregnant, I've thought, "I don't know this child. How come I love it and want it and am living and breathing for its emergence?" Well, as mothers we're programmed that way to fall in love with the unknown child. Now I feel you can extend that allurement toward the unknown person that you're becoming, toward the unknown creativity that's coming forth in you, and ultimately for the unknown world that's being created through all of us. That feminine ability to love the unknown in a very intimate way is very important.

Yes, and it's more than just a metaphor, because we're giving birth to something in ourselves and each other that we cannot see.

In the case of biological birth, we know at least a little what to expect in that we're giving birth to a biological organism. When we're giving birth to the universal being that we are and a new world that we haven't seen before, then that's where faith and the unconditional love of the unknown potential has to come in.

You've written about the power of memes and the memetic code as the shaping forces in a new evolutionary worldview. Can you talk about some of these memes that are shaping our perception and experience of the world right now?

I see four areas where memes are shaping the future of humanity right now: the evolution of the universe, the evolution of evolution, the evolution of society, and the evolution of the person. The basic meme of the evolution of the universe is that it is coming alive to ever more conscious life. The cosmos appears to many to be quintessentially a great unfolding intelligence. There is a developmental path encoded in the unfolding of the universe in which we are conscious vital elements. There's a set of memes right there—instead of saying that there's an intelligent God outside of our universe producing this structure, many thinkers and religious traditions suggest that there's an intelligent plenum out of which everything is arising.

In the case of the evolution of evolution, human beings now play an active and critical role not only in the process of their own evolution, but also in the survival and evolution of all of the living beings on this planet. The awareness of this places on humans a responsibility for their participation in and their contribution to the process of evolution. One of the memes that is shaping this is conscious evolution, the awareness of our contribution to the process of evolution, and the evolution of evolution itself. No matter what your background or belief system, the fact is that evolution is becoming aware of itself.

Yes, and that's an entirely new category of evolution.

It is, and consciousness accelerates the evolutionary process tremendously. We're now in a time when things are breaking down and speeding up at an exponential rate. My intuition is that we're going to see something radically new evolutionarily within the lifetime of many of the younger people living today. Biological evolution is very slow even considering punctuated equilibrium, but the advent of computer intelligence, robotics, nanotechnology, and genetic engineering brings something very new to the process. Evolution in the future is going to be accelerated—it's not going to be as slow as it's been in the past, because we're going to destroy our biosphere if we don't learn about it fast.

I think the process eventually can accelerate into unlimited unfolding, which goes way beyond *Homo sapiens* at this point. I mean, what's the form of body that a consciously evolving universal presence has? Is it light bodies? Is it silicon-based bodies? What is it? All of the great spiritual traditions have a description of some form of light body, so my intuition is that the human body will become ever lighter, and will be extended in intelligence.

And extended in extent as well. I'm thinking here of how the Internet and global communication extends our physical capacities and influence.

Yes, also in extent, and that consciousness will reside in ever-evolving bodies. I think there are many different options for life as we continue to speciate.

Yes, and something also evolves within the community as well, so that it's not a process of individual evolution, but a global process as well.

Right, and what form will the Earth community take? Or the solar system and the galactic community? Saying this right now, I feel attracted and drawn toward that emerging potential, and I think of that attraction as the generative impulse of evolution.

Now for this evolutionary process to continue in an optimal way, it makes a huge difference what memes we choose to develop. We're now at the point of being conscious of the fact that memes are chosen. I can choose to have a meme of violence and ethnic cleansing, or I can choose to have a meme of global cooperation, and I will behave very differently according to what memes I choose. We've had some terrible memes in the past.

I think we're currently in what I call a memetic gap, where the old memes from the past are fading, and the new memes have yet to take hold in our culture in a broad way. We're at a point similar to the Renaissance, when a new memetic code of innovation and secularism supplanted the old medieval Catholicism. Think of the difference between the medieval worldview and the Renaissance worldview.

The worldview that is currently being born for us is even more radical, because it's based on such huge new crises and opportunities. I would end with saying that one of the projects that most interests me right now is identifying and connecting the memetic codes that are arising in critical areas such as health, education, economics, science, and technology. As we see the outlines of a new memetic code take shape we can actually create the memes that we want. However, if we have the wrong memes, the self-destructive ones, we'll destroy our planetary life-support systems. This is a huge thing, and it makes all the difference in terms of what we want for our future.

Chapter 14

The Universe as a Living System: An Interview With Duane Elgin

Is the universe a collection of inert and dead objects, or is there evidence of greater organization and purpose in the cosmos? Ancient peoples worldwide have traditionally held that the universe is a living organism, infused with consciousness, intelligence, and purpose, but this view has largely fallen into disfavor with the rise of modern science. Do our beliefs about whether we are part of a living or a dead universe even matter? In his latest book, *The Living Universe* (Berrett-Koehler, 2009), internationally recognized author, educator, and media activist Duane Elgin argues that they do. How we feel about the universe has a tremendous effect on our outlook on life, he suggests, as well as the future that we collectively create together.

For more than three decades, Elgin has been at the cutting edge of research on the personal and collective aspects of the human journey. His first book, *Voluntary Simplicity* (HarperCollins, 1981 and 1993), pioneered the simplicity movement in the United States and abroad, promoting ways of living that are more sustainable and meaningful. His other books include: *Promise Ahead: A Vision of Hope and Action for Humanity's Future* (HarperCollins,

2000) and *Awakening Earth: Exploring the Evolution of Human Culture and Consciousness* (Morrow, 1993). With Joseph Campbell and others he co-authored the book *Changing Images of Man* (Pergamon, 1982).

Elgin has been researching the theme of a living universe for the past 27 years. In 1988 he published the lengthy article, "The Living Universe: A Theory of Continuous Creation" for the journal *ReVision*. In addition to decades of scholarship, Elgin brings 40 years of meditation to this exploration, as well as personal experience with parapsychological research in a scientific setting. For nearly three years in the early 1970s, he was a subject in experiments funded by NASA to explore our intuitive potentials. Results from these experiments (notably, "remote viewing") have been published in major scientific journals.

Elgin has an MA from the University of Pennsylvania and an MBA from the Wharton School. He was a senior social scientist with SRI International, where he conducted long-range studies and developed strategy for government agencies. He has also served as a senior staff member on the Presidential-Congressional Commission on the American Future. In 2006, Duane received the international "Goi Peace Award" in recognition of his contribution to a global "vision, consciousness, and lifestyle" that fosters a "more sustainable and spiritual culture."

Stephan Martin: Many people have spoken and written extensively about the "horizontal story" of the cosmos unfolding or evolving over billions of years. But you emphasize what you call the "vertical story" of the cosmos happening in the moment. Could you say more about that?

Duane Elgin: This is a key distinction that I think is extremely important. Many scholars focus on the evolution of the universe over billions of years—the horizontal rolling out of the universe through time, which I call the horizontal story. My focus is on the vertical story, which is the regeneration and re-creation of the entire universe in time—in every moment.

In your book, you make the point that if the entire universe is regenerating itself at the speed of light, it would be impossible to travel faster than the speed of light because you would then be exceeding the rate of manifestation. Because you cannot come into existence before you are regenerated and manifested by the universe, faster-than-light travel is impossible, just as modern physics predicts. You can't get ahead of yourself becoming yourself!

Yes, exactly. Although the story of the universe evolving through time is incredibly transformative in itself, what I am emphasizing here is not unfoldment *through* time, but continuous unfoldment *in* time. The idea that time itself is being created in the regenerative flow of the universe. It is a radically different perception to see the entire universe continually arising as a unified system, and this is where the notion of a living universe gains relevance.

In addition to insights from science, the world's spiritual traditions are uniformly and emphatically clear that the universe is being created moment by moment. Hinduism, Taoism, Islam, Buddhism, Christianity, and more teach that the universe is being re-created as an entire system at every moment.

It's interesting that you bring up the world's spiritual traditions, since in many of these traditions one of the purposes of meditation is to slow down the mind enough so that you can actually see the manifestation of the universe in every moment.

That's very true. I spent three years as a subject in several parapsychology experiments in a NASA-funded project at the Stanford Research Institute in the early 1970s. My core insight from this research is that our capacities of perception are more than equal to the speed of manifestation for the universe. Our physical senses may be limited to perceptions less than the speed of light, but our intuitive capacities are capable of perceiving the universe directly as an arising system in every moment. Because we are part of the universe and are interior to it, we can know it simply by resting in our own being and experience. When we do that, what we're resting into is the dynamic arising of the cosmos itself. That's why "Tantra" means thread, flow, continuity. To come into a Tantric appreciation of the universe is to ride the flow of creation.

To align oneself with it, so to speak.

Yes, and to consciously recognize that the universe is arising and that I'm riding the wave of its arising. I call this "reality surfing," moving with the arising of the universe in each moment.

So in this sense, we are not ultimately limited by the constraints of matter, of physicality.

No we're not. However, if we think all we are is just a bunch of biochemical reactions, then that self-limiting assumption will prevent us from investing the time and energy to look further.

Yes, but your research and experience with the world's spiritual traditions shows otherwise.

As I describe in my book *The Living Universe*, the world's wisdom traditions are emphatically clear that the universe is re-creating itself in its totality at an extremely high rate of speed. The "power of now" comes from the creation of the whole universe in every moment. If I'm in the center of that flow, there's tremendous power there. But if I'm strung out and stretched through the past, present, and future, then all that power is diluted and thinned out. It comes down to fully participating in the moment.

This idea of the universe being a living, dynamic entity that only exists in the moment brings into the conversation an entirely different definition of life than what is usually talked about in biology or in scientific thinking. If the universe is a living system, then what are we talking about when we talk about life?

That's a very good question, and the way I address it is to ask ,"What is a living system? What are its attributes? How would you know a living system if you saw it?" Although the nature of life is still widely debated in science, I've gone through an enormous body of literature and come up with five attributes that are generally widely accepted as defining a living system. So if we are to regard the universe as being alive in some sense, then it will satisfy those attributes.

Will these be the minimum criteria that will apply to the universe if it's to be considered a living system?

Yes, these are the most rigorous criteria for living systems that I can apply to the cosmos that are generally accepted by science. However, it is not my intention to scientifically *prove* that the universe is a living system; rather, I want to look at the direction in which the evidence is pointing. Here are core attributes that I see that suggests the universe is a living system:

1. The cosmos is a unified system that functions as an undivided whole.
2. The cosmos is continually regenerated by the flow-through of phenomenal amounts of energy.
3. There is a spectrum of consciousness with an accompanying capacity for choice at every scale of the universe.
4. The cosmos has freedom at its foundations. It is not a deterministic, clockwork system, but has the freedom to grow and evolve in unexpected ways.
5. The cosmos appears to be able to reproduce itself through black holes, the other side of which may be a white hole and the birth of a new cosmic system.

When we combine these, we can say: The universe is a unified and completely interdependent system that is continuously regenerated by the flow-through of phenomenal amounts of life energy whose essential nature includes consciousness or a self-reflective capacity that enables systems at every scale of existence to exercise some degree of freedom of choice. Overall, it seems proper, from a scientific perspective, to regard the universe as a unique kind of living system.

It is also a very ancient view to regard the cosmos as permeated by aliveness and this as the source of the constituent parts of the universe.

One view is that the foundations of the universe are non-living, so from non-life emerges life. Another view (that I hold) is that the foundations of the universe are alive, so from life emerges further life. In the latter view, aliveness is *both* fundamental and emergent—it is both permeating and sustaining the foundations of the universe, as well as an emergent property of self-organizing systems that have the capacity to reflect upon themselves.

Well, let's talk about life as a property of the whole a bit more. Is life a property of the universe as a whole, or does it arise from what cosmologists call the "multiverse" and spiritual traditions call the "mother universe"?

There appears to be a deeper field of aliveness that sustains countless cosmic systems: life within life within life. Current cosmology is opening to a multi-universe perspective and this view is congruent with a number of the world's wisdom traditions. Overall, my sense is that we exist in an unbounded and transparent field of aliveness that extends infinitely beyond our physical universe.

Many cosmologists think we live in a superspace or meta-universe with an infinite number of dimensions. I think it is important to recognize that we live, not in the 3,000th dimension or even in the 300thth dimension or 30th dimension—we are in the third dimension, which is only two steps above a black hole. My sense is that we are just getting to know what it means to live in a multidimensional reality. We are barely getting started on our evolutionary journey. If we assume that each new dimension provides an enlarged space for creative expression and learning, then with countless dimensions welcoming us with extraordinary opportunities for personal and social transformation, we appear to have an immensity of learning before us.

My sense is that the universe is creating self-organizing systems at every scale, from the atomic to the galactic, and we happen to be one of these systems that have the capacity for self-reflection. The universe is a garden for growing self-referencing, self-organizing systems in a context of great freedom, elegance, and beauty. As self-conscious organisms, we have the capacity to live within in a deeper ecology of life energy that reaches beyond the physical body, and to align ourselves with that larger ecology of aliveness.

It sounds as though you're talking about life as a field or a matrix of aliveness within which all these self-organizing systems are like eddies in a larger flow, and from which they ultimately derive their life energy.

Yes, I see life as both fundamental and self-emergent.

So you see aliveness as pervasive and present everywhere throughout the cosmos, even in empty space. Some spiritual traditions talk about space as the living creative potential of existence, and your thoughts sound similar to this.

Absolutely. I would suggest that empty space has even more potential in some respects than matter which has coalesced itself into a discrete form. The fabric of space-time is open potential, a dynamic transparency that's being regenerated at an extraordinary high rate of speed. Our ability to see through transparent space is a dynamically constructed capacity.

So are you saying that space is not inherently transparent?

I mean that the universe works tremendously hard to create what appears to us as the stillness of empty space. This became clear to me when I was involved with experiments in the parapsychology laboratory. I began these experiments thinking of myself as a separate entity whose task was to project energy from myself to a physical apparatus on the other side of the room. Over several years, I gradually realized that space is filled with a sea of energy and that the universe is continuously arising as an interdependent whole, and so what was really happening was that the apparatus and myself were participating in a dance of co-emergence together.

Your experience seems to show that if it's all arising together as a unity, then the idea that there are separate objects or entities is simply an illusion caused by our perception and perspective.

Exactly. Once again, this brings us back to the vertical dimension and the regenerative nature of the cosmos. It's very challenging to recognize our communion with the cosmos in the horizontal dimension of life, because the vast numbers of objects and activities naturally draw us into believing we are separate and differentiated from everything else. Therefore, all of the world's wisdom traditions point to the importance of being present in the NOW. If we are to experience the universe as a unified living organism, we can sit very quietly and ride the wave of existence, and it will become intuitively self-evident.

It's the difference between being *in* the universe and being *the* universe.

That's right. Part of the reason we usually don't see it this way is that our thinking conditions our perceptions, so if we think of ourselves as part of the dead matter floating around the empty space of the universe, then it will likely be a self-fulfilling prophecy. For a lot of people in the world, that's what's going on, but surveys show that approximately 40 percent of the U.S. adult population has had a mystical experience, some kind of experience of unity, oneness, and connection with the aliveness of it all. So it's not that we don't experience the universe in this way, but it's more likely that when we do, we simply don't recognize what's happening to us.

And as you point out, many people have these experiences of themselves as this larger reality, but they don't have a cosmology or worldview to fit them into, and so they dismiss their experiences. They might think they are going crazy, or that they can't share it with others because it's too weird, and so they don't get the validation that they're really having these deep insights into the way things really are.

That's exactly what I did in the beginning of laboratory experiments in parapsychology. Early on I discovered that I was resistant to a more spacious sense of "self." Deep down I wanted to discover a concrete sense of self—a bounded, definable sense of myself. What I discovered over a period of years is that the scope of our being is as big as the scope of our perception. When we experience this, it blows away a smaller sense of self.

This sounds like where cosmology and psychology come together. Psychologically, there is often the desire to have a stable sense of self or identity. But many of the great spiritual traditions claim that there is ultimately no separate sense of self. Look at Buddhism—once you start looking for a sense of self, where is it? You begin to see it takes the entire universe to create any part of it, including ourselves. So we really are much larger than we think.

If you look at the sizes of things in the universe, from the Planck length at 10^{-35} meters up to the size of the observable universe at 10^{28} meters, humans are a little bit on the big side of things. In other words, there is more smallness within us than bigness beyond us. We are literally giants in the cosmic scale of things! Now what does a giant do? Well, one thing a giant does is to overlook things that are happening on very small scales. So if the universe is regenerating itself at a very high rate of speed at the quantum threshold, it will be very easy to overlook that. You'd have to really pay attention to notice something like that. So we are essentially misperceiving who we think we are. We think we are tiny creatures in a vast universe and it turns out we are not.

The capacity to know ourselves and the universe directly is what I find to be one of the most empowering and radical aspects of the living universe hypothesis. If people don't have go outside themselves to try to fill themselves or to get love, then it's really an effective alternative to the problems of materialism that are dominating our culture today.

Completely. As you know, dark matter and dark energy comprise 96 percent of the known universe, so materialism is therefore the 4 percent solution. Consumerism is going to get you somewhere, but it's only going to get you 4 percent of the way. For the remaining 96 percent of the journey, we're going to have to go beyond the materialistic paradigm and into the invisible structures that make up the rest of the known universe.

Going beyond what we see with our eyes and instruments, and into what we actually know and feel intuitively about the universe.

That's right—it's a journey into our cosmic identity. The universe is creating self-organizing structures that have the capacity to "know that they know," as in the case with humans. With self-referential knowing, we are ultimately no longer bound by physical structures, and can move into more open, spacious, and free ecologies of learning, development, and being. As humans, we are learning to know who we truly are in a context of immense freedom and knowing. The universe is incredibly patient this way. It says, "I've got billions of years, so if you want to take a lifetime to know yourself fully, no problem. In fact, take a hundred or a thousand or more lifetimes to know and make friends with yourself." Recognizing ourselves as a stream in the greater aliveness of the living universe is not the end of the journey, but its barest beginning. Getting hold of ourselves as conscious beings closes the loop of self-recognition and provides a foundation for moving into more spacious ecologies of learning and discovery.

It sounds as though you're saying that in awakening to the aliveness of the universe within us, we can more fully participate in the co-creation of the universe in each moment.

Exactly. I think the purpose of our evolutionary journey is to progressively grow in self-recognition, understanding that with each stage of knowing ourselves, our freedom increases.

What do you think is most important for helping people see and experience the perspective of a living universe for themselves?

It's vitally important to develop a cosmology that accurately describes the universe so we can live in harmony with it. We are immersed in materialistic cultures that tell us the story of a dead universe where satisfaction is found through consumption. We are divided against ourselves and unable to live in harmony with the universe. A cosmology of a living universe is vital if we are to feel that we belong here and that our existence is purposeful. As we see that we are beings of cosmic connection who are learning to live in a living universe, we are motivated to live more sustainably on the Earth and compassionately with one another.

Chapter 15

The Universe, Reincarnation, and the Transformation of Humanity: An Interview With Christopher Bache

As an astronomer I'm used to thinking big, with big ideas about the universe and a big picture of our place in the cosmos, but my vision of the universe suddenly feels tiny once I start talking with Dr. Christopher Bache about what may really be going on. For more than three decades, Bache has investigated the nature of transpersonal reality on the largest scales and the relationship between the individual and that of the universal and the collective. Are we each separate individuals in a vast universe, or is the universe itself a vast collective consciousness that weaves humanity and all of our experiences together into an inseparable whole? Does humanity have a cosmic role to play in the evolution of the cosmos? Philosophers and mystics have speculated on these ideas throughout history, but few have explored them on with the intensity, rigor, and insight as Bache.

Dr. Christopher Bache has been professor of religious studies at Youngstown State University for more than three decades, where he teaches transpersonal studies, comparative spirituality, consciousness research, and Eastern religions.

A pioneer in the study of consciousness, he wrote his first book, *Lifecycles* (Paragon House, 1990), on reincarnation. His second, *Dark Night, Early Dawn: Steps to a Deep Ecology of Mind* (SUNY Press, 2000), focuses on the relationship of the individual to the collective from the perspective of non-ordinary states of consciousness.

He is also an adjunct professor in the Philosophy, Cosmology, and Consciousness program at the California Institute of Integral Studies in San Francisco and was director of Transformative Learning at the Institute of Noetic Sciences in Petaluma, California, for two years. The recipient of many awards for teaching, his latest book, *The Living Classroom* (SUNY Press, 2008), explores the dynamics of collective consciousness in the classroom.

Many of Dr. Bache's insights come from his personal experiences with sacred medicines throughout a 20-year period along with his current practice of Vajrayana Buddhism. His series of intensely transformative and evocative experiences are documented in his book *Dark Night, Early Dawn*, where he describes encounters with a spiritual reality that is remarkably similar to that described by the mystics of the world's spiritual traditions, as well as by other transpersonal psychologists such as Carl Jung, Ken Wilber, and Stanislav Grof.

Stephan Martin: Could you share something you've learned from your various experiences about the nature of the universe?

Chris Bache: The primary thing I may have to offer this discussion is a perspective that comes from my work with psychedelics. Because it reflects my individual journey, it may be risky to extrapolate information from it for others, but I take comfort in the broad resonance between my experiences and the hundreds of experiences documented in Stan Grof's work. He opened the door and created the fundamental framework I've built on. As I've grown older I've been able to look back on this 20-year period of engagement and get a better perspective on it.

What's coming through for you now as you look back on these experiences?

Well, for one thing, perhaps how stupid I was to push as far and as deep as I did, and how much I underestimated the depth of the journey and its cost.

[laughs] However, I now appreciate better that each of our journeys into the center of life is a singular journey. At the center of the universe is an infinite consciousness with infinite potential so vast that no one can hold the whole of it. A million individual journeys into the center elicit a million different aspects of infinite consciousness. Anything I have to offer comes from intuitions that have been shaped by my experience of this domain, as well as the guidance that has been given to me along the way by the universe.

Can you say more about the guidance and the perspective that's developed for you based on these insights?

Where to start? One of the recurring themes for me has been the patterns of the soul's development. Imagine a spool of kite string that you're winding round and round. The soul-process of collecting and accumulating experience takes place over hundreds of thousands of years of evolution and reincarnation, and what's being wound around the spool toward the end is some of the most precious stuff in the universe—human experience. It's very different, for example, than tree experience. As the soul winds more and more experience round itself, the system starts to glow until eventually it ignites. I think that's what the universe has been doing with us for millions of years, spinning us up on the inside, and now we're coming to critical mass.

Your work begins in some sense by pointing out that many individuals have experiences of an expanded reality, whether through dreams, synchronicities, or spiritual and mystical states, that don't easily fit into our culture's modern cosmological worldview. Based on this evidence, your work and the work of others in transpersonal psychology points to a vision of the universe that is much more comprehensive than that described by modern science, one infused with spiritual consciousness, expansive life, and universal intelligence. This sounds in many ways like the accounts of deepest reality described by the world's mystical traditions. Could you say something about this?

That's a good summary of the situation we're in. I think that the great spiritual masters saw something that is fundamentally true about the universe. Physics in some ways is catching up with parts of their vision. Their fundamental vision is that the universe is alive, with the vast majority of it's aliveness not visible to our naked eye. Think about the recent finding in astronomy that 96 percent of the universe is invisible. We're essentially floating on an ocean of invisible light.

Just as the mystics relate, we're finding that the universe is saturated with layers upon layers of intelligence, and it has plans and strategies we're just starting to get glimmers of. The genius that surrounds and permeates us has been billions of years in the making, and maybe includes universes that existed before this one. We're just beginning to wake up to the complexity of it all.

The universe is alive and it's spiritual as well as physical. It's exploding all around us, shattering us into bigger and bigger visions and understandings of ourselves. Because our core awareness is rooted in something that is beyond space and time, we can't really die. This part of us was never born—it just becomes more complex over time.

The astrophysicist Bernard Haisch, who is also included in this book, has theorized that all physical phenomena arise out of the zero-point field, which is essentially a sea of light.

That corresponds with my experience. It's been my experience that in sustained inner work, the universe reveals itself in stages. As my work progressed through the years, deeper layers of the universe showed themselves. In the early stages, the experiences moved beyond the material world into the psychic and soul domain. Then the unfolding continued beyond soul reality into layers of archetypal reality and the deep structures of the subtle realms. Then it continued beyond this to the deity realms, the god realm, and deeper still to the domain of pure light. This light was then refined and purified at deepening levels until it became a field of pure Diamond Consciousness. Beyond all visible light there was a domain where light purified into an energy so refined that it became invisible. Pure invisible potentiality, what some call the Void.

From this perspective, then, there are many layers of reality between the Void and the manifest physical world. That's the way it has appeared to me, at least. It's as if the archetypal realm is like a field of giant trees growing out of this ground of light and pure consciousness, with the tips of their leaves eventually reaching into time and space.

It sounds as though this is the underlying field that is giving rise to space, time, and our everyday embodied experience.

I think so. It's exciting that physicists are pointing in this direction with concepts like the quantum field and the zero-point field, which they describe as having the qualities of light and nonlocality. If physics is describing something like this lying at the foundation of physical existence, it is coherent with the vision of reality that surfaces in deep transpersonal experiences.

It's interesting that the universe would use the same dynamics at all these various levels. For me, that's astonishing in itself!

That's when you begin to know you're looking at something really important, when you find it operating at multiple levels—at the physical, mental, and spiritual levels.

I think this same principle of repetition of design at multiple levels applies to the concept of reincarnation. Reincarnation is simply one instance of a larger pattern in nature—nature recycling its learning. It builds on itself. The universe recycles everything, including human learning. It's incredibly efficient. You don't need to get too personal about it.

What's exciting is that this continual compounding of experience is building up inside each of us. For this reason alone, I don't think we can stop an awareness of rebirth from eventually rising inside people. The longer we accumulate life experience, sooner or later we will become aware of this compounding within us. And once people see it, it's going to become obvious that this is simply one more pattern of learning in a self-evolving, self-arising universe, part of evolution's thrust toward greater complexity. I think it's going to become an unstoppable idea in history.

It sounds as though this is something that the universe wants us to know. The fact that these kinds of insights are arising all around us seems to be part of the universe's self-revelation, its desire to know itself in a deeper way, to use somewhat anthropic terminology.

Yes. The universe is pouring its secrets into us every moment. What are we? We *are* the universe, and the larger universe is downloading as much information into us as we can take in. Every time we have a little deeper insight, it is giving us more information. We are the universe becoming aware of its larger self.

I think that there is so much joy in the spiritual domain that humanity is finally getting old enough that we can begin, just begin, to touch the edges of the intelligence that has been birthing us these many billions of years. I think there's tremendous joy, because even if we are just waking up, It knows fully what we are. The image that keeps coming to me is of God holding us as delicately as a mother holds her new baby. But God has to be careful not to touch us too directly, not to allow us to feel His/Her full love for us, because if we felt that great love, the energy would be so strong it would send the baby into paroxysms of pain. The fact is that we're just now getting strong enough to be able to withstand more contact with the Divine Mind without shattering.

It reminds me of the image that we talked about earlier with the cocoon of our essence being wrapped more and more with the kite string of human experience, so that we eventually become stronger and able to embrace more of this reality.

Yes, but how long does it take? This awareness is opening in so many people that I think we are coming to a moment in time when an earlier crop of soul consciousness is beginning to be harvested into something greater. You know, you plant something in the ground and you have to wait months for it to mature. Human experience has been planted in the universe, and the universe has waited 100,000, 200,000 years for it to sprout. Now there seems to be some kind of ripening taking place, some massive underground awakening.

I've heard some people say that more people are waking up these days than at any other point in history.

I agree. I think that there's a quickening or ascending energy rising from the depths so that we are collectively coming to a kind of psychic boiling point. As our collective unconscious comes to a boil, our entire political and social system is going to start to cook ferociously, and all that energy is going to churn each of us at very deep levels. Our collective unconscious is not going to be the quiet partner it has been in the past, but will be much more active and arousing.

It's going to turn up the heat, so to speak.

It's going to turn up the heat, throw us into collective labor, and send us into convulsions that will force us to throw off the past and create a new present. It's going to draw all of us together into a massive realignment, with an accelerated learning curve. It's going to be a near-extinction event, I fear, a massive interruption of life as we know it. Large nation-states and global economies may fragment in this process. I just don't see any other way.

However, I deeply believe that out of this crisis something new and better will arise. We know we have great potential that can rise to great heights when under duress, and I deeply trust the intelligence and wisdom that's carried us 13.7 billion years to where we are today. So if we're coming into global crisis, we must be ready. We may feel stupid and clumsy in the face of all this, but there must be a large enough reservoir inside the human heart to allow us to become more than we were.

I hope there is, and your transcendent vision of the universe sounds like something people need right now, given the current world situation and the kind of guidance that many people are yearning for.

You know, a crisis is the worst time to start looking for a new philosophy. Ideally, you should have your philosophy in place before a crisis hits. It worries me that many people are going into this transformation standing on such weak theological ground. What do they have? Most of our churches are deeply alienated from their time in history.

The knowledge of the natural world is our new religion. It's what we truly believe and trust in. It's where our greatest talent is focused and what our children go to college to learn. I don't think we're going back to the religions of the past, and I don't think we're going to give up science in going forward. What I suspect is going to happen is that we'll bring the deeper spirituality of the old religions forward, but in a post-religious form. We're on the verge of the birth of a new spirituality, which will include science while simultaneously opening more intimately to cosmic and divine genius. The depth of what is alive inside us will sooner or later overtake us.

It sounds as though one of the elements of this coming transformation is a shift in authority, where people will no longer derive their knowledge of reality primarily from external sources such as science and religion, but will begin to investigate their own experience directly to see what is true. I wonder if you see this as part of this synthesis of science and religion that is coming.

Yes. And I think our experience is showing us that the inner universe is as "large" as the outer universe is. And this is coming as a big surprise to us; it wasn't supposed to be this way! We thought we could tuck our minds into an envelope the size of our brains, a mental envelope that contained the sum total of our physical senses. What we're finding experientially, however, is very different. Consciousness is vast. And whether it's discovered through meditating on a mountaintop, ingesting psychotropics, or having a near-death experience, in each case you find a vast reality within.

I think a sophisticated version of the perennial philosophy will emerge in a new global form. There will also be an appreciation of the fact that the individual is a fractal being that resonates and vibrates within the larger collective. So as the collective goes through *its* turning point in history, each one of us goes through our own *soul* turning point as well. We take our underlying pivot from the larger universe, and our individual transformations simultaneously ripple out into the field of the universe.

I feel very strongly that each of us is connected to specific people through the tissue of time and space. We may not know many of them, but we are connected by threads that run through the hearts and minds of specific persons. Through these specific beings, we are connected to the family of humanity as a whole. When we rise to the challenge of our individual lives, when we do what it is we are here to do, it sends a pulse of light and life along these filaments that nourishes everyone we are connected to and helps them achieve what they are being called to do. Likewise, if we fail, it lowers our collective energy. We are truly and deeply all in this together.

How the individual is embedded in the collective and how the collective is nourished by the work of the individual are some of my preoccupations. I'm interested in what happens when a collective system reaches a critical bifurcation point where it becomes nonlinear and more unstable and more subject to change. Systems theory and chaos theory tell us that at these critical points of stress and compression, systems become extremely susceptible to influence. Small influences can have large outcomes. If this is so, then in this time of global crisis, even a small number of people doing the right thing may crystallize a positive outcome for humanity. I believe that these "seed people," persons who have accomplished within themselves what the world is trying to accomplish collectively, are distributed throughout the entire system.

The seeds of the future are already here among us, here in the younger generation, with some working to clear out old ideas from the past and others bringing in new ideas from the future. I personally feel myself to have been more involved with detoxifying and purifying the past than bringing in the future, but when I look around, I see many people who already have new ways of thinking within them, persons whose consciousness is not encumbered with the old patterns. For example, when did you start thinking like this, being interested in the relationship of the individual to the universe?

I think I've been pursuing the questions "What is the universe?" and "What is my role in it and my relationship to it?" for most of my life. These two questions I think drew me initially toward studying science, and later philosophy and consciousness studies, and they have been with me ever since in subtle and not so subtle ways.

Yes, and if you are asking these questions, then there are lots of other fractal forms of "you" asking them as well. And if you can answer them, then it will help all of us answer them. Your insights, whether expressed publicly, physically, or even psychically are shared instantaneously with everyone else who is asking these kinds of questions, like interconnected neurons in an enormous brain.

I like the image of neurons that you use, because if we're all elements in a larger global brain then it seems that not all of the neurons have to have to wake up individually for there to be a cascading change of awareness in the brain itself.

Yes, you only need to hit the critical mass to begin the cascade.

A related concept to what we've been discussing is the idea in your work of a universal field of consciousness that includes and yet transcends the physical universe. So the deeper nature of the universe is like that of a single integrated living organism, a field of experience that remembers, learns, and grows from the experiences of many individuals over many lifetimes. Can you say more about your insights and perspective on this?

In so many ways and in so many different cultures throughout history, people have talked about the universe as being alive, as being a single great living organism. This becomes especially apparent in non-ordinary states of consciousness, in which one sees that the universe is alive on more levels than we had previously imagined. But staying just with our scientific knowledge, our understanding of the universe has grown to the point that we can reconstruct the general sequence of events that produced us step by step through 13.7 billions years of evolution. If we study this chain of events carefully, sooner or later we are brought to our knees, struck dumb by the sheer intelligence and genius of the physical universe. Then we have to consider the genius of whatever it was that birthed the physical universe in that fireball of unimaginable creativity we call the Big Bang.

I think our scientific knowledge has exploded so fast these past three centuries that it has left all our gods in the dust, every one of them, and they're still panting to catch up. Now we need an understanding of God that is at least as big as the universe that science is showing us. Historically, our concept of God has always been proportionate to our knowledge of the universe. We are now living intellectually in a universe many orders of magnitude larger and more complex than the universe we previously lived in.

So it seems that the two go together, so that with each revolution in knowledge, our images of both God and the universe shatter together.

Yes. We've reached a point where science is our culture's true religion. And just as we've reached this point—being the most educated, most knowledgeable, most organized human beings ever to exist on the planet—we're about to be put through a meat grinder! We're going to be put through an ordeal of such magnitude that it will change us forever. Once we pass through this ordeal, we will be different people from who we are now. We will find that we are living with a different standard of "common sense," a different level of compassion, and a different set of rules for life. People will overcome their surface political differences in the interest of mutual support and common survival. From this process a new human will emerge—and much more quickly than we would have expected. I think the prototype of this emerging human is found in the great saints and geniuses of history.

This new human will mark a new plateau of human evolution—a radical discontinuity from the old. I think that many people are intuiting and feeling this shift from different perspectives and are using the language that's available to them to describe it. That's what I'm doing. I come out of religious studies and psychedelic research, and so I'm using that language to give voice to something that others are trying to express in other ways.

All the components of what is emerging are within us now, and, surprisingly, I feel that most of the work that's needed for this transition is already done. The work has been done over countless millennia by the slow, patient process of evolutionary reincarnation, strengthening individuals and bringing us to where we are now.

Bringing the system to critical mass is like a small bomb sitting on top of a big bomb. The big bomb is all the knowledge and experience and qualities of soul that have been gathered over time, and this is what's going to be pressurized by this critical time. The foundation for the radical change that is now upon us has been laid by all the experiences over hundreds of thousands of years that each one of us is carrying.

It's exciting to me that many people today are having similar visions of something large coming. I personally feel the need to think and talk with other people about the nature of this future human. The more clearly we see what's coming, the easier it will be to understand the gravity of what we're dealing with right now. I believe what's coming is the most extraordinary form of human being, a human being that has qualities very different from those that dominate us now. It's like we're all *Homo erectus* sitting around watching *Homo sapiens* emerge—it's that big an event. Nine months of gestation and one day of labor. The long gestation has already taken place, and this is the day of labor.

We can't fully see what we're becoming. I was talking with Pete [Russell] the other day and he observed that everything is accelerating so fast that we can't plan even 10 or 20 years out at this point. It's truly an intense time.

And our inability to plan in such a rapidly transforming world is such a break with the rational mind that wants to predict the future in a linear way based on the past.

Absolutely. The ground comes out from under our feet and we go into a free fall.

In some ways—and this is going to sound strange—it's been healing to have all of this finally begin, because it's been crazy-making to have had the experience that it did happen—to have touched that future time when it has already happened—and then to come back and live the last 10 or 15 years leading up to this transition. Most of the world around you is saying that this is not going to happen, that it's not real, but deep down you know that it *is* real. It's not that I would wish this pain on anyone, but when people start to be aware that it's actually happening, it removes some of the dissonance for me.

I wonder if there's something about the collectivity of the suffering and the transformation that can help here as well, to see that we're not each going through this process alone as separate individuals.

I think we can really open up to that if we become sensitive enough to listen to the very back of our minds. If you listen very carefully, you can hear the suffering of all the world's poor inside you. They're all there because, really, there is only one Mind. If the world starts to change, if we genuinely start to take care of the world's poor, putting them to bed every night with a full stomach, then we won't be hearing them suffering in the back of our minds every night. We'll have a different feeling as our baseline.

When we truly begin to understand that we're all in this together, we'll begin to recognize that the quality of our lives and our individual well-being rests upon the quality of life around the planet. A new common sense will become the norm, in the same way that democracy became a new standard in the world after centuries of monarchy. A new way of thinking will come forward.

This inner transformation that's happening now is going to ignite a fire in our culture, and vice-versa. They affect each other and are interdependent.

Yes, we're going through the inner fire and the outer fire together—they are two sides of the same fire. The next book I want to write is a fresh look at reincarnation, because the academic community is so far behind the curve on this point. I want to take the discussion of rebirth to the next level. Given the high caliber of the evidence that exists today for reincarnation, we need to ponder more deeply the implications of living in a universe that is perpetually gathering more and more experience to itself over time.

It won't be long before we'll be able to step back and appreciate what's been accomplished through this historical crisis and what we've gained from it. I really do believe that once we begin to experience the new human that's coming forward, we will retroactively understand the significance of what we've been going through. Right now we don't have a clue, and it scares us.

We may not see how all the pieces fit together yet, but we can all feel that we're on the edge of something big. When we can't ignore each other and we can't convert each other, we're going to be rammed together, and out of this convergence something profound will emerge. I like to remind my students that out of all the possible combinations their soul-stream might have brought forward from thousands of years of rebirth, they were chosen to be in the ringside seat at this critical time in history. It's quite an honor and quite a responsibility.

And our soul chose not only here and now in this time, but in these very circumstances.

Yes, everyone's soul did! In my journey work, the universe sometimes gave me mantras to work with, and one was: "Every being is perfect and deserves my complete respect." Each one of us is a warrior. You don't get to enter time and space without making certain commitments. People may not remember doing so, it may be buried deep inside us, but just to be here is a remarkable accomplishment in itself and quite a privilege.

And reincarnation keeps diversifying and drawing us out—there's no box or packaging that we as humans can stay in. Interracial marriages, intergender relationships, interfaith partnerships—the combinations are exploding.

In the years since I've come back from these journeys, it gives me great peace to carry a larger vision of what's happening to us and where we're going. I sometimes get overwhelmed by all the suffering, as many of us do. I have to deal with dark days, knowing that this transformation is coming and the magnitude of what it will involve, but I find stability in the larger vision of what's being birthed through this suffering. To hold all of it in my heart, it helps to know its purpose. It truly does change a day of mere pain into a day of labor. Working with psychedelics has given me a certain perspective on the wave of transformation that's crashing down on us, but in the end, we'll all be tumbling through it together. As the wave rolls over us, it will be confusing and hard as hell.

It seems that even advance knowledge of the wave coming doesn't spare you from having to go through its crashing down.

Yes, and it is a time of great leaders and lots of them. We'll need millions of people stepping forward, and I believe that they're here. I don't know what will become of the vast reservoirs of hate that are burning like oil fires in different parts of the world. I don't know how we're going to handle the enormous mountains of injustice that divide the haves and the have-nots of the world. I don't know how we're going to bring about a fair and just economy. I can't imagine how we're going to do these things.

What I keep coming back to is the visionary experience that I laid out in *Dark Night, Early Dawn*—that just when we thought everything was lost, the storm passes and there are survivors. When we reconnect after the catastrophe, we find a new beginning dawning around us, reflecting new values that we forged within ourselves during the crisis. In that process we rise to a level of self-realization that's extraordinary. We let go of our past in a way that takes us into a new maturity. Our hearts hurt so much that they tear open, allowing us to see into time and across borders in a new way. There's a period of grace, repentance, and stepping into a new reality.

From a deeper spiritual perspective, I think we're going to empty the *bardo*, clearing out the soul-baggage of our fragmented past. When this happens, there will be greater transparency between the world of spirit and the world of embodiment. The collective human mine-field will become clearer, more coherent, and less fractured by the distortions of our history reverberating in the *bardo-field*. That was Robert Monroe's vision of a possible future in *Far Journeys*. When he went into a time about 1,500 years into the future, he saw a future without the *bardo*. I think that's a very powerful vision, because it represents a radical maturing of humanity. We won't need those levels of the *bardo* anymore because we won't be as limited as we were when we generated them.

It's like a shell that we sloughed off.

Yes. We'll finally integrate all the pieces of our lives. The universe is all energy, and the *bardo* is filled with the energy of living soul-fragments. We'll integrate that energy so that it's all within us now. It's a time of soul-retrieval, where we're pulling all this energy back into us. It's like a vast cloud precipitating big water drops, with people incarnating more and more of their history into themselves until eventually they become whole and clear.

I really think this is the crash and burn century. How long will it take before we turn it around? Will it have bottomed out by the end of the twenty-first century? Will we have made the pivot? However long it takes, when we start to come out of it, we will be completely changed from what we were at the beginning of the descent. In that free fall of history, that's when the compression is going to hit.

And from a big-picture perspective, all the time it takes to do this is just a flash in the pan. If the universe is anything, it's patient, so it will take as long as it needs to. Maybe this is an ongoing cosmic process, so maybe it will happen again and again, ad infinitum...

Yes. The universe thinks in a time frame that boggles the imagination. A million years here and a million years there, that's ok. Have they got it yet? I'll be back in a few million years! [laughs] Maybe for this new being to come forward, it will take several contractions. We just don't know. I'm hoping for a quick resolution, for an intense, short labor, but you never know.

None of us knows what it's going to be like when a whole planet goes into crisis. A storm or a war can throw us into crisis, but a whole planet going into crisis at the same time, all wired with the Internet and television?—it's never happened before. It's a one-of-a-kind event, and *so we should expect a one-of-a-kind outcome*. If we embrace change, we will move through it more smoothly. If you know you're going into whitewater, you can prepare for it. Let life change you.

I'm afraid where I live, people are buying guns. They're scared. The churches are still preaching a philosophy of theological self-isolation. Clearly we're not awakened yet. We're sleepy, in a daze, mesmerized by malls and television, thinking we can still hold on to the old order.

Can you talk about what's needed in our culture to support this transformation?

There is no one answer to that question. I think we each need to focus on the part that is ours to do. This is our collective task and how we will move through it. The part that interests me personally is exploring the possibilities that can come from the skillful integration of psychedelics into philosophy. I think this represents a turning point of great significance, a new way of doing philosophy—by systematically reflecting on deliberately induced non-ordinary states of consciousness. We haven't done this before, not since the ancient Greeks. The vision that emerges from entering into this deeper communion with the universe looks at historical events from a deeper perspective, looks at time and space from a spiritual perspective.

When all is said and done, what psychedelics is giving us, I think, is the opportunity to deepen our experience of the universe's experience of itself. To be able to actually experience how the universe experiences itself beyond us. Intellectually, we're seeing the universe and understanding it through mathematics and physics and the other sciences, but with these sacred medicines we can actually *experience* how the universe experiences itself. Our capacity for doing this is expanding exponentially at the same time that our understanding of physics is expanding exponentially.

To actually experience the genius of the universe, to feel its depth, scope, and richness, answers many questions, and these answers do not conflict with scientific knowledge. The resurgence of psychedelics is one more lightning bolt hitting us as the pace of change accelerates. There's no way that we can continue to keep this experience from the people.

There are hard times ahead and there are great times ahead. Everybody wants their life to count for something as part of a larger order. The birth of a new humanity is as good a larger cause as any I've seen. That's an event I want to be a part of!

Chapter 16

The View From Space: An Interview With Edgar Mitchell

S eeing the Earth from space in 1957 was the beginning of a new stage in the history of the world. For the first time, humans saw the Earth as a single integrated system from a cosmic perspective. Economic, political, and cultural boundaries all disappear when our blue globe is glimpsed from space, and the words *fragile*, *interconnected*, and *unity* appear often in the descriptions of men and women viewing the Earth from space for the first time. So many astronauts have reported having spiritual epiphanies and euphoric experiences of "cosmic consciousness" while in space that some have dubbed this phenomenon "The Overview Effect," referring to the expanded universal perspective that space travel can provide.[8] One individual whose life was altered forever by such an experience is the astronaut Dr. Edgar Mitchell.

Dr. Edgar Mitchell is a scientist, naval officer, test pilot, astronaut, and author. A passionate and intrepid explorer of both the frontiers of outer space and the latent capacities of the human mind, he has dedicated his life to exploring and expanding the horizons of human knowledge about the universe in a way few others have.

Raised in Texas and New Mexico, he had an interest in science and engineering from an early age, and earned a Bachelor of Science degree in industrial management from Carnegie Mellon University. He later earned a BS in aeronautics from the U.S. Naval Postgraduate School and a Doctor of Science in aeronautics and astronautics from MIT. He was also later awarded honorary doctorates in engineering from New Mexico State University, the University of Akron, Carnegie Mellon University, and a ScD from Embry-Riddle University.

Following his career as a test pilot and aviator in the Korean War, Mitchell was selected as a NASA astronaut and served as lunar module pilot for Apollo 14, becoming the sixth person to walk on the moon. Upon his retirement from the Navy in 1972, he founded the Institute of Noetic Sciences (IONS), a nonprofit organization dedicated to studying the nature of consciousness and the frontiers of the human mind. He later also co-founded the Association of Space Explorers, an international organization of astronauts dedicated to promoting space exploration, science and technology education, and environmental awareness.

Dr. Mitchell is the author of *Psychic Exploration: A Challenge for Science* (G.P. Putnam's Sons, 1974) and *The Way of the Explorer, Revised Edition* (New Page Books, 2008), as well as many articles in professional and popular journals on space exploration, quantum physics, consciousness studies, and the common ground between science and spirituality.

He has received many awards and honors including the Presidential Medal of Freedom, the USN Distinguished Service Medal, and three NASA Group Achievement Awards. He has also been inducted into the Space Hall of Fame and the Astronaut Hall of Fame, and was been nominated for the Nobel Peace Prize in 2005.

Stephan Martin: Very, very few humans have traveled as far out into the universe as you have, and so you are in a unique position to share insights and reflections about the universe and our role in it. I wonder if you could speak a bit about how your experiences with space exploration have shaped your ideas and perceptions of the universe.

Edgar Mitchell: Let's first put it in perspective. At the beginning of the space age, with the launch of *Sputnik* in 1957, it was certainly the conventional wisdom, in science, religion, and politics, that we were completely alone in the universe. Our knowledge of the heavens was essentially about as sophisticated as "God in heaven, men in the middle, and everything else below." We really didn't know much beyond that.

The Big Bang theory had been formulized only about 30 years before, with Hubble's observations of galactic redshifts having led to the idea of an expanding universe with its origin as the Big Bang. Now in the past 50 years of the space age, and with the results from the Hubble Space Telescope and other observatories, our minds are being blown by what is actually out there. We're being pointed to seeing the universe in a totally different way than ever before.

So, it's all continually changing. The big, quick answer is that the universe is far more complex and far more vast than we ever thought possible. Our science is still far from complete, and likely flawed in quite a few important ways.

In my lectures I often relate that my great grandparents came across from Georgia to west Texas after the Civil War to start a new life. Railroads weren't complete across the West. They went by covered wagon and on horseback. Automobiles had not been invented, electrical lights had not been invented. My father was born shortly after the Wright brothers made the first flight, and in a short time after that, I went to the moon. So, from covered wagons to going to the moon in less than 100 years is what the late 19th and 20th century was all about.

Before that, the Phoenicians began their first ship explorations across the Mediterranean four or five thousand years ago, and about that same time or a little later the South Sea islanders started exploring the Pacific in dug-out canoes. In my parents' generation we went into the air, and then in my generation we went off the planet altogether.

But in my opinion, even with all that progression of our development and our exploration of this planet, we're still just barely out of the trees. But right now the issue of the sustainability of our civilization is in question, and this is now one of the greatest challenges that humans currently face. If we make it past this coming century we will have to learn to be cooperative and live together in peace. We're just not going to make it in the current paradigm, with killing each other over religion, border wars, and similar things. We just won't make it.

Many people talk about how a larger shared perspective on the universe can lead to a common understanding of ourselves and our situation on Earth beyond our relatively minor points of disagreement and difference.

That is the main thing that came out of the space experience for me—the epiphany that gave me hard data that the universe is totally interconnected, and that we are all part of the same cloth, as it were. Seeing that the molecules in every one of our bodies were created in star systems long ago.

Could you talk a little bit about your epiphany in seeing and experiencing this for yourself on your return trip on *Apollo 14*?

After the work on the surface was done, and we were coming home, my mission was essentially complete. I was still the systems engineer on a well-functioning spacecraft, monitoring dials and conducting a few more experiments, but at this point I could be pretty much a tourist. While getting my PhD, I had studied astronomy at MIT and Harvard, and so I was aware of the very little that we knew at the time about how star systems form, how matter is formed in the universe, and how we had only very recently realized that the atoms in our bodies were created in stars long ago.

While we were coming home, the spacecraft was rotating to maintain thermal balance, and that allowed the Earth, the moon, the sun, and the stars to come into my view in a 360-degree panorama every two minutes, which is a pretty powerful sight. Now remember that in space, because you're above the atmosphere, you can see 10 times as many stars as you can from the ground, and so the stars you see are brilliantly bright.

And suddenly it settled in, a visceral moment of knowing that the molecules in my body, the molecules in the spacecraft, and the molecules in my partners had been prototyped and manufactured in an ancient generation of stars. It was not an intellectual realization, but a deep knowing that was accompanied by a feeling of ecstasy and oneness that I had never experienced in that way before.

"In an instant, I knew for certain that what I was seeing was no accident. That it did not occur randomly and without order. That life did not, by accident, arise from the primordial earthly sea. It was as though my awareness reached out to touch the furthest star and I was aware of being an integral part of the entire universe, for one brief instant…. Any questions that my curious mind might have had about our progress, about our destiny, about the nature of the universe, suddenly melted away as I experienced that oneness. I could reach out and touch the furthest parts and experience the vast reaches of the universe. It was clear that those tiny pinpoints of light in such brilliant profusion were a unity. They were linked together as a part of the whole as they framed and formed a backdrop for this view of planet Earth. I knew we are not alone in this universe, that Earth was one of millions, perhaps billions of planets like our own with intelligent life all playing a role in the great creative plan for the evolution of life."[9]

This experience continued for three days while coming home, and whenever I looked out the window and wasn't distracted by my duties this experience of ecstasy and interconnectedness returned. I've continued to experience it on certain occasions and sometimes in meditation, and so it's stayed with me ever since.

This experience really altered your view of the world and your direction in life forever after, didn't it?

Yes, very much so. After I came back I started doing research to find out more about this experience. I started digging in the science and psychological literature, but I could not find it. I went into religious literature of various traditions, and I could not find it there either. I appealed to scholars, primarily anthropologists, and historians over at Rice University near the Houston space center campus, asking them to do some digging to see if they could find anything on this experience, but ancient literature didn't help either. Finally one of them came back with a description of the experience described by the Sanskrit word "samadhi." In samadhi, you see things with your eyes as separate, individual things, but you experience them viscerally and internally as a oneness, a unity accompanied by bliss and ecstasy. When they described that to me I said, "That's it," and I was relieved to finally have a name for it. After that I took the opportunity to research different cultures throughout the world, and throughout the next few years I had the privilege of talking with Tibetans, Buddhists, Sufis, Christians, kahunas, and medicine men about my experience.

Did you find they were familiar with that experience?

Of course, and I found that every culture has its own version of it. I think that this kind of mystical, explosive experience and these types of deep insights into the nature of Mind and consciousness is the basis of religion in every culture. What happened in the West was that Rene Descartes successfully got the Church off the backs of the intellectuals in the 1600s by postulating that body and mind, physicality and spirituality, belong to different realms of reality that do not interact.

This was the beginning of the Enlightenment.

Yes, and the good side of the Cartesian duality was that it got the intellectuals away from the inquisition, and kept them from burning at the stake. Giordano Bruno was the last one to take the heat for that. But for 400 years science labored under the idea that Mind, consciousness, and spirit were subjects for philosophy and theology. Only material things mattered in science.

Even through the late 19th and early 20th centuries, with Maxwell, Einstein, and others, physicists had assumed the Cartesian duality was fundamentally true, and refused to look at consciousness and Mind until it smacked them in the head with quantum mechanics.

This was the main reason you founded the Institute of Noetic Sciences in 1972 shortly after your return from space, to bring the study of consciousness and subjectivity into the scientific realm.

Yes, after my experience in space I realized that our science was far from complete, and that the study of consciousness, as well as science, was crucial to our understanding of the universe. One of the main research objectives was to understand the relationship between subjectivity and objectivity from a basic science point of view, and to realize that all of our subjective experiences require interpretation. We find in our scientific experiments that we do not get direct knowledge, but we receive information that has to be put in context, and the interpretation of experience is what consciousness studies is really all about.

In your book, *The Way of the Explorer* (New Page Books, 2007), you present your dyadic model, in which information, experience, consciousness, and knowing are the primary elements of the universe.

Yes, in my dyadic model, energy and information are a dyad, two basic elements of the universe that represent two different faces of the same reality. Information is simply patterns of energy, and so the universe is essentially organizing information and energy over time into increasingly complex structures. Information is also the basis for knowing, which is a property of all matter, from atoms to humans, all of which share the capacity for consciousness or basic awareness in varying degrees. All experience, including all of human experience, is essentially information or energy arranged in a particular way in this model. Energy is also the basis for all matter, so matter and energy are also another dyad and therefore two sides of the same coin.

You also make the case that intentionality and volition are a basic dyad of the evolutionary process as well.

Yes. We have demonstrated fairly conclusively that through intentionality and volition we have the capacity to influence physical matter with the mind. This has been done repeatedly in laboratories and even through Faraday cage barriers, which demonstrates that intention and awareness are not electromagnetic phenomena only, but are a basic property of things. This basic capacity of matter for knowing may be a property of quantum entanglement, and therefore nonlocal.

These experiments are well documented and good science, so I see two of the major contributions of the 20th century as scientists going into space for the first time and becoming space-farers, and the discovery and use of quantum science to understand awareness and perception in a radically different way than in conventional classical science. The discovery of the quantum, nonlocal aspect of our existence has a direct bearing on our perceptual framework and agency in the world, which physical scientists have denied for all of the 20th century until very recently.

In your dyadic view, knowing is both fundamental and nonlocal everywhere in the universe, and you describe deep knowing, or communion with the universe, as one of its fundamental dynamics. Can

you talk about why the universe wants to experience itself ever more deeply?

Well, we often describe intuition, or our innate capacity for knowing, as our sixth sense. But we now understand that this kind of knowing is rooted in the quantum world, at a level even beyond atoms, so we should really be calling it our first sense! This aspect of nature was around before our solar system even existed, long before we evolved to develop any of our other senses. All of our sensory mechanisms are based on the properties of our planet—the density of our atmosphere, the amount and wavelength of sunlight we receive, and the acoustic properties of the atmosphere have all shaped our biological makeup and the forms that our senses have taken.

Our five normal senses are therefore very much tied to this Earth, but the quantum sense that intuition represents is not—it is more fundamental than all these. I root the capacity of basic awareness in quantum correlation, the property of a pair of entangled quantum particles to remain interactive and correlated even at large distances from each other.

So let's call the basic awareness that quantum entanglement represents the most fundamental act of knowing possible, with all other forms of knowing beyond that arising from molecular complexity. As we become more complex in our physical organization, our ability to use information grows accordingly, and so we see that there are different levels of awareness possible, from plants to animals up to *Homo sapiens*, where self-awareness emerges.

Now the research of Walter Schempp and others strongly suggests that a great deal of information in the universe may be nonlocal in nature and holographic. Some scientists now even see the entire universe as a hologram. I do not, but that it uses holographic principles as information. Further research suggests that biological evolution is not random, but is driven by a nonlocal learning feedback loop with the environment. So nature and the universe may be learning as a whole over time and retaining this information for future use.

The ancients called this the akashic record, a holographic record for all experiences in the universe that grows and evolves over time.

So, is this in some sense like a cosmic memory or Mind?

That was the ancient view of it. In more recent times, Rupert Sheldrake has incorporated similar ideas in his theory of morphogenetic fields. The quantum hologram is providing a mechanism for the basis of his research and that of others. In other words, nature does not lose its experience.

It's a very ancient view that the universe is like an organism, and it sounds like you're suggesting that it's an organism that's learning over time. Do you see an innate intentionality or direction for this learning? Is it tending over time to come to greater consciousness?

I don't know, and you can speculate on that about as well as I can. Something else that comes out of the mathematical formalism of the quantum hologram in addition to this cosmic memory is the suggestion that nature may be continuously creating matter. I would even postulate that dark energy and dark matter may really be protomatter, matter in the process of coming into being.

That's amazing! Is it coming into being out of the zero-point field?

Yes, dark energy and dark matter might really be protomatter before it starts to be formed into solar systems and galaxies.

The astronomer Fred Hoyle promoted a theory of continuous creation of this sort for many years as an alternative to the Big Bang theory. So I wonder if conservation of energy and matter, which are cornerstones of our current theories of physics, may only apply on a local level.

Yes, conservation of energy and matter are attributes of a closed system, but our universe may not be a closed system, and if you consider the Big Bang, that energy had to come from somewhere.

It's an exciting idea that the universe is not a contained phenomenon, but is continually in the process of emerging something new and increasingly enlarging our context for thinking about it. Can you tell us anything more about the cutting edge of your research these days? How has your theory of the universe evolved since you first developed your dyadic model in *The Way of the Explorer*?

The main thing is to keep pressing on, and to learn more about our mutual interaction with the universe. We need to better understand how our mind and our collective mind influences the behaviors and environment around us, because the research shows that it clearly does. We don't have a good model for how this works just yet.

So if matter is being continuously created, and if it can be influenced by Mind, then I wonder if we are shaping its form in very subtle ways with our minds, whether consciously or unconsciously.

It could very well be. What we may be doing is imprinting into it some kind of memory, information, or idea of some sort.

What is it that you think people don't generally recognize about the universe?

The main thing is that the power of Mind and consciousness is much stronger than we have previously thought. I also hold to the idea of the universe as an intelligent, self-organized, creative, learning, informational, interconnected, and interactive evolutionary system. The notion of a grandfather God pulling all the puppet strings is really pretty passé. The universe is an evolutionary system that continues to learn and create as it goes along. It doesn't seem to have started out with a full-blown blueprint, as far as I can tell.

And it doesn't seem to need a fixed plan to get where it's going.

Exactly. It goes where we as a local species direct it to go, whether consciously or unconsciously.

I think you make an important point, with shifting the responsibility for the direction of things back to our shoulders.

Yes, and that's what comes out of all these studies in consciousness research—that our responsibility for how things continue to be is right here. It's not out there somewhere in the form of God or extraterrestrials or something.

Chapter 17

Light, Consciousness, and the White Hole in Time: An Interview With Peter Russell

❝For the rest of my life I want to reflect on what light is," said Einstein to his colleague Wolfgang Pauli in 1916. At the heart of many of the universe's enigmas lies the mysterious nature of light. It seems to transcend time, space, and matter, belonging to a realm all its own, and making it the object of speculation by scientists, philosophers, and theologians for centuries. It's no wonder that nearly every spiritual and religious tradition around the world has held light in equally high esteem, linking it in various ways to the ultimate nature of consciousness and the divine itself. Yet whatever light is, we are that, proposes mathematician, physicist, and consciousness researcher Peter Russell, who has studied light and consciousness from both scientific and spiritual perspectives for more than 30 years.

Russell is the author of more than seven award-winning books and videos on topics such as the relationship between science and religion, the nature of consciousness, and the awakening of a new global culture. His books and videos include *The Global Brain*, *The White Hole in Time*, *The Conscious-ness Revolution*, and *From Science to God: A Physicist's Journey Into the Mystery of Consciousness*.

He has degrees in theoretical physics, computer science, and experimental psychology from the University of Cambridge, England. There he studied with renowned physicist Stephen Hawking and later did foundational work in developing computer technology that would become the basis for modern virtual reality environments. After Cambridge, he went to India to study meditation and Eastern philosophy, and after his return he began conducting research in the psychophysiology of meditation at the University of Bristol.

For more than 20 years he has worked with large companies and corporations to introduce innovative practices in creativity, self-development, sustainability, and stress management into the workplace. His primary interest currently is toward a deeper understanding of consciousness and the spiritual and evolutionary significance of the times we are passing through.

Stephan Martin: I'd like to start with a topic that you point to many times in your writing, which is the difficulty of integrating consciousness into our current scientific theories about the universe, which are largely based on materialism. In response to this situation, you suggest that consciousness may not be a property of matter, as our current theories propose, but that consciousness itself may be a primary property of the cosmos. Can you say more about the role of consciousness in the physical world?

Peter Russell: If the physical universe is entirely composed of insentient and unconscious matter, as the current scientific worldview holds, then how does consciousness and subjective experience happen? Dead and insentient matter in a complex arrangement such as a brain should not give rise to sentience, since it wasn't there to begin with. Yet somehow out of insentient matter comes consciousness and subjective experience, which are entirely different phenomena than insentient matter.

People often explain this by suggesting that consciousness is an emergent property of matter, that it emerges when matter reaches a certain degree of complexity. But emergence here doesn't explain the appearance of a completely different type of phenomenon, and because we unquestionably have sentience and conscious experience, this presents a big anomaly for the current scientific paradigm.

We're in the midst of a paradigm shift in which anomalies such as these are still trying to be explained in terms of the old paradigm. People are still trying to think up ways in which inert matter could give rise to experience. They're still trying to patch up the old system and make it work in light of new data that suggest otherwise.

One thing we all know absolutely for certain is that we are conscious. In fact, without consciousness there'd be no science, because it's through conscious experience that we understand and learn about the world. So in a sense, all of science takes place in the mind, because it's the mind understanding, forming hypotheses, theories, and coming to conclusions. It all happens in the mind and yet the mind is the one thing that science hasn't studied extensively.

The alternative paradigm that is being proposed by myself and others is that consciousness or mind is an innate capacity and potential for subjective experience that is always present in the universe. So consciousness or mind doesn't come out of the brain, but the brain simply modifies or gives shape to pre-existing consciousness, and this is the fundamental difference.

As life has evolved, organisms, sensory organs, and nervous systems have become increasingly more complex, and so the contents of consciousness and the forms that the mind can take have become more complex. In this view, even simple bacteria might have some very, very faint glimmer of consciousness— nothing like what we would call self-conscious awareness, but they may have a very faint sense of their chemical environment, some very simple form of consciousness. That's the basic shift, that everything has some capacity for conscious experience. When you make that shift, it doesn't change anything at all in terms of physics or biology, but it changes our assumptions about where experience comes from. It overcomes this whole problem of how insentient matter could ever give rise to something that is its total opposite.

If consciousness is a fundamental quality of the cosmos, then it must be there in everything—not just bacteria, but below that in the virus, and then below that in amino acids. In this new paradigm, there's no place to really draw the line between consciousness and insentience, as our current scientific worldview does. The capacity for experience is always present as a fundamental quality of the cosmos, and it gets filled out as systems become more and more complex.

So in a sense the whole spectrum of complexity of life is really the infinite gradations of this capacity for consciousness or awareness. You've just made a very important point in stating that this alternative view is not inconsistent with our current scientific theories, but it presents a larger view that embraces our subjective and personal experience. I want to go back to an important point you touched on previously, which relates to everything in the universe appearing as forms in the mind. You've written extensively about this, so I wonder if you could say more about how the universe actually exists inside of us.

Yes, this is an absolutely fascinating thing that the scientific worldview completely accepts, but it never looks at its ramifications. What we know is that when we experience the world with sight, what actually happens is that photons are hitting our retina and stimulating electrochemical impulses that are then analyzed by the brain, and out of that a picture forms that appears as an image in the mind. So we have a visual experience that is integrated with sound and touch and all the other senses to create a very convincing multidimensional, multi-sensory picture of the world. What we don't realize is that it's only a picture of what is out there, but it's so convincing that we make the error of thinking we're seeing and experiencing the world directly. But we undeniably know that what we're actually experiencing is just the image that appears in the mind. This is true not just of sensory experience, but of all our experience. Thoughts, beliefs, memories, and everything we experience is something that is appearing in the mind.

Immanuel Kant realized in a major breakthrough for philosophy more than two centuries ago that we never actually know the world itself directly. We make inferences about the world, and based on these inferences we then have an experience of the world. This is what science does—it collects experiences of the world, and from those experiences, it makes inferences about the nature of physical reality, about what is out there giving rise to our experience. So you can say that the process of science is testing those inferences, checking them out with other people, and coming to a consensus understanding of the nature of the physical world.

But it's important to recognize that all of this understanding is always based upon experiences in the mind. A lot of the problems and contradictions that arise in modern physics come about when we forget that this is what's really happening. It's becoming clear that the way things appear in the mind is not always the way things are in the physical world.

The simplest example is that of color. When we see the color green we are experiencing light of a certain frequency or photons of certain energy. The light itself isn't green. There's no such thing as a green photon, it's just a photon of a particular frequency that when experienced by the eye and brain gives rise to a certain experience of greenness in the mind. This is true of all experience; what is out there is unlike what we're actually experiencing in the mind. When we don't see this, we make the mistake of projecting our own experience onto our understanding of the world.

Another classic case of this is with atoms. We experience little hard balls in our world, so when we first thought of atoms, of course we thought they were like little hard balls. We later realized they were composed of sub-particles, so then we imagined they were collections of particles, like little balls, because that's what our experience of tiny particles is like in the physical world. Then we later realized they weren't solid things at all, and so we started thinking maybe they're more like waves, which again is an idea that comes from our everyday experience. So what we're doing is taking ideas from our everyday experience and trying to fit the physical world into these ideas.

I think the only way we can truly describe the world is through mathematics. Anything other than that is a model, which is inevitably based on an interpretation of the mathematics. It's an approximation in which we say "it's like this, but not really." So I think that whatever the real nature of reality, a dolphin scientist or an extraterrestrial scientist on some other planet must also agree. They may have very different brains and see very different pictures of the world and come up with very different models, but whatever the world is really like must be beyond the models that come from the human mind.

This is a fundamental point that is continually missed when we try to understand the universe. We have this very anthrocentric view that the physical world is something like the way it appears inside the human mind, forgetting that the world is filled with other kinds of minds. The dolphin mind is going to have a very different view of the world: it doesn't experience gravity in the same way, being more or less weightless, and it "sees" with sound much better than it sees with light, so its picture of the world is going to be quite different than ours, but it's just as real and authentic. We make the mistake that believing that our view is *the* one, the only right one.

Yes, and this goes back to the tremendous importance of understanding the nature of Mind. We have such a very basic understanding of the mind, and so it seems that the less we understand the mind, the less we understand the world, as the mind is the ultimate filter for our experience.

Yes, and I'm currently working on a new book in which the mind and experience is the fundamental reality. In this view, everything that exists is a form or entity in the mind, and so the entire cosmos is just pure Mind reflecting through a multiplicity of minds.

In this view, all of atomic physics holds up—you've got electrons and baryons and all that stuff, but they're all just different types of entities of experience, and so we end up with a model in which matter only exists in the mind and our direct experience of the universe is primary. We've made the assumption that the world "out there" is material in nature, and what I'm saying is that it is actually mental in nature. When we drop the assumption that it is material in nature, and just accept that it is only mental in nature, then all of physics still absolutely holds true, but it's measuring mental entities rather than physical particles.

Interesting! So everything we call physical objects in the world are really forms in the universal Mind and our physics is basically the relationships between those forms in this universal Mind. I can see how the view of everything as the same substance of experience overcomes the duality of our conventional view in which matter-mind and inner-outer are so intractably different. Another place where you bridge the inner and the outer world is in your discussion and exploration of light. You've explored in your book *The Science of God* that our experience of the world happens when the light of the outer world meets

the inner light of our awareness. I wonder if you can say a little bit more about this and the relationship between the two.

It's interesting that we use the word *light* in both senses. We talk about light as a physical phenomenon, such as the light from the sun or a lamp, and we also use the word *light* at times to describe our inner experience. Now we should remember that just as we were discussing earlier with color, the experience of light is not the same thing as light itself, and although there are fascinating parallels between physical light and the light of our consciousness, we need to be clear about which one we are referring to at the time.

When we talk about the light of consciousness, we often say things like "the inner light" or "seeing the light" when we feel inspired, or things like "the lights went out" when we fall unconscious. There is a long tradition in many spiritual traditions that the mind is lit from the inside, that it has its own self-illumination that we sometimes call the light of consciousness. This is really the essence of experience, because when we have an image in the mind or we experience a feeling, we could say we are aware of it because it is lit by consciousness. Everything we experience is a form consciousness takes on as an image in the mind, and so everything we experience is lit by that light of consciousness, and so in that sense, it is an absolutely universal phenomenon.

Now when we go into the physical world, every interaction above the level of atoms is mediated by light. Photons are the universal principle here because any energy exchange above molecules is mediated by light, so everything we know in a sense—every activity, every interaction, every exchange of energy—is a form taken on by light in the physical world.

Also, if you look at the implications of Einstein's special theory of relativity, the faster you go, the slower time goes and the shorter distances become, and if you could ever travel at the speed of light, time would stop and distances in the direction of travel would contract to zero. However, because light has no mass, by definition it always travels at the speed of light. So if we look at the universe from light's point of view, it implies that light itself is not traveling in time or space. Because light has no mass, it is not in space, and since it is not in space, it takes zero time to travel, so it's actually a direct interaction between the point where it is emitted and the point where it is absorbed.

This implies that light doesn't actually travel anywhere because it doesn't experience space or time, and so it doesn't actually need to be a wave or a photon. From our point of view, we see light traveling through time and space, and we project onto it that it must be either a wave or a photon, because it seems to act sometimes like one and other times like the other. We think it's one or the other or that it's both, but if light could speak, light would probably just laugh and say "How crazy! I don't need to be either one—that's just your projection, your mind, your experience."

So once again, we're projecting our own concepts on this phenomenon called light and trying to make it fit our everyday experience. All the while, its true nature lies hidden and much deeper than this.

Yes, and so we can say that light from its perspective is outside the realm of space, time, and matter. Now let's come back to the mind and take a look at the mystical experience of pure consciousness. When the mind settles down to a state of complete stillness, there's no thought and no activity, and what the mystics report again and again is that there's just an eternal sense of presence, where time disappears and there's no sense of location in space.

Because consciousness is not material, it has no mass, and yet out of consciousness comes all of our experiences of space, time, and matter. But its deeper nature lies beyond space, time, and matter, so it seems to me there is a close parallel between the true nature of the light of consciousness and the true nature of the light of the physical world. We make the mistake with both of assuming that they belong to our everyday world, but they are both beyond all of our concepts of space, time, and matter.

Once again we're back to the basic paradigm we started with, the belief that the material world is the real world. What light seems to be telling us is that the material world is a description of but one level of reality, and that the true nature of light lies beyond it. So whatever the absolute nature of the world, it lies beyond concepts and matter, but the first level of manifestation into our everyday world of space, time, and experience seems to be one of light or luminosity.

Many of the world's spiritual teachings affirm something similar to this, with statements like "let there be light," or "in the beginning there was light," and mystics talk about a white or golden light that can appear in the mind as the faintest level of consciousness or the first level of manifestation. So both science and spirituality seem to be two sides of the same coin with respect to light, and this seems to be one area where the inner mental world and the external physical world overlap.

And many of the world's spiritual traditions speak of an eternal world not as a world of infinite time, but as a world outside of or beyond time, which seems to be what you're pointing to here. The other interesting point you raise is that the experience of ourselves through the light of consciousness is instantaneous and unmediated, just as light's experience of itself traveling between two parts of the cosmos is instantaneous and unmediated. So the light of consciousness and the light of the physical world behave very similarly from the perspective of subjective experience.

Yes, time is just a construct in our minds in the sense that we are only ever in the present moment, but in the present moment we construct a timeline, have memories, and think into the future, but it's all actually taking place out of time.

Yes, and all of this is being mediated by the mysterious phenomenon that we call light.

And, God is light. It's one of the characteristics often ascribed to the Divine, so the deeper nature of the world is somehow closely linked to the Divine light.

Fascinating! Because we've been talking about consciousness, and just touched on the development and evolution of the universe briefly, I wonder if we can explore the question of whether there's a direction to the evolution of consciousness over the history of the universe.

If we are going to be strict in terms of our use of language, I would say that consciousness itself doesn't evolve, because the way I've been using the term is that consciousness is the capacity for experience. Because that capacity is always there, it doesn't evolve, but the experience of it does. So I would say that there is the evolution of experience, which is closely linked to the evolution of the mind.

However, the essential quality of the mind, which is awareness, is always present, and so I would say that the direction of the evolution of the mind is toward increasing intelligence, which I define as the ability to organize and use information. For example, a very simple cell is intelligent insofar as it may be sensing its environment, responding to it, avoiding toxic substances, etc.... That's intelligence at a very basic level. Now that intelligence has evolved to what we call human intelligence, which is much more multifaceted, but I think it still comes back to a basic capacity of being able to take in information, organize it, and extract from it new principles, which can then be applied in order to further our own well-being.

So is intelligence in this context similar to the contents of consciousness, in that there are infinite gradations of this intelligence going back throughout time?

Yes, I would say so. Whereas the capacity for consciousness is always present, there are infinite gradations in the forms that appear in consciousness. For example, the sensory forms you find in very simple creatures are very, very simple, but as the senses have evolved and the nervous systems have evolved, so have these gradations developed in terms of the content of consciousness.

The best way to put it might be that the capacity for consciousness is universal, the gradations are in the content of consciousness, and then the way those contents are organized is the intelligence, with infinite gradations of intelligence, and I would say that is the direction of evolution.

Now in some of your earlier books you've also explored the possibility that evolution might actually be speeding up toward a new stage of development. You've speculated that evolution might be accelerating toward a temporal singularity that you refer to as a white hole in time, and I wonder if your current thinking is still resonant with that idea.

Yes, yes, yes! Very much so. This idea comes out of the observation that evolution generally speeds up as it progresses. The reason for this is that as you develop more complex levels of evolution, there's a feedback system that makes future evolution easier and faster.

Multi-cellular organisms evolve because the arrangement of the cells and the organs evolve, rather than through the development of new types of cells. A heart cell in a human being is very similar to a heart cell in a pig, which is why we can transplant a pig's heart into a human being. The level of organization of the organs between the two is different, and it's that organization that can evolve much faster, because you don't have to wait for a new cell or new organs to evolve. So when we look at the history of evolution, we see it takes billions of years for simple cells to evolve, and then it gets increasingly faster with complex organisms.

Human beings have been around for just one ten-thousandth of Earth's history, and yet what has happened in human culture has been enormous in that short time. If we take the last few thousand years, and then the last few hundred years, or even just the last 10 years, we see tremendous acceleration of progress based on this principle. A good example is the information revolution that has followed the industrial revolution. The industrial revolution took a while to really settle in because we had to invent factories, build them, and then create the means for mass distribution, and it took a hundred years to lay all that infrastructure down. When the information revolution came along, we didn't have to reinvent factories to produce computers—we knew how to do that and also how to distribute them. So the information revolution happened much faster and is pushing change much, much faster. It's a universal trend that the rate of progress accelerates—it's just positive feedback in the evolutionary process.

I see the development of human consciousness accelerating in the same way for similar reasons. We are all rapidly learning from each other. So any breakthroughs in understanding, about how to liberate the mind or how to become mentally healthier, are shared within our culture extremely quickly. Information on the Internet is shared much faster than it was through books or word of mouth. The more we learn, the faster we wake up, and the more we have to share. So you've got this same positive feedback loop happening today with the awakening of consciousness, meaning it's going to get faster and faster.

This seems to resonate with many people's experience with saying that their lives are speeding up so fast that they have a hard time even catching up with them.

Well, clearly we're all experiencing the pace of life speeding up, and I think there are several reasons for this. One is that change is happening much faster these days, so we're having to adapt to new situations and challenges much more quickly than previously. We also are getting busier and busier. There's so much more to do in each day because we *can* do so much more. It's ironic actually—we're consciously speeding our lives up in many ways based on the idea that the more we do, the happier we'll be. But also I think people are noticing that their own inner process is speeding up as well. People often tell me at workshops that they've been through more shifts of awakening in the past two or three years than they had in the previous 10 or 20.

In some sense it's like we're feeling the evolutionary pressure to expand our capacities through this speeding-up of our daily lives, and it sounds as though, from what we've been discussing, that this trend will only increase.

This is the white hole in time that I've talked about in an earlier book. The idea of the white hole in time is a parallel process to the evolution of a star becoming a black hole. A star goes through various stages of birthing, beginning with burning hydrogen into helium, which typically takes 5 to 10 billion years. Then, when the hydrogen burns out, it starts burning helium, and it goes through about 5 or 6 various elements, with the ashes of one process leading to the next.

Yes, hydrogen forms helium, then carbon, neon, oxygen, and silicon, as parts of the whole sequence, with each stage burning faster and faster in a shorter amount of time.

Yes, and ending up with iron, at which point it can't go any further. So the star collapses, then, if it is sufficiently massive, explodes as a supernova. What's left behind after that is a black hole, which is a very stable state. It goes through this faster and faster acceleration toward this stable state of a black hole.

It struck me that the evolution of the mind, or the evolution of intelligence, runs a similar course. It gets faster and faster, and we seem to be heading toward a similar moment of almost infinitely rapid evolution of intelligence.

This could be the awakening of the human mind breaking through into something entirely different, just as a black hole is a completely different state than the star it was previously. I think that this would be like Teilhard de Chardin's noosphere or even his idea of Christogenesis, the collective spiritual awakening of humanity, although he saw that as happening thousands of years into the future.

Right, what he called the Omega Point.

Yes, the Omega Point. Interestingly, Teilhard didn't take the acceleration of the evolutionary process into account. I don't think it was apparent to him when he wrote the *Phenomenon of Man* and the *Future of Man*, but later in his life after televisions and computers came along, he made the comment that these developments bring the Omega Point much, much closer through the sharing of information. I think if he had included this accelerating trend, he'd have seen that all that development, which he imagined would take another 10,000 years to happen, would actually happen in the next 20, 30, or 40 years.

And just like a black hole, we have no idea what's in store for us with this acceleration of intelligence. I mean is it infinite intelligence? Is it collective spiritual awakening? It's hard to say.

Yes, it's like the other metaphors I've used—how can a caterpillar guess what it's going to be like as a butterfly? I think we can get some sense for saying what it might be like if we look at the lives of the great saints and the enlightened people throughout history, with their sense of freedom and all that love in their hearts. What would it be like if the whole of human culture was founded on that?

It's a wonderful image.

Or it could be something even far more strange than that. For example, we might move into something equivalent to a collective near-death experience. This might have similar stages to what individuals report from near-death experiences, such as stepping outside the physical body, moving into an experience of light, along with feelings of infinite peace, love, and light where there is no longer any fear of death.

It could be that at the white hole in time, this might happen on a collective level, where we all somehow simultaneously transcend our physical bodies and come together in a collective experience of awakening or transcendence. We have no way of really understanding what it would be like. But it's a possibility that we cannot exclude, and I'm just pointing to a possible direction things could take.

Yes, and it also sounds as though it's something we can trust as part of the natural process in the unfoldment of the universe, even if we have no idea where it's going or what things might be like on the other side. Thank you for sharing this broader view.

Chapter 18

The Archetypal Cosmos: An Interview With Richard Tarnas

A re humans the product of random processes in a purposeless universe, or is there an underlying meaningful order to the cosmos? For much of human history, there has been a profound and meaningful relationship between the events of human culture and the larger patterns and cycles of the cosmos. Yet in the modern era, words such as *alienated, meaningless, insignificant,* and *mechanistic* have been used to describe the relationship between the human and the larger universe. We seem to have gained an immense perspective in our scientific study of the universe, but I wonder if we have also lost something equally valuable as well. Many would suggest that the sense of alienation, isolation, and existential emptiness that some experience in modern society are symptoms of a profound disconnection between themselves, the natural world, and our greater cosmic context.

But does it have to be this way? Is it possible to live in a modern technological society and have a meaningful relationship with the cosmos? Cultural historian Dr. Richard Tarnas thinks that we can. The development of the modern sense of self, he suggests in his groundbreaking work *Cosmos and Psyche*, is not an accident, but is the result of a great arc of development that spans the entire length of Western cultural history. He makes the case in great detail that our sense of self and our relationship to the world and cosmos are inextricably interconnected, so that a shift in either will dramatically affect both. Tarnas believes a more integral worldview is possible, a radical revisioning of ourselves and the cosmos that interweaves both together in a meaningful way. It was in search of this integral worldview that I began the final interview for this book in conversation with Tarnas.

Dr. Richard Tarnas is a cultural historian, writer, and professor of philosophy and psychology at the California Institute of Integral Studies in San Francisco, where he is a founding director of its graduate program in Philosophy, Cosmology, and Consciousness. He is also adjunct faculty at Pacifica Graduate Institute in Santa Barbara, where he teaches in the clinical and depth psychology programs. Tarnas graduated cum laude with an AB from Harvard in 1972, where he studied cultural history and depth psychology. He received his PhD from the Saybrook Institute in 1976 and was director of programs and education at the Esalen Institute, where he lived for more than 10 years, and studied with Joseph Campbell, Gregory Bateson, Huston Smith, Stanislav Grof, and James Hillman.

Dr. Tarnas's first book, *The Passion of the Western Mind*, is a narrative history of the Western worldview from the ancient Greek to the postmodern era that became a bestseller and has been widely adopted as a classroom text in many universities. His most recent book, *Cosmos and Psyche: Intimations of a New World View*, challenges the basic assumptions of the modern worldview by exploring consistent correlations between planetary movements and significant events in human history from an archetypal perspective.

Tarnas's work investigates and celebrates the deeper aspects of the human psyche embedded in a cosmos saturated with intelligence, consciousness, imagination, and meaning. His work has been widely praised as a foundational step toward an integral worldview that embraces philosophy, religion, science, nature, and culture in a meaningful relationship with the cosmos.

Stephan Martin: Depth psychology and its archetypal perspective has a long and distinguished lineage that stretches back from Freud and Jung and evolves through Stanislav Grof, James Hillman, and now through yourself and many others today. One of the themes of this approach is the exploration of a profound relationship between individual consciousness, cultural movements, and an archetypal psyche embedded in the universe itself, an *anima mundi*. Could you talk a bit about the nature of these relationships and some of the discoveries that have led to this new understanding of the universe?

Richard Tarnas: It all begins with Freud and Jung's opening of the unconscious that brought about such a profound deepening of the modern psyche's experience of itself and of its inner reality. Freud first opened the door to these depths with his recognition of the psychological power of the biological instincts, and particularly the role of the libido in shaping the unconscious. Jung broadened and deepened Freud's work by relating the unconscious to the archetypal dimension, thus reconnecting the human psyche with its spiritual ground.

These developments were taking place during the early and middle part of the 20th century, when the modern psyche found itself in an increasingly problematic state of alienation and disorientation from any meaningful connection with itself, the world, or the cosmos. To use Max Weber's term, our cosmology had been profoundly "disenchanted." As a result of the Scientific Revolution and subsequent intellectual developments, the modern psyche found itself without any sense of an underlying cosmic order that comprehends and gives coherence to human existence, a worldview that has informed virtually every culture prior to the modern.

Nietzsche recognizes this when he talks about the death of God, the destruction of the metaphysical world, the wiping away of the horizon of meaning, the perceived cosmic order that has always encompassed human existence prior to this era. In *The Gay Science*, when he announces the death of God, Nietzsche writes, "What were we doing when we unchained this Earth from its Sun?...Where are we going now? Is there still any up or down? Are we not straying as through an infinite nothing? Do we not feel the breath of empty space? Has it not become colder? Is not night continually closing in on us?" That sense of the endarkenment of the cosmos and the disenchantment of the world is the beginning of the late modern condition that anticipates and precedes Freud and Jung.

And this condition continues today in our postmodern culture, as many struggle with the great underlying schism between the inner world and the outer cosmos. The richness of the inner tradition in modern Western culture has its roots in the Romantic tradition with Rousseau, Goethe, Coleridge, and Blake, right on up through the 1960's psychedelic counterculture and beyond, and is reflected in the insights of depth psychology, the archetypal perspective, transpersonal consciousness research, and other forms of exploration of the inner world. This internally oriented perspective has been largely at war with the more outward-turned aspect of the modern self that comes from the Enlightenment and the Scientific Revolution, which generally views the cosmos as a disenchanted phenomenon in which unconscious, mechanistic forces of matter and energy have randomly evolved in such a way that the oddity of human consciousness accidentally emerged as an epiphenomenon of impersonal processes.

You might say that the Romantic tradition in the modern sensibility represents the modern soul, while the Enlightenment and scientific aspect represents the modern mind, and so there has been this polarized tension within the modern self between its heart and mind. This is the great schism in our contemporary worldview, the great contradiction between the rich meaningful inner world of the self and what is perceived as an impersonal and purposeless cosmos devoid of intrinsic meaning. Our profoundest values, our spiritual aspirations, our moral and aesthetic sensibilities, our psychological depths have no place in the disenchanted modern cosmos.

One of Jung's great contributions was to begin to reconnect the inner world with the outer cosmos in a meaningful way, particularly through his observations of and reflections about the phenomenon of synchronicity. In turn, beginning in the 1960s, Stanislav Grof synthesized Freud's and Jung's work, bringing together the biological and the spiritual realms with his understanding of the archetypal death-rebirth process and the tremendous impact of biological birth and death on the human psyche and spiritual condition. This was a great advance for the field of transpersonal psychology and a considerable source of healing for a modern psyche embedded in a disenchanted worldview.

During my work with Grof for my doctoral dissertation in psychology, we were working in the field that is now known as consciousness research. We were searching for a deeper and more holistic understanding of the human condition, but also seeking to understand certain paradoxes and perplexities that had arisen with Grof's research with psychedelics. I should mention that, because Grof is a psychiatrist, he had a special government dispensation under the auspices of the National Institute of Mental Health to continue working with psychoactive substances in a therapeutic setting for several years after they had been banned from mainstream culture. His research in this area had begun in the mid-1950s in Prague and continued into the 1970s.

What we were investigating was why the same person could take the same psychoactive substance, whether it was LSD, psilocybin, or mescaline, and have radically different experiences at different times. Similarly, how was it that the same substance, the same molecule in the same quantity, could induce the most ecstatic, spiritually transformative states for an individual at one time, and absolutely hellish states of despair and seemingly irremediable psychotic panic at others? No conventional psychological tests such as the Rorschach, the MMPI, or the TAT had proved to have any predictive value in understanding these differences.

Now Jung, one of the most distinguished figures in the psychological profession, had left hints and suggestive comments in some of his letters and writings that he noticed there were remarkable correlations between the planetary alignments at a person's birth and the basic archetypal dynamics in their psychic constitution. He also found that the motions of the planets in the sky relative to where they were at a person's birth seemed to coincide with the shifting activation of different archetypal complexes in the course of a person's life. I later found out from those who knew Jung personally that Jung found this correspondence so convincing that in his later years he was consistently using astrology as a uniquely helpful therapeutic indicator with all of his patients. In the mid 1970s, when we were at Esalen, Grof and I met an astrological researcher who persuaded us to consider the possibility that planetary transits coincided with the shifting quality of individuals' experiences. Given as well Jung's observations of these correlations between a person's inner process and the planetary positions in the sky, Grof and I wondered if this might be a potential explanation, however far-fetched, of the radically different experiences people had in these types of sessions.

So as skeptical as I initially was about astrology, I learned how to calculate birth charts and transits, and began to see if this approach might shed any light on this problem that Grof and I were working on. Because our modern prejudice against astrology is so strong, you really can't take anyone else's word for its validity. You must test it with the rigor that you can directly confirm, working with evidence with which you have a direct, intimate connection.

It's very interesting that you were initially so skeptical of astrology and this more cosmic archetypal perspective even after it came recommended, as it were, by a giant in the field such as Jung.

Yes, astrology really represents the gold standard of superstition for our culture. But I now realize that, as with many things in life, those things of deepest value are often the most scorned in the conventional perspective, with the greatest mysteries continuing to loom right in front of us, encompassing the whole sky so to speak.

To our astonishment, we discovered that a wide range of individual experiences were consistently synchronized with the ongoing planetary movements with respect to the Earth. We first looked at our own sessions, which we had very good records for, and also those of Grof's patients over many years, and from this large database of experiences we found that these powerful, nonordinary states of consciousness seemed to have an underlying connection to certain archetypal principles that correlated with the planets. Moreover, the ongoing movement of these planets relative to each other and to the Earth seemed to be strongly correlated with collective human experiences and cultural movements on a global scale. It seemed as if there were fundamental archetypal principles at work on individual, collective, and cultural levels that were not simply human constructs, but were in some sense universal and connected to the macrocosm itself.

This insight unfolded gradually as we were taking in more and more evidence and were seeing how comprehensive these patterns were and beginning to understand the nuances of these archetypal correlations. We came to see that what Jung had been looking at as the collective unconscious and the archetypal unconscious was not only a human phenomenon, but was in some sense embedded in and expressive of the cosmos itself.

It was as if the cosmos was ensouled and that the human psyche was in some sense an expression of and grounded in a cosmic psyche, in an *anima mundi*, or soul of the world. The evidence seemed to point to something that many shamanic, mystical, and esoteric traditions had been suggesting all along, namely, that the cosmos itself is profoundly ensouled and imbued with purposes and meanings within which the human is a co-creative and essential participant, and not simply an isolated oddity in a vast cosmic void.

It's all the more startling that the discovery of this kind of cosmic order was initially found by investigating the inner world so deeply through non-ordinary states, as if the inner world of the psyche and the outer world of the physical cosmos are two sides of the same mysterious phenomenon.

The other important point I see here is that this synchronous relationship between the cosmos and human experience is an "acausal" relationship, to use Jung's term. It's not a mechanistic type of direct influence in that there isn't a channel of energy coming from Saturn to influence one's life, which is the usual critique of astrology by mainstream science. It's much more subtle and profound than that.

Yes, that's right. Jung used the word *acausal* to refer to meaningful coincidences in which external events perfectly paralleled certain inner events without any apparent linear causal connection between the two. But he was using the word "cause" here in the very narrow sense that the modern mind tends to restrict it to, which is essentially what Aristotle would call "efficient causality"—a kind of linear, mechanistic, billiard-ball causal understanding. But Aristotle and the Greeks after him had a more sophisticated understanding of causality than we generally do today, and they recognized several other forms of causality. For example, Aristotle attributed the "formal cause" to that which gives pattern and structure and form and meaning to something. This kind of causality in fact seems to be what is at work here in synchronicities and astrological correlations, in that there is some underlying patterning to the universe that provides a correspondence between, say, certain positions of the planets Pluto and Uranus and periods of tremendously intensified revolutionary, social, and political phenomena in human culture. I explore this in careful detail in the book *Cosmos and Psyche*, but briefly, I would say here that from this point of view it seems as if there is a formal cause at work in the cosmos that manifests as meaningful form or pattern of experience.

Jung found that the most powerful synchronicities tended to occur at times of important transformation, such as crises, births, deaths, and so on. He noticed that in these moments a kind of larger purpose was being served, moving the individual consciousness toward increasing wholeness with itself and with the cosmos. This purpose, this teleological impulse at work within the synchronicity, represents what Aristotle would call the "final cause."

Astrological correlations certainly do not represent mechanistic causality, as you rightly said. There doesn't seem to be anything like electromagnetic radiation or gravity waves that are moving from the planet Saturn, Venus, or Pluto to the Earth and making Saturnian or Venusian or Plutonic things happen. Mars as a planet is not making this person angry right now. It's not that kind of simplistic, mechanistic causality at work here, but it rather seems to be more like the formal and final causality that Aristotle proposed.

You might wonder that if this is true, then what about free will? Actually, with our understanding of archetypal dynamics and archetypal causation we find that there's nothing predetermined in a literal and concrete way about how a particular planetary alignment is going to express itself, so to speak, in a concrete event. One cannot look at a birth chart and say, "This person is going to be good," or "This person is going to be bad." Rather, we see that these archetypal principles have a multiplicity of meanings that they can potentially express, a wide range of ways in which they generally can express their particular character—ways that can be creative or destructive, noble or ignoble, profound or trivial, but still true to the complex nature of the archetype involved.

So what we find is that astrology and the kind of archetypal perspective that we've been researching does not seem to be *concretely* predictive, but is instead *archetypally* predictive. Our freedom of will allows us to bring consciousness to the situation, and this capacity of human autonomy is the crucial element that allows the situation to actualize and flourish in relationship to these archetypes. Without that freedom of choice, we'd be looking at a deterministic, fatalistic system in which we're just puppets of these archetypes. But being conscious of them actually increases human freedom and allows us to bring an intelligent participation to the enactment of these archetypal principles in our lives.

Would you say that it depends on our attitude and our availability to the archetypal realm as to whether these potentials become activated within us and in our lives?

It doesn't seem to depend on our attitude as to whether they will come through. They come through whether or not we are aware of them, and whether or not we believe in them. One didn't have to believe in the correlations with the Uranus-Pluto cycle to be in a very intense, revolutionary Paris in 1789, or again in Berkeley or Paris in 1968.

What the archetypal astrological perspective does is that it extends the basic depth psychological project of Freud and Jung in a powerful way into the cosmological domain. As we become conscious of all that is unconscious within us, we move beyond being puppets of these powerful unconscious forces, and towards being conscious participants in relationship with them. I think having an astrological awareness of them can augment our conscious relationship to them, but they're going to come through one way or another no matter what. For example, they tend to be enacted more destructively when one is in denial of the shadow side of a particular complex. But you don't have to know astrology to bring forth highly creative, life-enhancing expressions of these forces. This happens all the time. I doubt that Beethoven had much astrological knowledge, but his life and music represent a beautiful illustration of the archetypal dynamics of his type of birth chart because of what he did with the energies and potentials that he was carrying within him.

Now given the relationship of these archetypal cosmic forces to cultural movements and cycles in human history, can you say something about the archetypal significance of our time now with respect to our relationship to the universe? It seems as though the rediscovery in Western culture of a meaningful relationship with the universe has a particular trajectory in human history, one which arcs through Freud, Jung, Grof, Hillman, and now yourself. Is the universe in some sense calling Western culture back to itself?

I see this particular trajectory of recovery of the *anima mundi* and the reconnection of the human psyche with the soul of the cosmos as very significant, but ultimately as but one part of a much larger transformation of consciousness that virtually every field of human activity seems to be going through right now. Physics, biology, ethics, business, ecology, cosmology, philosophy, medicine, and every other field is experiencing comparable breakthroughs and transformations. All of these together seem to be pointing to a larger awakening of the Earth, of the birth of a new kind of planetary consciousness that is not only recognizing the embeddedness of humanity with all other forms of life in the larger Earth community, but also a new kind of planetary consciousness of the Earth within its cosmic setting.

It's not unlike those experiences of a new consciousness that registered for people after seeing the first photos of the Earth taken from space. It's interesting that so many astronauts had powerful, mystical, and spiritually transformative experiences while they were in space, as if some new perspective on the cosmos was awakened in them by their journey beyond the Earth. It's almost as if they awakened from a kind of trance of disenchantment, separation, and fragmentation into a larger sense of numinous cosmic wholeness.

This growing awareness suggests that some kind of gradual revelation, some kind of transformative vision of within the human, is taking place. The cosmos itself through the human being is awakening to itself in a new way. From this point of view, human beings are not separate entities that live on the Earth and in the cosmos. Rather, human beings *are* the cosmos, *are* the Earth in human form, and our human consciousness is in some sense the universe's consciousness in its human inflection. Our creative imagination and our spiritual aspirations—these are the universe's creative imagination and spiritual aspirations coming into new expression and new modes of being in this moment. So the sequence of insights and breakthroughs that we were describing earlier from Freud through Grof is part of a much larger awakening that many, many people, disciplines, religious traditions, scientists, human rights activists, ecological activists, and others are currently participating in.

I think that many people are feeling the groundswell of a new kind of consciousness being born at this time, and we may have to wait until later in order to fully appreciate the deeper significance of what is happening right now. But there does seem to be a kind of quickening, a certain kairos of the moment at this point in terms of human and Earth history.

There is the sense of something awakening and being born, but this is also intertwined with a profound sense of something in the world passing and dying away. Much of what is passing away may be very valuable to us and connected to ways that currently shape our identity and the essential structures of our reality and ways of being in the world. Many of us have been thinking about these things for decades, but even in the last six months there seems to have been an acceleration of the collapse of existing structures across the board—political, economic, social, ecological, and psychological—an intensification of the forces of change that can be both destructive as well as creative.

I want to hold the sense of this coincidence of opposites, that death and birth are happening simultaneously, and while it's true that some things are being joyfully left behind, there are also some genuine losses that are rightly experienced as tragic. From a spiritual perspective, it's part of the death-rebirth mystery that one really does have to die in a fundamental way to be reborn; one has to experience a kind of tragic loss in order to experience a spiritual dawn. It is not a simple climbing of a cognitive ladder where one leaves behind outmoded identities while journeying steadily upward into expanded states. It's a much more taut, complex drama that is unfolding.

It sounds much closer to the archetypal Hero's Journey where obstacles, trials, and triumphs are all interwoven into a complex narrative.

Right, and it's not the Hollywood hero that has one triumph after another and is everybody's favorite from beginning to end. It's that deeper sense of the hero who is really defined by death, by the courageous willingness to totally transcend oneself and sacrifice oneself in the service of the larger life. It is the sense of the Hero archetype who is in this sense deeply united with the Great Mother archetype in both men and women—they both sacrifice themselves and give of their essential being so that new life can emerge. Out of the tension of opposites and in the course of the death-rebirth transformation these two are reconciled, Sun and Moon, and out of that mysterious unity the birth of a new being takes place.

All of which fits with our experiences of both gain and loss during this profound moment in history. Could we go a bit further here and talk about the new sense of self or identity that is emerging for the human right now?

There's a certain tendency within new-paradigm thinking of wanting to "get beyond" the so-called Cartesian/Newtonian paradigm and go towards the embrace of the oneness of things and so on. This perspective can be very disdainful of modernity, Descartes, patriarchy, Christianity, modern science, rationality, and so on. What I have been gradually coming to understand is that all these developments are ultimately interconnected with the emergence and embodiment of this new form of consciousness that is currently arising.

In the end, it is incoherent and self-contradictory to say that everything is part of the underlying unity except for the modern Cartesian, mechanistic perspective, or patriarchy, or Christianity, or something like that. Each of these has their noble and significant side, as well as their shadow side, and what I think has been going on is that the West has been on a kind of hero's journey, where it has brought wondrous things into the light, but has also created tremendous suffering in its shadow. This journey, this narrative trajectory that has been unfolding for Western civilization for centuries is both dynamic and traumatic and seems to be now climactically bringing forth the possibility of a new mode of consciousness that will preserve the noble side of this long, traumatic trajectory and will at the same time bring about a fundamental transcendence of it.

By transcendence I mean that humanity—as individuals, as a civilization, and as a species—will come into a new mode of relationship to the whole and with the ensouled cosmos and the Earth community. As we move out of that one-sided identification with the Cartesian rational ego and into a holistic participation with the whole, it will not be in a way that submerges the individuality of the part, but instead in a way that reconnects the individual with the whole in an I-thou relationship, rather than the I-it relationship that has been the dominant mode in the past.

It's very hopeful to see that we're all involved in and working towards this larger perspective that seems to be at the same time happening on its own.

In a sense, what I've just described is an archetypal narrative in itself, a myth in the grandest sense, and I'm suggesting that we may be at the point in our collective journey where one of the great challenges before us as human beings is to open up to the possibility that the cosmos itself is informed by archetypal and mythic meaning. Narrative trajectories and great stories imbued with purpose and meaning are not the exclusive possession of the human being, but instead may express the very essence of the cosmos. We may have to consider the possibility that the universe may not be an unconscious, purposeless void within which we alone carry meaning and purpose, which is a fairly hubristic assumption. We may have to open up to the possibility that the cosmos is informed by some kind of profound intelligence, which is realizing itself through the human being, as well as through every other form of its speciation.

Now for many years, physicists such as Einstein and many others have had the intuition that the universe isn't just completely unintelligent, but is instead informed by some kind of supreme mathematical intelligence. When Stephen Hawking talks about understanding the mind of God that rules the universe, he's combining older biblical ways of describing divinity with the mind of a mathematical physicist. What I'm suggesting is that even this perspective is still too limited, and I think we need to awaken to the possibility that the universe is informed through and through by a kind of intelligence that is not only like the mind of Einstein, but also like that of Shakespeare. That is, the cosmos seems to have a profound spiritual, moral, and aesthetic dimension to it, with a depth, majesty, and imaginative magnitude that we only glimpse in the greatest works of art that human beings have ever brought forth. We need to consider that the universe is not only a great work of art, but is also the artist itself.

So in this sense the perspective of a narrative drama that has moral, imaginative, and aesthetic dimensions to it is what is unfolding in the universe through us in our moment in time. We seem to be in the midst of a mysterious death-rebirth process of the universe awakening to itself through us, with a new kind of planetary consciousness emerging. Along with this is the recovery of the *anima mundi* and the emergence of a new way of relating to this soul of the universe in a co-creative way.

All this—this myth, this archetypal narrative, this hero's journey of transformation, initiation, and awakening—is perhaps expressive of the very nature of the cosmos itself, rather than something projected from the isolated corner of human psychological subjectivity onto a meaningless cosmos. I am trying to suggest that we open up to the possibility that the cosmos is in fact capable of carrying out that kind of high drama with that kind of profound meaning and that kind of compelling narrative, unfolding it all out of its very essence. The reason we as human beings are so drawn to these kinds of narratives, dramas, tragedies, romances, and divine comedies is that we in our attraction are being lured by the very nature of the heart of the universe that is revealing itself through us.

The scope, magnitude, and majesty of what you are proposing is much more than an anthropocentric or human-centered view, it's a cosmo-centric view that looks at things from the perspective of the cosmos itself and sees the role that humans are playing in a larger drama.

Exactly. It doesn't deflate the human being to being entirely peripheral, but recognizes humans as one of many centers in the cosmos. There are many centers in the universe, just as there are many stars and many planets. We live in an omni-centric cosmos, and so the human being in a sense is one center of cosmic meaning and the Earth is another center of cosmic meaning and there are many other centers throughout the universe. We need to create new words to express this new and richer sense of meaning and perspective. One of the best I've heard was coined by the great Spanish-Indian philosopher Raimon Panikkar. He uses the word *cosmotheandric*, combining the universe, the divine, and the human into one inseparable whole.

It's a beautiful phrase that really captures in this moment what is being born. Thank you for sharing your insights and perspective.

Conclusion

The night sky is different now. More fluid. Less certain. Even more magnificent.

Paradoxically, the more I talked about the universe with people of diverse orientations, I slowly began to experience the disturbing—yet strangely exciting—feeling that I knew less and less about it. As an astronomer, I've studied the universe my entire life. Now I find myself in the awkward position of being unable to explain the universe even to a child. I am like a tailor who has measured the height, inseam, and girth of a client he has stitched for cycles of seasons, yet he still knows nothing about him personally—after all, there's only so much to extrapolate from the size of a waist.

The realization that I know very little about the universe has been oddly comforting. As it appeared progressively less like what I had thought, I found myself more at home in it. As its mystery was magnified, its gravitational pull drew me deeper into awe, wonder, and amazement. Having given up my most cherished beliefs about the ways things are, I am now free to imagine and experience myself in ways previously impossible.

Then can we say nothing at all about what the universe is? To simply say, shrugging, "It's a mystery," and continue brushing the dog or loading the dishwasher denies the depth and richness that is constantly speaking all around us. Yet to say anything at all about the universe can seduce us into thinking we know what it is, that we can box it into words and place it like a butterfly in a display case, unfluttering.

But we must try.

The understandings articulated in these Cosmic Conversations are paradoxical, enigmatic, and even contradictory. They present a challenge to constructing a single unified model of the universe. From the perspective of science, if the universe is only matter and energy, then what are we to make of the religious and spiritual traditions that perceive a nonphysical or spiritual dimension to reality? Denying this viewpoint would cut us off from the rich well of meaning and guidance from the wisdom traditions of all the world's cultures. Conversely, suggesting that the universe is ultimately nonmaterial and denying the physicality of the world is not only philosophically naïve, but potentially dangerous (especially when trying to cross a busy intersection).

Rather than debating the "correctness" of the scientific or the spiritual or the cultural views of reality, I suggest another possibility. Instead of either/or approaches that exclude—the universe as matter or spirit, alive or inert, purposeful or random, real or imaginary—what if it could be all of these, and more? What if the universe is so rich and multivalent that no single tradition, discipline, or individual has the capacity to circumscribe or encompass it fully? Because these diverse perspectives coexist in and arise out of the same universe, then from the universe's perspective they must each contain some truth to them.

As an experiment, let's try a both/and approach, combining the richly diverse insights and perspectives expressed in these conversations to see what emerges from this synthesis. If we do this, some statements we might make about the universe from this expanded and inclusive perspective include:

1. The universe is not a thing or a collection of objects, but is a unified living process continually flowing and arising in each moment. (Elgin, Drolma, Ali and Johnson)
2. Life is not an emergent phenomenon, but is woven into the fabric of the universe itself. (Gardner, Elgin, Bache)

3. The fundamental "stuff" of the universe is not matter or objects, but may be energy, light, consciousness, mind, or something even more mysterious. (Haisch, Wolf, Radin, Elgin, Zuavala, Drolma, Ali and Johnson, Russell, Mitchell)

4. We are not *in* the universe, but we *are* the universe, or expressed even more personally, we are Universe. (Swimme, Dowd, Hubbard, Bache, Mitchell, Gardner)

5. The universe is infused with intelligence, purpose, and guidance that reveals itself through nature and the events of our lives. (Haisch, Dowd, Elgin, Bache, Horn, Mitchell, Teish, Zavala, Tarnas, Ali and Johnson)

6. We are the continuation of an immense evolutionary process that continues to express and reveal the universe's unfolding potential. (Swimme, Hubbard, Gardner, Bache, Mitchell, Russell)

7. How we approach the universe makes a difference, in what we perceive, the language we use, and how we create a meaningful worldview from our experiences. (Swimme, Wolf, Radin, Primack and Abrams, Tarnas)

8. There is a boundless spiritual reality that enfolds and includes the universe of phenomena that we experience. (Haisch, Drolma, Ali and Johnson, Elgin)

9. The universe is a very deep and profound mystery. (Everyone!)

These insights and revelations seem to express merely the beginning of what could ever be said about the nature of the universe. To paraphrase Einstein, the most incomprehensible thing about the universe is that it is endlessly comprehensible. We are not likely to run out of words or ways to describe it anytime soon.

So what to make of this? How do these insights shift our relationship to the universe and ourselves?

First, we find ourselves living in an omnicentric, multiperspectival cosmos. Because everywhere is the center of the universe's dynamism, creativity, and action, we can learn about the cosmos from every location within it. We can discover the universe in laboratories and observatories, but also in our own backyard, in our churches and temples, and in each other. Not only are professional scientists experts on the universe, but so is every living thing. Children, elders, trees, and stars are all radiating "Universe!" every moment of every day. When I told my ecopsychologist friend Tina about this book and the people I would be speaking with, she immediately asked, "Aren't you going to interview any redwood trees?" In this cosmic perspective, every single thing that exists is precious, not only for what it is but also for the unique perspective it brings to the conversation about the universe.

The second radical insight to emerge from these conversations is that, because we find ourselves not only to be *in* the universe but that "we are Universe," then all these understandings about the universe apply equally to us as well. We, too, are an endlessly flowing, mysterious process that is evolving with intelligence, guidance, and purpose while increasingly revealing the elaboration of our innate potential.

Asking "What is the Universe?" as a personal inquiry is another way of asking "Who am I?" As our understanding deepens, we will surely ask, "If I am at least this, and almost certainly infinitely more, then what does this mean for my life, my relationships, my way of living in (and *as*) the world?"

One final discovery we might take from these conversations is that asking the question "What is the Universe?" is itself an answer, a reply from the heart of the cosmos. The universe is a not a thing or an event, but is the living process of revelation and questioning itself. Not only is the universe *what* is revealed by asking the question, but it is also the *process* of inquiry itself. It is the origin, goal, and activity of discovering itself. Beginning, end, and middle all rolled into one. The universe is what is seeking, what is being sought, and the seeking itself.

We ask the question "What is the Universe?" because it is the universe that asks the question in us, through us, and as us. We ask "Who am I? What am I? Where do I come from and where am I going?" The universe, like all its progeny, wonders as we do, for we are the starry night itself come to human form to ask these questions. And the answer comes in the smile of a newborn, the flight of an eagle, the perpetual rhythm of the tides, and the profound silence of the stars.

Only now have we lived long enough in this evolving cosmos to become both the questioners and the answer. We ask these questions and have these cosmic conversations because we are wonder itself, cosmic fire stirred through billions of years of evolution to finally stand under the night sky and ask itself "Who am I?" And out of silence arises the reply: I am the birds and the trees, the effulgent Earth, the whirling stars and galaxies, the flowing cosmos having come to form.

In the night sky tonight the stars are no longer distant point-like objects, but reminders of the vast and creative mystery shining forth from everywhere.

Notes

1. Robert Lawrence Kuhn, "Why This Universe? Towards a Taxonomy of Possible Explanations," *Skeptic* 13 (2007): 28–39.

2. Werner Heisenberg, *Physics and Philosophy*, New York: Harper Torchbooks, 1958.

3. Swami Muni N. Prasad, *Chandogya Upanishad*, New Delhi: Dk Print World, 2006.

4. Hua-Ching Ni and Fu Lao Wang, *Hua Hu Ching: The Later Teachings of Lao Tzu*, Boston: Shambhala, 1995.

5. Joseph Epes Brown, *The Sacred Pipe: Black Elk's Account of the Seven Rites of the Oglala Sioux*, Norman, Okla.: University of Oklahoma Press, 1989.

6. For one perspective on this, see Jared Diamond, *Collapse: How Societies Choose to Fail or Succeed*, Boston: Penguin, 2005.

7. Paul H. Ray and Sherry R. Anderson, *The Cultural Creatives: How 50 Million People Are Changing the World*, New York: Harmony Books, 2000. Recent research by Paul Ray suggests that the number may be closer to 70 million in America and rapidly increasing worldwide. See "The New Political Compass," *www.culturalcreatives.org/thoughts.html* (accessed May 6, 2009).

8. Frank White, *The Overview Effect: Space Exploration and Human Evolution, Second Edition*, Reston, Va.: American Institute of Aeronautics & Astronautics, 1998.

9. This description is quoted from Mitchell's narrative account of his experience in space called "The View from Space," and is used by permission of the author. The full account can be heard on Edgar Mitchell, *The View from Space,* Sheilah Mitchell Productions, compact disc.

Bibliography

Almaas, A.H. *Inner Journey Home: The Soul's Realization of the Unity of Reality.* Boston: Shambhala, 2004.

———. *The Pearl Beyond Price: Integration of Personality into Being, an Object Relations Approach.* Boston: Shambhala, 2000.

———. *The Point of Existence: Transformations of Narcissism in Self-Realization.* Boston: Shambhala, 2000.

———. *The Unfolding Now: Realizing Your True Nature through the Practice of Presence.* Boston: Shambhala, 2008.

Bache, Christopher M. *Dark Night Early Dawn: Steps to a Deep Ecology of Mind.* New York: State University of New York Press, 2000.

———. *Lifecycles: Reincarnation and the Web of Life.* New York: Paragon House Publishers, 1994.

———. *The Living Classroom: Teaching and Collective Consciousness.* Albany, N.Y.: State University of New York Press, 2008.

Brown, Joseph Epes. *The Sacred Pipe: Black Elk's Account of the Seven Rites of the Oglala Sioux.* Norman, Okla.: University of Oklahoma Press, 1989.

Chardin, Pierre Teilhard De. *The Future of Man.* New York: Image, 2004.

———. *The Phenomenon of Man.* New York: Harper Perennial Modern Classics, 2008.

Diamond, Jared. *Collapse: How Societies Choose to Fail or Succeed.* Boston: Penguin, 2005.

Dowd, Michael. *Earthspirit: A Handbook for Nurturing an Ecological Christianity.* Mystic, Conn.: Twenty-Third Publications, 1991.

———. *Thank God for Evolution: How the Marriage of Science and Religion Will Transform Your Life and Our World.* New York: Plume, 2009.

Elgin, Duane. *Awakening Earth: Exploring the Evolution of Human Culture and Consciousness.* New York: William Morrow & Co, 1993.

———. *The Living Universe: Where Are We? Who Are We? Where Are We Going?* San Francisco, Calif.: Berrett-Koehler Publishers, 2009.

———. *Voluntary Simplicity, Revised Edition: Toward a Way of Life That Is Outwardly Simple, Inwardly Rich.* Brattleboro, Vt.: Harper Paperbacks, 1998.

Gardner, James N. *Biocosm: The New Scientific Theory of Evolution: Intelligent Life Is the Architect of the Universe.* Makawao, Hawaii: Inner Ocean Publishing, 2003.

———. *The Intelligent Universe: AI, ET, and the Emerging Mind of the Cosmos.* Franklin Lakes, N.J.: New Page Books, 2007.

Haisch, Bernard. *The God Theory: Universes, Zero-Point Fields, and What's Behind It All.* San Francisco, Calif.: Weiser Books, 2009.

Hawking, Stephen. *The Universe in a Nutshell.* United States and Canada: Bantam, 2001.

Heisenberg, Werner. *Physics and Philosophy: The Revolution in Modern Science.* New York: Harper Perennial Modern Classics, 2007.

Horgan, John. *The End of Science: Facing the Limits of Knowledge in the Twilight of the Scientific Age.* New York: Broadway Books, 1997.

Horn, Gabriel. *Contemplations of a Primal Mind.* Gainesville, Fla.: University Press of Florida, 2000.

———. *Native Heart.* New York: Paraview Special Editions, 2003.

———. *The Book of Ceremonies: A Native Way of Honoring and Living the Sacred.* Novato, Calif.: New World Library, 2005.

Hubbard, Barbara Marx. *Conscious Evolution: Awakening Our Social Potential.* Novato, Calif.: New World Library, 1998.

————. *Emergence: The Shift from Ego to Essence*. Charlottesville, Va.: Hampton Roads Publishing Company, 2001.

————. *The Hunger of Eve: A Woman's Odyssey Toward the Future*. Harrisburg, Pa.: Stackpole Books, 1976.

Kuhn, Robert Lawrence. "Why This Universe? Towards a Taxonomy of Possible Explanations." *Skeptic* 13 (2007): 28–39.

Martin, James. *The Meaning of the 21st Century: A Vital Blueprint for Ensuring Our Future*. Boston: Riverhead Trade, 2007.

Mitchell, Edgar. *The Way of the Explorer: An Apollo Astronaut's Journey Through the Material and Mystical Worlds*. Franklin Lakes, N.J.: New Page Books, 2008.

————. *The View from Space.* Sheilah Mitchell Productions. Compact disc.

Morin, Edgar. *On Complexity*. Cresskill, N.J.: Hampton Press, 2008.

Ni, Hua-Ching, and Fu Lao Wang. *Hua Hu Ching: The Later Teachings of Lao Tzu*. Boston: Shambhala, 1995.

Peat, F. David. *Blackfoot Physics: A Journey Into The Native American Universe*. San Francisco, Calif.: Weiser Books, 2006.

Penrose, Roger. *The Emperor's New Mind: Concerning Computers, Minds, and the Laws of Physics*. New York: Oxford University Press, 2002.

Prasad, Swami Muni N. *Chandogya Upanishad*. New Delhi: Dk Print World, 2006.

Primack, Joel R., and Nancy Ellen Abrams. *The View from the Center of the Universe: Discovering Our Extraordinary Place in the Cosmos*. New York: Riverhead Books, 2006.

Radin, Dean. *Entangled Minds: Extrasensory Experiences in a Quantum Reality*. New York: Paraview Pocket Books, 2006.

————. *The Conscious Universe: The Scientific Truth of Psychic Phenomena*. New York: HarperOne, 2009.

Ray, Paul H., and Sherry R. Anderson. *The Cultural Creatives: How 50 Million People Are Changing the World*. New York: Harmony Books, 2000.

Russell, Peter. *From Science to God: A Physicist's Journey into the Mystery of Consciousness*. Novato, Calif.: New World Library, 2004.

———. *The Global Brain: The Awakening Earth in a New Century*. Edinburgh: Floris Books, 2008.

———. *The White Hole in Time: Our Future Evolution and the Meaning of Now*. New York: HarperCollins, 2007.

Swimme, Brian. *The Hidden Heart of the Cosmos: Humanity and the New Story*. New York: Orbis Books, 1999.

———. *The Universe Story: From the Primordial Flaring Forth to the Ecozoic Era—A Celebration of the Unfolding of the Cosmos*. San Francisco, Calif.: Harper San Francisco, 1994.

———. *The Universe is a Green Dragon: A Cosmic Creation Story*. Rochester, Vt.: Bear & Company, 1985.

Tarnas, Richard. *Cosmos and Psyche: Intimations of a New World View*. New York: Plume, 2007.

———. *The Passion of the Western Mind: Understanding the Ideas that Have Shaped Our World View*. Chicago, Ill.: Ballantine Books, 1993.

Teish, Luisah. *Carnival of the Spirit: Seasonal Celebrations and Rites of Passage*. New York: HarperCollins, 1994.

———. *Jambalaya: The Natural Woman's Book of Personal Charms and Practical Rituals*. New York: HarperOne, 1988.

———. *Jump Up: Good Times Throughout the Seasons with Celebrations from Around the World*. New York: HarperOne, 2000.

White, Frank. *The Overview Effect: Space Exploration and Human Evolution, Second Edition*. Reston, Va.: American Institute of Aeronautics & Astronautics, 1998.

Wolf, Fred A. *Taking the Quantum Leap: The New Physics for Nonscientists*. New York: Harper Perennial, 1989.

———. *Mind and the New Physics*. London: William Heinemann, 1985.

———. *The Dreaming Universe: A Mind-Expanding Journey Into the Realm Where Psyche and Physics Meet*. New York: Touchstone, 1995.

———. *The Yoga of Time Travel: How the Mind Can Defeat Time*. Wheaton, Ill.: Quest Books, 2004.

Index

About the Author

Stephan Martin, MS, is an astronomer, educator, and writer who has taught astronomy and physics at colleges and educational centers across the United States for more than 20 years. Growing up under the dark starry skies of the Everglades and Keys of South Florida, he developed an interest in astronomy and the mysteries of the universe from an early age.

His graduate and subsequent astronomical research has focused on dark matter, spiral galaxies, and studies of the solar corona. His writing and research have appeared in a wide variety of scientific and cross-disciplinary venues, including *The Bulletin of the American Astronomical Society* and *Shaman's Drum Journal.* He lives with his wife in Westport, Massachusetts.